TERPSICHORE
AT LOUIS-LE-GRAND

Baroque Dance
on the Jesuit Stage in Paris

JUDITH ROCK

TERPSICHORE AT LOUIS-LE-GRAND

*Baroque Dance
on the Jesuit Stage in Paris*

THE INSTITUTE OF JESUIT SOURCES
Saint Louis 1996

Studies Composed in English

Published by

The Institute of Jesuit Sources
3700 West Pine Boulevard
Saint Louis, MO 63108
 tel: [314] 977-7257
fax: [314] 977-7263

Library of Congress Catalogue Card Number 96-79049
ISBN 1-880810-22-0

For
William Carroll, S.J., 1913–1984
who shared his research on the Jesuit theater
and urged me to undertake this project

Lyn Farwell, S.J., 1940–1986
who made possible the restaging of L'Espérance
and my second research trip to France

Marc Hoël, S.J., 1927–1995
Director of the Jesuit Cultural Center
at Les Fontaines, Chantilly, France
where I did much of the research for this book
and whose community corrected my French, encouraged me daily
danced with me
and became my French "family"

contents · · · · · · · · · · · · · · · · · ·

illustrations · · · · · · · · · · · · · · · · ·

following page 112

Illustrations reproduced by permission of Musée Carnavalet, Paris.

Introduction · · · ·

THE SETTING

Beaux Arts, who follow in my suite,
know Terpsichore by her voice:
assist me in my plans—
and be worthy of my choice.

By tragic drama's clamor
my sister, Melpomene, has tired you;
Dance, and Music, and the Chorus
give the theater its glamor.

—Words of Terpsichore in *L'Espérance*

Any art form is inseparable from its time and place. In order to become "spectators" at the ballets produced at the Jesuit college in Paris between 1660 and 1762, we need to see, hear, smell, and feel the college—which was the context for the ballets—and the city—which was the context for the college.

The College

By 1560, twenty years after its official papal sanction, Ignatius of Loyola's Society of Jesus was teaching in Paris. Its fledgling school, located on the rue de la Harpe, near the left bank of the Seine, was called Clermont.[1] Needing more space, in the spring of 1562 the

---

[1] Although in her article "Pierre Beauchamps and the *Ballets de Collège,*" Régine Astier refers to "two Jesuit schools: the Collège d'Harcourt and the Collège de Clermont" as the two centers of Jesuit education in Paris, the only evidence I have found that could be taken to support this assertion is the Philidor collection of musical scores, which includes ballets performed at Harcourt among "Les Ballets des jésuites" (Jesuit ballets). Within the Philidor collection, however, some scores are designated as "Ballet des jésuites" and others as "Ballet d'Harcourt." In Sommervogel's Jesuit bibliography, when the compiler wishes to indicate that a member of the order taught in Paris, he

1

college moved to two houses on the rue Croullebarbe, in the Saint-Marcel district. On July 2, 1563, the Jesuits found what was to be their school's permanent location on the rue Saint-Jacques, in the left-bank parish of Saint-Benoit.

The college settled in a neighborhood of colleges. Along the rue Saint-Jacques were the Colleges of Montaigu, Sainte-Barbe, the Lombards, and the Dominicans. The College of Cholets was to the south of Clermont, that of Mans to the east, and Marmoutier College was to the north. Across the street was the Sorbonne, the University of Paris.

At first, Clermont's façade was pierced by small shops whose brightly colored signs all but obscured the college entrance; in all, eighteen shops occupied the frontage between the two streets that then bounded the Jesuits' property. Between 1578 and 1647 the order managed to buy or rent nine of these shops. Between 1643 and 1682 the growing school annexed three of its immediate neighbors, Mans, Marmoutier, and Cholets. To provide a place for student vacations, around 1630 the college purchased a country house at Gentilly. Eventually Clermont engulfed twenty-eight small colleges, some because they were defunct or nearly so, and others as a result of inheritance, sale, or litigations.[2]

In accord with the practices of the Society of Jesus, instruction was offered free of charge.[3] The earliest fathers even acknowledged the possibility that they and their twenty or so students might live by asking for alms from door to door in their quarter, although that custom had never been much in repute in Paris. But by 1571 three thousand students were attending Clermont's classes. In 1593, as the number of students in all the Jesuit colleges continued to increase, the

---

says that so-and-so served at "le collège de Paris" or simply "à Paris." It is clear from the biographies of professors like Gabriel Le Jay and Charles Porée that he is referring to the college of Clermont. Likewise, Louis Desgraves, in his bibliography of college-theater pieces, *Répertoire des programmes des pièces de théâtre*, identifies Clermont as "le collège des jésuites." He lists Harcourt simply as "Collège d'Harcourt." According to Emond, Harcourt was founded in 1280 by Raoul d'Harcourt, archdeacon of Rouen, and was, with Clermont/Louis-le-Grand, one of the ten "grands collèges" of Paris; it offered a full program of instruction, including theatrical presentations. On the basis of this and other evidence, it is clear that the Jesuit college on the rue Saint-Jacques was the only Jesuit college in Paris.

[2] G. Emond, *L'Histoire du Collège de Louis-le-Grand, ancien collège des jésuites à Paris, depuis sa fondation jusqu'en 1830* (Paris, 1845), 370–77.

[3] Ibid., 11.

order's superiors decided that each large college must have a minimum revenue of twenty thousand livres.[4] By 1688, in addition to its swarms of day students, called *externes*, the rue Saint-Jacques school had five hundred and fifty boarding students, called *pensionnaires*. Though this growth marked the success of the Society's educational enterprise in Paris, it meant that, in spite of increased revenues from the annexed schools, a never ending search for patrons and funds occupied the college's administration.

Accounts of how the miracle happened differ, but by 1682 the Paris college had acquired no less a personage than the King as its patron. Long an enthusiastic member of the rue Saint-Jacques theater audience, Louis XIV declared the college a royal foundation. Its name was changed to Collège Louis-le-Grand, a bust of the king was set up in the garden, and the new patron undertook to make up the deficit in the schools's theatrical expenses. The college-ballet program for August 5, 1682, is the first to reflect Louis as the new patron and the school as his namesake; in a burst of gratitude and relief, the fathers called the ballet *Plutus, dieu des richesses* (Plutus, god of wealth).

The Jesuit college in Paris was one of several Jesuit institutions occupying a recognized place in the city's world of theater and fashion. The professed house and its adjoining Church of Saint Paul and Saint Louis were located on the rue Saint-Antoine, in the well-to-do Marais district. The church, whose services the King attended, enjoyed the reputation of being the "church of the Opéra," because so much of its music was performed by that theater's personnel. It was said that those who were unable to go to the Opéra performance at the Palais Royal could always make up for their disappointment by attending vespers at Saint-Louis.[5]

The City

When Louis became patron of the college, Paris was still a small city. What is now its heart was then its outskirts: both the Louvre and the Tuileries were almost outside the city proper when Louis XIV came to the throne.[6] In spite of its sprinkling of grand

---

[4] Gustave Dupont-Ferrier, *La Vie quotidienne d'un collège parisien pendant plus de 350 ans: Du Clermont au Lycée Louis-le-Grand, 1563–1920*, 3 vol. (Paris: De Brocard, 1921), 92.

[5] Robert Lowe, *Marc-Antoine Charpentier et l'opéra de collège* (Paris: Maisonneuve and La Rose, 1966), 26.

[6] Fernand Braudel, *The Structures of Everyday Life* (New York: Harper and Row, 1979), 520.

royal buildings, like the new Palais Royal and the renovated Louvre, much of Paris was built of wood, and some of its buildings still had thatched roofs. Indoors, lighting came from candles or torches, and heat—when there was any—came from huge, inefficient fireplaces and tiny charcoal braziers. In the depths of a hard winter, the water and wine froze even on the King's table.

Paris was a busy trading center, and the Seine was full of commercial traffic. Oddly enough, the river was used hardly at all for public transport. Unlike the Thames, it was not plied by water taxis and noble barges. Its quays were busy with trading in hay, wheat, lumber, and everything else the city needed; but the domestic traffic of Paris jammed the streets. Horses, carriages, and public horse carts clogged the roadways. The worst traffic jams occurred around two in the afternoon, the dinner hour. At night, especially in winter and on moonless nights, this tide of people and horse-drawn vehicles subsided. The only street lighting came from scattered lanterns, and that only from September through May. Even when the street lanterns were lit, they were extinguished at midnight. Very early in the morning the tide of traffic rose again, as thousands of peasants came in from the surrounding countryside with produce and other goods to sell. They went to the enormous market at Les Halles and to the smaller market for game on the quai de la Vallée; indeed, they ventured all over the city shouting, "Live mackerel! Fresh herrings! Baked apples! Oysters! Portugal, Portugal!" (which at that time meant oranges).[7]

Despite the press of traffic, riding was probably more pleasant than walking. Paris had no sidewalks until the end of the eighteenth century. The gutter—which was in many cases also the sewer—ran down the middle of the street; after any moderately heavy rain, it overflowed. Though the water closet had been invented in England in 1596, in Paris it was still extremely rare; the norm was the chamber pot emptied haphazardly out of the window. The streets began to be cleaned after 1666, and every morning a reeking cart came slowly up the rue Saint-Jacques hill to collect the household offerings. But still, say diaries and other documents of the period, the stench permanently attached itself to everything.

The city was small enough that certain regular events affected most neighborhoods. For instance, debts were paid—in coins, not banknotes—on the tenth, twentieth, and thirtieth of each month; on those occasions porters could be seen carrying huge sacks of money to and from rue Vivienne, the financial center. When a sought-after

---

[7] Ibid., 502.

aristocrat came to town, theaters often closed, because managers knew that most of their potential audience would go to wait on or at least try to catch a glimpse of the celebrity. And on Thursdays the theaters were closed because that was the bourgeois' day for walking—especially to visit the college and university neighborhood.[8]

This baroque world did not look, sound, or smell like our own world. But how deep did the differences go? How alien or at home would we feel if we were suddenly set down on the rue Saint-Jacques before the Jesuit college? One of the best ways to get a physical feel for a vanished time is to survey a random sampling of its more ordinary cultural details: to study, for example, the baths, deaths, police, fashion, table manners, and drinks of the period.

In the seventeenth century baths were generally regarded as medicinal, to be resorted to only in illness. In the next century, however, swimming in the Seine became popular. The *Nouveau Mercure* for August 1719 included a popular drinking song about the new practice. The gist of it was that the singer was only too willing to let all Paris plunge into the river; he, meanwhile, would stay firmly at table, swimming in a river of wine![9] Partly as a result of the popularity of swimming, perhaps, Parisians looked on baths with increasing favor as the eighteenth century progressed.

The mildly improved personal hygiene of the eighteenth century does not seem to have affected the Paris death rate. Some twenty thousand people died there every year, and between seven and eight thousand unwanted babies were annually abandoned.[10] The city's first lieutenant of police was appointed by Louis XIV in 1667. Watching politically suspect persons—including intellectuals and writers—was as much a part of his job description as catching robbers and murderers.

Fashion was serious business for Parisians of rank and fortune, and even more serious business for those who wished to be regarded as persons of rank and fortune. Clerics were as concerned as anyone else. When an Italian priest arrived in France in 1664, public ridicule

---

[8] John Lough, *Paris Theater Audiences in the Seventeenth and Eighteenth Centuries* (London: Oxford University Press, 1957), 85.

[9] *Le Nouveau Mercure*, August 1719. The original reads as follows: "Tout Paris dans la Seine / Va se plonger tour à tour. / Pour moi sans tout de peine / Je me baigne chaque jour: / Constamment je garde la table / Et je mi ris de leur erreur: / Charmant Bacchus, dans ta liqueur, / Je trouve un bois plus agréable. / Je bois si long tems et si bien, / Que je nage au milieu du vin" (149).

[10] Braudel, *Structures of Everyday Life*, 491.

soon forced him to assume the fashionable dress of his French colleagues. He lamented as follows:

> I had to give up my sugar-loaf [hat] . . . my coloured stockings and
> began to dress entirely in the French fashion, [with] a Zani hat with a
> narrow brim, a wide collar which made me look more like a doctor
> than a priest, a cassock which reached only to mid-thigh, black stock-
> ings and narrow shoes . . . with silver buckles instead of laces. In this
> costume . . . I could hardly believe I was a priest any more.[11]

In the seventeenth century, when wigs became fashionable, at first
the church protested, and then engaged in prolonged controversy
over whether a priest could officiate at Mass wearing a wig that hid
his tonsure. As Braudel recounts, a fashionable lady of the eighteenth
century could spend five or six hours dressing, surrounded by
servants and a hairdresser, while she chatted with visitors, including
her priest (330).

More so perhaps than any other single fact about or artifact
from baroque Paris, the ordinary table fork startles us into realizing
the distance separating that time and our own. Invented in Italy
during the Renaissance, the table fork spread north very slowly.
Anne of Austria, Louis XIV's mother, ate with her fingers all her life.
Louis, likewise, never used a fork, and enjoyed the reputation of
being able to eat chicken stew with his fingers without spilling a drop
(206). Of his courtiers, the only one who bothered with the finicking
Italian invention—though not in Louis's presence, since the King
forbade forks at his table—was the Duke of Montausier, who was
described as being "of formidable cleanliness."

In the mid–seventeenth century, chocolate was introduced in
France, tea was known (but generally distrusted until some years
later), and coffee was becoming the favorite new Parisian drink. The
first coffee stall was at the Saint-Germain Fair on the Left Bank in
1672, and in 1686 one of Paris's most famous cafes, the Procope, was
opened; it remains there to this day. The Procope was a few blocks
from the Jesuit college, near what was then the elegant center of
town, the Buci crossroads and the approach to the Pont Neuf. Front-
ing on the rue des Fosses-Saint-Germain, today the rue de l'Ancienne
Comédie, the new cafe was helped to succeed by business from the
Comédie-Française, which soon took up residence in its new quarters
across the street.

During the hundred years that concern us, Paris's three major
theater troupes took shape: the Comédie-Française, which grew in
part out of Molière's company; the Comédie-Italienne, the result of

---

[11] Ibid., 321.

various sovereigns' invitations over the years to companies of Italian players; and the Paris Opéra, which developed from the royal academies of music and dancing, established by Louis XIV in the 1660s. Though theater was to a good extent represented in Paris at the beginning of the seventeenth century by scatological farce, by about 1630 it was becoming the province of serious and respectable persons. As Corneille, Racine, and Molière staged their works and as the ballet became the theatrical passion of the century, the theaters, including the theater of the Jesuit college, emerged as a constellation of important places on the social and cultural map of Paris.

This Study

The purpose of this study is to make available for English-speaking readers a survey of dance at the Jesuit college in Paris between 1660, when ballet was emerging as the favorite theater form of the French capital and court, and 1762, when the Society of Jesus was expelled from France. This research is offered as a contribution to a better understanding of the role played by the Paris college ballets in the history of Western theater dance and in the history of the relationship between Christian theology and the performing arts. Some dance historians have considered the Jesuit theater as either too minor in its influence or too specialized in its intent to merit serious study. Artists and scholars in theology and the arts have, for the most part, been unaware of the Jesuit-college ballets. I hope that this study, the work of one who is both a performer and a researcher, will prove useful to performers and researchers in both groups as they reevaluate the Jesuit ballets or approach them for the first time.

Although the Jesuit college was called Clermont until 1682, in the body of this book I have called it, for the sake of convenience, by its subsequent name of Louis-le-Grand. I have referred to the hundred-year period covered as "baroque," although that confusing term is used for different periods in the history of different art forms. In dance history it indicates the period beginning around 1660 and extending into the second half of the eighteenth century.

Because Louis-le-Grand was in Paris and was closely connected with the court and with the major figures who shaped baroque dance, its theater appears to be the most important of the French college theaters in the study of dance on the Jesuit stage. Unfortunately, the comprehensiveness of its archives does not match its historical importance. The archives for many of the other hundred or so French Jesuit colleges and their theaters are more complete than are Louis-le-Grand's.[12] Because this is the case and because the Paris college clearly was the arbiter of theatrical fashion and taste for French Jesuit ballet, I have at points come to conclusions about the ballet at Louis-le-Grand on the basis of what is known about the ballet at other French colleges.

Most of the sources for this research are in French. In many instances I have made my own translation of the material; where possible, I have included the original French in the accompanying note. Where this was not possible, I have indicated my responsibility for the translation with the words "translation mine." In every case I have retained the period spelling in French quotations.

The French college ballet, as we shall attempt to demonstrate, is the result of several influences and lines of development. Historically, it is the descendent of the medieval school theater. Culturally, it is a response to the upper-class French enthusiasm for dance, which reached its zenith under Louis XIV. Philosophically, its roots are in the humanist branch of the Catholic Counter-Reformation, a period during which the Catholic Church was engaged in intense self-examination in the aftermath of the Protestant defections.

Though school theater was centuries old in Europe, and though other colleges also produced ballets, the Paris Jesuit theater was unique in bringing the college ballet and the college opera to new heights of lavishness and sophistication. Louis-le-Grand's role in college theater was comparable to that of the Comédie-Française in secular theater.[13]

Although in many provincial towns the Jesuit theater was the only permanent local theater, in Paris it was part of the network of court and professional theater productions. Jesuit-college ballet and court ballets are an important additional source of information about dance on the Jesuit stage in Paris. Full-blown court ballet had been thriving in France for seventy years when Louis XIV began his reign. Productions were mobbed, when as many Parisians as possible tried to squeeze into the Salle de Bourbon in the Louvre, where the ballets were given when the court was in the city. The audience was not specially invited; to attend, all that was necessary was to be well

---

[12] Robert Lowe, "Les Représentations en musique au Collège Louis-le-Grand, 1650–1688," *Revue d'histoire du théâtre* 10 (1958): 26.

[13] Ibid., 205.

dressed and ruthless enough to elbow one's way through the throng. A passage in *Francion*, a popular book of the time, describes a character's fight to reach the Salle de Bourbon, where he finally sits thankfully on the floor. Behind him, a cramped musician uses his shoulder for a hat stand and his back for a music rack.[14]

Louis XIV made his *gloire* the central point of his ballets at court, and in their theater the Jesuits retained the ballet's function as eulogy of the monarch. Far from discarding them in times of political danger, rulers devoted additional attention to the ballet as a means of consolidating their threatened power. In the midst of the civil war of the Fronde, the thirteen-year-old Louis, symbolically surrounded by an ensemble consisting of his brother, the counts, marquis, and dukes of France, made his dance debut in the *Ballet de Cassandre* on February 26, 1651. Between February and September of that dangerous year, at least four major ballets were given at court, as well as a spur-of-the-moment effort created in twenty-four hours and put on in the gardens of the Palais Royal.[15]

A seventeenth-century Jesuit dance historian and ballet producer, Claude François Menestrier, connects politics with the new vitality of the French theater arts in his time. He says that after the King "gave peace to all of Europe" with the Treaty of the Pyrenees in 1669, he established academies of painting, sculpture, architecture, physical science, mathematics, and music to help France recover from the war. Significantly, the academy of dancing had been established nine years before, and now Louis wanted to continue encouraging the wellborn to acquit themselves creditably in the sciences and arts—including public theater presentations—without incurring any blot or stain on their social status.[16]

Politics, the King, and the court gave impetus to and embodied the fervent enthusiasm for theatrical dancing. But, fundamentally, it was a case of contemporary attitudes, interests, technical developments, and the needs of the upper strata of French society converging like the lines of a stage design on one scenic point—the ballet. Jean Loret, seventeenth-century chronicler of the Paris social scene, raises the curtain for us.

---

[14] Margaret McGowan, *L'Art de ballet du cour en France, 1581–1643* (Paris: Centre nationale de la recherche scientifique, 1963), 229.

[15] Marie-Françoise Christout, *Le Ballet de cour de Louis XIV, 1643–1672* (Paris: Editions A. et J. Ricard et Cie, 1967), 58.

[16] Claude François Menestrier, S.J., *Des représentations en musique anciennes et modernes* (Paris, 1681), 236.

Last month, on the very last day,
I went to the Jesuits, to see their play.
A tragedy it was, in a lively style
and, to make the audience smile,
there were pleasant interludes of ballet.
The tragedy subject was out of the Bible,
The Book of Kings, that tale without rival
of highly placed souls, well born and well bred.
What chapter? I never heard it said. . . .
Père Darrouy, the learned doctor,
was the tragedy's noble and dignified author. . . .
And in the entre-acte ballets—*so* well danced—
was one of the very best dancers in France.[17]

---

[17] Jean Loret, *La Muze historique*, ed. C. L. Livey (Vichy, 1878), Letter 35, Saturday, September 3, 1661. The original reads as follows: "De l'autre mois, le dernier jour, / je fus au Jésuites, pour / y voir une Pièce Tragique, / Compozée en stile énergique. / . . . des entr'Actes plaizans / Comme on en fait-la tous les ans.

"On a pris ce Sujet plauzible / au Livre du Roys, dans la Bible, / (le grand Livre des Gens-de-bien) / Chapitre, je ne scay combien. . . .

"Père Darrouy, profond Docteur, / En est le noble et digne Autheur. . . . Et les Balets entrelacez / Fort agréablement dancez, / Se trouvant, il est, d'assurance, / Un des adroits Danseurs de France."

one ·

THE BALLETS AND THEIR RAISON D'ÊTRE

"Outward show . . . gives a second life to all things."
God . . . has sanctified ostentation by
creating light (and thus glitter) first of all.

—Germaine Bazin, *The Baroque*

The Ballet's Beginnings

Claude François Menestrier, S.J. (1631–1705), who has been called the first ballet historian, published his definitive treatise on dance at Paris in 1682. He tells us that ballet is

> a movement of the whole body fitting chosen subjects or things to be represented, at a chosen speed and musical meter, and to the sound of instruments or the voice; and all these things together make a pleasing harmony of movements of the body which represent various things to the audience, and by these figured imitations of things natural and moral, create clever images.[1]

At Louis-le-Grand, the Jesuit college on the rue Saint-Jacques in Paris, the ballets began as "intermedes" for the school's Latin tragedies, produced every year in August. These intermedes were

---

[1] Claude François Menestrier, *Des Ballets anciens et modernes selon les règles du théâtre* (Paris: René Guignard, 1682): "un mouvement de tout le corps accommode a certains sujets ou représentations, a certains temps, a certaines mesures, et au son des instruments ou de la voix et de ce tout ensemble il se fait un concert agréable des mouvemens de tout le corps qui représentent quelque chose aux yeux des spectateurs, et font des images scavantes par ces imitations figurées des choses naturelles et morales" (199).

lighter intervals of dancing, singing, speaking, and instrumental music placed between the acts of the somber drama.

The Jesuit educational guidelines of 1599, the *Ratio studiorum*, allowed the presentation of tragedies and comedies in the Jesuit colleges, provided five conditions were met: Performances must be infrequent, in Latin, on sacred subjects, with no feminine roles, and accompanied only by Latin intermedes of the most rigorous propriety.[2] However, as contemporary observers commented, there were the Jesuit educational rules from Rome, the French interpretation of them—and their Parisian interpretation!

Happily for dance in Paris, all five rules were stretched nearly beyond recognition at Louis-le-Grand. In some years, half a dozen major theater productions were mounted. Comedy was played in French by 1699, and by 1704 at the latest, French tragedy was being acted. Feminine characters were cast in most years, and by 1650 danced intermedes with French songs and words were delighting the college's cosmopolitan audience.

As early as 1622 entertaining intervals had begun to appear between the acts of the Latin tragedies that were the staple of the Jesuit college stage.[3] These pauses in the main theatrical action were composed of speech, song, instrumental music, and dance. Though the term "ballet" was not in general use in the French Jesuit theater until the 1660s, the first definite intermedes of which we have records included dance. In 1638 a Louis-le-Grand celebration of Louis XIV's birth was called a "ballet," and the term appears to have been in continual use at the college after 1651.[4]

To us a "ballet" is one complete dance production, like *The Nutcracker*. But the word can be confusing in period references, because it was used in two ways, especially in the seventeenth century. It could mean the dancing that took place between one act of a tragedy and the next; that is, one interval of dance or one intermede. It could also mean *all* the dancing between all the acts of a tragedy; that is, a complete set of intermedes. Jean Loret, the mid-seventeenth-century reviewer of the Paris social scene, used the term in the first way in his account of the production at Louis-le-Grand in August 1663. He wrote that not only had the Jesuits' students acted very well

---

[2] Dupont-Ferrier, *La Vie quotidienne d'un collège*, 286.

[3] H. M. C. Purkis, "Quelques observations sur les intermèdes dans le théâtre des jésuites en France," *Revue de l'histoire du théâtre* 18 (April-June 1966): 182.

[4] Robert W. Lowe, *Marc-Antoine Charpentier et l'opéra de collège* (Paris: Maisonneuve and Larose), 176.

in the tragedy *Theseus,* they had also, "with great assurance," danced "four ballets." By "four ballets" he meant the four intermedes, consisting of dance, music, and poetry, which alternated with the five acts of the tragedy.[5] Loret's "four ballets" made up a complete set of thematically related intermedes called *Ballet de la Verité* (Ballet of truth), whose four parts were called "Truth Disguised," "Truth Driven Away," "Truth Sought," and "Truth Found."[6]

Meant originally to reward the audience for its attention to the difficult Latin tragedy, the intermedes at Louis-le-Grand developed in three directions. One line of development led to ballets related thematically to tragedies and called *ballets d'attache*, like *La Verité*. Another became intermedes primarily for voice and instruments, like those presented with the tragedy of *Joseph vendu par ses frères* (Joseph sold by his brothers) in March 1698. The third was full-blown baroque opera, like *David et Jonathas* (David and Jonathan), composed by Marc-Antoine Charpentier and presented with the tragedy *Saul* in February 1688. Predictably, intermedes of all three kinds became the main attraction to the rue Saint-Jacques theater, until in August 1701 the ballet itself, *Jason, ou la conquête de la toison d'or* (Jason, or the conquest of the golden fleece), had its own musical intermedes, called *récits en musique* or musical narratives.

Lyric theater was the coming thing in Paris, and the Louis-le-Grand faculty, part of that "new wave," produced a variety of dance, music, and poetry on their college stage. By 1685 the college was in an artistic ferment of theatrical production and aesthetic philosophy.

The Ballets and the Classical Aesthetic

The professors at Louis-le-Grand were Christian-humanist educators. The syllabus they offered their students showed many characteristics of the humanism of the Renaissance. Though Renaissance humanism is still popularly labeled anti-Christian, many scholars now believe that it sprang from a commitment to traditionally Christian moral and religious values.

> Much of the rebirth that Humanists sought was a rebirth of good moral standards in public life and the rebirth of an education that would promote genuine piety. Contrary to public opinion, the Renaissance was, in many ways, a religious and moral Renaissance. Humanist spirituality had an activist character and was appropriate for lay

---

[5] Loret, *Muze historique*, Letter 31, August 11, 1663.

[6] Lowe, *Marc-Antoine Charpentier*, 177. Ernest Boysse, *Le Théâtre des jésuites* (Paris: 1880; reprint ed., Geneva: Slatkine Reprints, 1970), 146f.

people and even clerics whose lives were spent in the service of family, Church, or country. It was perhaps the first time that on a large scale Christian spirituality was articulated by and for people who did not live in a cloister.[7]

Among the cardinal characteristics of this new spirituality were optimism, affirmation of the physical world, and an emphasis on the human aspects of divine revelation. The baroque spirituality of the Jesuits likewise focused on this world, rather than the next, as the theater of revelation.

The Jesuits at Louis-le-Grand shared their contemporaries' intense interest in formulating and practicing a classical aesthetic. This attempt to base the European arts on the thought and theory of the ancient world reached its highest development in France in the seventeenth century.

Baroque classicism came to the Jesuits and their theatrical colleagues as filtered through the early Christian era and the Italian Renaissance. The classical-humanist aesthetic was based on Aristotle, passed on by Vitruvius, shaped by Alberti and many others in the fifteenth century, and endlessly elaborated in the sixteenth. Seventeenth-century writers on the arts did not see themselves as presenting a new theory; they would not have said that they represented a ground-breaking thrust in aesthetics, nor would they have wanted to occupy such a position. They understood their work as a careful and confident stating of eternal truths. Even in the major aesthetic debate of the century—Who has made better art, the ancients or the moderns?—neither side doubted that contemporary artworks should be solidly built on the principles of the ancients.[8] All followed the rules of the Greeks and Romans because all considered them the surest foundation for masterpieces. Historian André Maurois has said that the mark of a classical artist, according to Valéry,

> is that he seeks not "to make the new" but "to make enduringly," which means fashioning a masterpiece which shall be independent of circumstance and of date. La Rouchefoucauld observes himself, but analyses within himself the everlasting man; Racine transposes dramas of his own time into ancient or biblical tragedies.[9]

---

[7] John O'Malley, S.J., "The Jesuits, St. Ignatius, and the Counter-Reformation: Some Recent Studies and Their Implications for Today," *Studies in the Spirituality of Jesuits* 14 (January 1982): 16.

[8] Ladislas Tatarkiewicz, "L'Esthétique du Grand Siècle," *Revue du dix-septième siècle*, 1966?, 23.

[9] André Maurois, *A History of France*, trans. Henry L. Binsse (n.p.: Minerva Press, 1960), 223.

This theorizing bore a different relationship to the creative work in literature than it did to the creative work in the other arts. In literature, the classical theories preceded the artworks—such as Racine's tragedies—which exemplified them. In the other arts, including dance, the reverse was true. For example, in visual art, the classical theories of the 1660s *followed* Poussin's paintings of the 1640s. In his first theoretical work on the ballet, written in 1658, Menestrier tells us that he has been moved to try to identify the principles underlying this art form as a result of working on his recent ballet, *L'Autel de Lyon* (The altar of Lyon). The establishment of the Royal Academy of Dancing and the Royal Academy of Music in the 1660s, the decade of the Grand Siècle that saw the height of aesthetic theorizing, bolstered technical standards and helped create the critical climate for the steady flow of books on dancing that appeared during the next hundred years.

The classical aesthetic of the seventeenth century had eight major points:

1. Beautiful things are objectively beautiful, beautiful in themselves. Beauty is *not* in the eye of the beholder.

2. Beauty is the result of order, of the proportion of parts and the harmony of details.

3. Our reason as well as our senses allows us to perceive beauty. Therefore, in order to respond to the arts, we must understand, as well as see and hear.

4. The creation of beauty is the purpose of art; the ability to create beauty is the result of knowledge and understanding as well as of technical skill.

5. Truth is a necessary prerequisite for beauty; an artwork must be faithful to what it seeks to imitate.

6. Art is the imitation of nature: nature is perfect, and the human body is the most perfect of all natural things.

7. Nonetheless, the artist can perfect nature.

8. Art attained perfection in the ancient world, and therefore we cannot do better than to imitate what the ancients did.[10]

The discussion that centered on the idea of imitating nature was complex. The painter Poussin, also a theorist, distinguished between the *aspect,* or simple appearance of a thing, and its *prospect.* By "prospect" he meant what appears when a thing is contemplated or thought about; that is, the abstraction of something from nature

---

[10] Ibid., 24f.

into a truth. Similarly, Roger de Piles spoke of the *first truth* of a thing, or what is revealed by a faithful copy of nature, and the *second* or *ideal truth,* which is inherent in natural objects. Understanding these conceptions of layers of truth in nature is the key to understanding both the allegorical dimension and the style of seventeenth- and eighteenth-century ballets.

In poetry (by which baroque theorists meant not only verse but imaginative literature in general), "truth" came to mean a kind of ideal truth which was called *vraisemblance.*[11] Difficult to define in either French or English, this word carried an idea dominant in theatrical theory. Sometimes it was used to mean "things as they ought to be," and sometimes it referred to an agreement with public opinion. The point seems to have been that the truth could sometimes be the naked truth, so to speak, and therefore unpleasant or scandalous, unworthy to be shown. When that was so, the appropriate choice, according to the rubrics of the classical aesthetic, was to show the truth not as it was—desperate and starving peasants, for example—but as it ought to be or as the theatergoing public had decided to pretend that it was—happy rustics and graceful shepherdesses, for instance.

Although the classical aesthetic was not created by the theorists of the Grand Siècle, they did tend to emphasize four points that previous centuries had overlooked. First, they stressed that art demands *grandeur:* sublimity, noble subjects, beautiful sentiments, illustrious actions. Second, they insisted that art must have a *moral value.* This second point is especially important for an understanding of the Jesuit ballets. Relating the arts and moral messages was a nearly universal artistic practice in this period. The Jesuits' fidelity to this dimension of their theater reflected their commitment to contemporary aesthetic principles as much as it reflected their commitment to a particular religious worldview.

The third idea characteristic of seventeenth-century classicism was that the ordering principle of art is *bienséance* or *convenance.* Probably the clearest indication of the meaning of these words is their Latin translation as *decorum.* The fourth idea, that *allegory* is an essential part of art, had perhaps the greatest impact on the ballets. Though visual allegory had been used for centuries in Europe as part of public celebration and spectacle, it assumed a new place in aesthetic theory in the later 1600s.[12]

---

[11] Ibid., 26.

[12] Ibid., 27f.

The thought that circled around these principles of classical aesthetics evolved in two ways. Those who took the liberal direction held that there was, after all, some beauty contrary to nature, that artists could sometimes take liberties with the rules, and that the rules themselves were not infallible. Those who took the conservative direction, including the Jesuits, held that the classical rules were definitive, were based on the best authority, and were infallible.

Contrary to what we might expect, this conservative aesthetic position did not stifle the Jesuit theater, because the classical canon of moderation was gradually being replaced by another taste characteristic of the seventeenth century—the new or "baroque" taste for variety and spirituality. In the course of the century, this new taste modified the old ideal and ensured the popularity of the ballet, which, though it remained paired with the classical tragedy, became the star of the Jesuit stage.

Between 1658 and 1760, at least ten books and treatises were published in France on the history and theory of theatrical dancing. There were also many technical books by dancing masters, as well as collections of new dances, most of them social. The dances were published in the dance notation created by Pierre Beauchamps and popularized by Raoul Feuillet. Feuillet's book, *Chorégraphie, ou l'art décrire la dance, par caractères, figures et signes démonstratifs* (Choreography, or the art of writing dance, by means of characters, figures, and signs), was published in Paris in 1700.

More general treatises on theater, both for it and against it, were also being written. One of the less well known antitheater books is *Nouvelles réflexions sur l'art poétique* (New reflections on the poetic art), written by the Oratorian priest Bernard Lamy and published in 1668. Lamy, opposed to imaginative art forms as morally dangerous, represents the minority opinion in this period. The other side of the question was represented by writers like the Jesuit Joseph Jouvancy, dramatist and teacher of rhetoric at Louis-le-Grand, who included a section on correct tragedy and theater practices in his 1685 work on rhetoric, *Ratio discendi et docendi*.

Of the ten French books on the history and theory of dancing, seven were by ecclesiastics:

1658: Claude François Menestrier, S.J., "Remarques pour la conduite des ballets" (Remarks on directing ballets), in *L'Autel de Lyon* (Lyon) (The altar of Lyon)

1668: L'Abbé Michel de Pure, *Idée des spectacles anciens et nouveaux* (Paris) (The theory of ancient and modern theatrical productions)

1681: Menestrier, *Des Représentations en musique* (Paris) (On musical productions)

1682: Menestrier, *Des Ballets anciens et modernes selon les règles du théâtre* (Paris) (On ancient and modern ballets according to the rules of the theater)

1715: L'Abbé d'Aubignac, *La Pratique du théâtre* (Amsterdam), first published in 1657 (The practice of the theater)

1724: Jacques Bonnet, *Histoire general de la danse* (Paris) (A general history of dancing)

1725: Gabriel Le Jay, S.J., "De choreis dramaticis," in *Bibliotheca rhetorum* (Paris) (About dramatic ballets, in The library of rhetoricians)

1732: Charles Porée, S.J., *Discours sur les spectacles* (Paris) (A discourse on theatrical productions)

1750: François Riccoboni, *L'Art du théâtre* (The art of the theater)

1760: Jean Georges Noverre, *Lettres sur la danse et les ballets* (Stuttgart and Lyon) (Letters on dancing and ballets)

Five of these ten works were by Jesuits from Louis-le-Grand. One of them, Porée, emphasized the points of his discourse with a ballet, *L'Histoire de la danse* (The history of dance), performed at Louis-le-Grand in August, 1732.

Of the remaining five books, four were reviewed by the Jesuits in their influential journal *Les Memoires de Trévoux*. In March 1716 the editors wrote of d'Aubignac's book that if the practices of this excellent book were followed, the ancient world would have to envy France the perfection of its theater.[13] This endorsement was followed by twenty-two pages of closely reasoned argument on the classical theory of theater as it was then being debated by d'Aubignac and his adversary, M. Menage. The review of Bonnet's history of dance enthusiastically recommended the book to the public. "A title like this ought to unwrinkle the foreheads of readers, and make them feel something of the gaiety and playfulness which even the idea of the Dance naturally brings with it."[14] In February 1750 the Jesuits reviewed Riccoboni's book, and in July 1756 also commented on a treatise concerning the stage machinery at the Opéra-Italien. In his *Lettres sur la danse*, published in 1760, Noverre regretted that he seemed to give his subject undue importance, but recommended the

---

[13] Article XXVI.

[14] Ibid., May 1724, article XXXIX, p. 850.

book for its beautiful edition and good style.[15] The journal continued to be published after the Jesuits ceased to edit it in 1762, and maintained its tradition of bringing works on the theater to the attention of the public.

Considered by some dance historians to be the most complete and original work on dance from the seventeenth century, Menestrier's *Des Ballets anciens et modernes* is the major primary source on Jesuit ballet theory and practice. Menestrier is like an architect, however. His interest is in the overall design, shape, and impact of the finished product. The specifics of the technical dance vocabulary and of its accompanying music he leaves to the ballet masters and composers, who are more or less like carpenters building according to his plan.

In part, his 1682 book is a restatement and enlargement of his 1658 "Remarques." The modern researcher tends wholeheartedly to echo Le Jay, who, while basing his own comments on Menestrier, also complained about his predecessor's lack of organization and wished that the book had not been "such a cornfield of ballets."[16] Nevertheless, Menestrier represents the later-seventeenth-century theoretician-practitioner as he relates his own and others' ballet-production practices to the classical aesthetic.

Des Ballets anciens et modernes was intended to be part of a monumental work, never completed, called *Philosophie des images* (The philosophy of images). For Menestrier, ballets are "images of action." The elder brother of music, painting, and poetry, ballet is unlike any of these arts, and therefore needs its own rules. These rules are to be based on the practices of the ancients and the dictates of reason and taste.

He begins by describing the place of ballets or "figured dances" in the Greek theater—in tragedy and comedy, and in the prologues of musical productions. Having legitimized ballet by finding its origin in the ancient world, he explains that dance used to be part of Judaism and Christianity, but that

> [w]e no longer dance as part of our religious practice . . . as do the infidels. . . . We content ourselves with creating honest theatrical presentations that form the body to noble action and decorum. We present them in public celebrations, and often under the veil of ingenious allegories representing the events which create the well-being of

---

[15] Ibid., April 1760, 936.

[16] Gabriel Le Jay, S.J., "Liber de choreis dramaticis," *Bibliotheca rhetorum* (Paris: 1725), 801. Unpublished translation by John Rundin.

the state, so that the people will enjoy all the sweets of these events, made more tangible by the attractions of pleasure and entertainment.[17]

He tells us that the ancients called the arts, including dance, the "Monkeys of Nature," because one of their primary functions is to imitate things in the natural world (3). But the ballet goes farther than the other arts because it not only expresses how things look and how they are arranged but also, by its movement, expresses their soul, or *inner* nature. Menestrier jokes that the god Proteus, who could imitate and become anything he chose, was just a good dancer (42).

The author's explanation of how ballet expresses the inner nature of things is a somewhat startling combination of seventeenth-century physiology and classical aesthetics. He says that the ballet's unique power of expression derives from the intimate relationship of dance and music. Physical expression is the result of sound hitting the eardrum, which sets up a reaction in the nerves, causing movement and therefore dance. Music causes dance as a small stone cast into a fountain causes ripples. Just as the stone and the water constitute two movements—the stone sinking to the bottom and the water rippling—so the music penetrates to the soul by means of the imagination and movement ripples through the body by means of the nerves (196f.). The combination of these two movements creates harmony, an essential element of ballet.

Harmony in ballet, then, is created not just by the blending of instruments and voices but by the blending together of sound and body. The four harmonic parts of music, as conceived by the Greeks, match the four-part harmony found among the different parts of the body. These body parts have different proportions and move at different speeds. (He does not name these body parts, but seems to mean head, arms, torso, and legs.)

Because dance is the movement of diverse body parts, it should be accompanied by a *group* of instruments, rather than by one instrument alone. Though he finds all instruments appropriate for use in ballets, he, like most of his contemporaries, feels that the violin is the

---

[17] Menestrier, *Ballets anciens et modernes*, preface: "Nous ne faisons plus des Actes de Religion, des danses comme on fait . . . les Infidèles, nous nous contentons d'en faire des divertissements honnêtes pour former le corps a des actions nobles, et de bienséance. Nous en faisons des rejouissances publiques, et souvent sous des allégories ingénieuses on représente les événements qui font le bon-heur de l'Etat, pour en faire gouter aux peuples toutes les douceurs, sous les appas du plaisir et du divertissement qui les leur rendent plus sensibles" (5).

best, since it can play many different types of music. Perhaps, he speculates, it works so well for dance because its strings are made from the bodies of animals, and therefore its sound is especially effective in producing expressive movement in the human body (201f.).

However, most instruments can be used to accompany ballets, since natural movement is caused by "les esprits" or "spirits." "Spirits" are not beings from the world beyond, but something more like what the nineteenth century might have called "animal spirits"— impulses arising from our physical nature. These "spirits" are light, nearly always in motion, and round, like a ball, so that they can receive the impressions caused by any type of instrument (200). The nature of the instruments will dictate whether these "spirits" move slowly or quickly, which means that the creator of the ballet must choose instruments for their ability to inspire expression appropriate to the particular parts of the ballet. He suggests trumpets, drums, and cymbals for the dances of soldiers, flutes and musettes for shepherds and peasants, the lyre for serious dances and dances of the gods, little bells and Basque drums for comic dances, and castanets for Spanish dances.

Whatever instruments are chosen, the music of a ballet is made to fit the dance, not the other way around. This is to ensure that it fits the movements and passions expressed in the dancing. Menestrier repeatedly decries the growing interest in "la simple danse" or pure dance, which he contrasts to ballet. By pure dance he means dance which does not express the inner nature of things, dance for its own sake. In his time (as in our own) and despite the classical aesthetic, nondramatic dance represented one line of development within the art form. De Pure, Menestrier's contemporary, noted this tendency, as did Bonnet, who commented in 1724 that it was particularly true of social dance. As Menestrier saw it, the difference was that the nondramatic dancers would rather perform beautiful steps and rhythms than give themselves the trouble of expressing anything (163). Since the theoretical point of seventeenth- and eighteenth-century theater dance was, in general, to express the human passions, Menestrier's position was that of the dance "establishment." Any lessening of the emphasis on expression seemed a threat to "real dance." In his opinion, the best ballets show all three basic kinds of human feelings— anger, love, and reason, and their characteristic movements (176).

Menestrier divides a ballet into qualitative and quantitative parts. The qualitative parts have to do with the ballet's subject: its choice and its "form" or "invention," by which he means the way the subject is presented. What is important to him about the choice and treatment of a ballet's content is not unity of action, but unity of subject. That is, anything goes as long as it can be related in some logical way to the ballet's stated theme. This attitude is markedly different from the assumptions of most twentieth-century choreographers about the making of a ballet. The focus today is generally on unity of action when there is a dramatic theme; what happens next must follow in some degree from what happened before. For Menestrier, however, the important thing is that all of the ballet's parts be *thematically* related to each other. At first glance, they do not seem particularly related to the modern reader. For example, in the ballet *Night*, which Cardinal Mazarin produced in 1653 and which Menestrier regards as having unity of subject, there were dances for gods, thieves, heroes, shopkeepers of Paris, hours, shepherds, and the rising sun, because all those characters could be made to relate to the idea of nighttime.

A ballet's subject can come from history, fable, natural history, morality, or the author's own imagination.[18] Historical subjects include the siege of Troy, the rescue of Rhodes, the capture of Thebes, the education of Achilles, the victories of Alexander, the building of Athens, and so forth. Fable or myth suggests the judgment of Paris, the story of Niobe, the metamorphoses of Acteon, the story of Narcissus, the wedding of Peleus and Tethys, the Cretan labyrinth, and the birth of Venus. Subjects invented from morality and the natural world include the vagaries of disguised love, lovesickness, success in the world, night, weather, age, proverbs, pleasures, blindness, illness, fashion, curiosity, and games. From the choreographer's own imagination might come a ballet of invented incidents in relation to the Saint-Germain Fair, the street-cries of Paris, or the Carnival season. All of these themes will make good ballets, but the last three sources—the natural world, morality, and the imagination—offer the most ingenious possibilities.

Though he is writing about ballet in general—ballet produced at court, in theaters, and in colleges—he recounts that at Louis-le-Grand, most of the ballets in his time are philosophical. That is, they express the causes, effects, properties, and principles of things. In them, the natural world is skillfully presented by means of theatrical craft and invention. He tells us that some of the recent college ballets in this category have been *Curiosité* (Curiosity), 1670, *Les Songes*,

---

[18] Claude François Menestrier, "Remarques pour la conduite des ballets," *L'Autel de Lyon consacré à Louis Auguste* (Lyon: Jean Molin, 1658), 51.

(Dreams), 1671, *Comètes* (Comets), 1665, *Illusion*, 1672, *L'Empire du soleil* (The empire of the sun), 1673 and *La Mode* (Fashion), 1675.[19]

The "economy" of a ballet, Menestrier says, consists in the right distribution of a whole in all its essential parts—its causes, effects, properties, circumstances, and events. It is a drawing together of story, example, and imagination around a single subject, so that a pleasing and ingeniously developed production is created (135). After the subject is chosen, the ballet's "economy" is built up by means of figure, gesture, and movement. All of these elements contribute to the ballet's harmony.

"Figure" is another difficult term to define from context alone. Menestrier seems to mean two different things by it: the ballet's roles or characters, and also the floor pattern traced by the dancers in relation to one another on the stage (139, 178). When he writes about theory, he apparently intends the first meaning; the second (which is the usual sense of the term in baroque dance) he seems to mean when he is discussing what he has done in specific ballets. He states that an infinite number of figures (presumably in both senses) can be invented, because ballet can express an infinite number of things.

His understanding of "gesture" and "movement" emphasizes the distance between his century and ours. For the contemporary choreographer, to talk about gesture and movement is to talk about the heart of dance. What matters most, first and last, is what the dancers *do*. For Menestrier, that is both true and not true. It is true insofar as it is movement that expresses reality; it is through the movement of the body that the ballet imitates the action and feeling of the natural world. However, the movement is *only* important because it is expressive. He repeats himself more than once on the difference between ballet and pure dance as he drives home his point that expression is what matters.

> [P]ure dance is movement that expresses nothing, observing only an accurate cadence with the sound of the instruments by means of simple and figured steps and phrases, while *the ballet* expresses, according to Aristotle, the actions, manners, and feelings of human beings.[20] [emphasis added]

---

[19] Menestrier, *Ballets anciens et modernes*, 67.

[20] Ibid.: "[l]a simple danse est un mouvement qui n'exprime rien, et observe seulement une juste cadence avec le son des instrumens par des pas et des passages simples ou figurez, au lieu que le Ballet exprime selon Aristote les actions des hommes, leurs moeurs, et leurs passions." (158)

It must be stressed, however, that ballet and pure dance share the same movement vocabulary. A ballet is the *movements* of pure dance serving the classical goal of *expressing* the natural world's inner nature and truth—and therefore beauty.

> The movements of the body are the harmonic movements, the steps and actions of dance: to step forward and backward, *trousser* [used here to mean a dance step, possibly a bend of the knees; one literal meaning of this verb is "to fold"], to turn, to jump, to rise onto the toes, and so forth.

> The expressions are the actions that denote character, like the actions of someone rowing a boat, falling asleep, getting drunk, and the like, and the figures are the various arrangements of dancers, who face front, back to back, in a circle, on an angle, in a cross shape, in an X shape, in a crescent shape, turning, pursuing and fleeing each other, and weaving in and out.[21]

Menestrier and most of the dance theoreticians—except those who were also themselves dancing masters, like Rameau and Noverre— simply assume the technical vocabulary. They note it as the province and business of the dancing master, who will, like a skilled crafts- person, construct a part of the edifice the ballet creator has imagined. This is why in most of these works on ballet theory, we look in vain for technical descriptions of dance steps. Those whose main concern was ballet as exposition of the classical aesthetic—and therefore as expression of the soul—regarded the technical vocabulary of baroque dance as an important means to an even more important end. The seventeenth century was in some ways the most hierarchical of centu- ries, and human endeavor did not escape classification into more and less worthy pastimes and vocations. Nearly always, theory was valued over practice—as it usually still is in academic circles. The review of François Riccoboni's *L'Art du théâtre,* which appeared in the February 1750 issue of *Les Memoires de Trévoux,* explicitly stated this attitude. Though the Jesuit reviewer has several favorable things to

---

[21] Ibid.: "Les portemens du corps sont les mouvemens harmoniques, ou les pas et les actions de la danse, comme couper en avant, en arrière, trousser, pirouetter, sauter, s'élever, etc.

"Les expressions sont les actions qui marquent, comme les actions des Rameurs, des endormis, des personnes prises de vin, etc., et les figures sont les diverses dispositions des danseurs, qui dansent de front, dos contre dos, en rond, en quarte, en croix, en sautoir, en croissant sur une ligne, en évolu- tion, en se poursuivant, en fuyant, en s'entrelassent les uns dans les autres" (158).

say about the book, he comments that the author "has written for a woman, and he only proposes details of practice."[22]

Dismissive as it is of women and dancing instructors, this comment holds one of the keys to the complex attitude of many ecclesiastics over the centuries toward the theater arts and their practitioners. Too often dance historians have assumed that any suggestion of indifference, superiority, or negativity toward the arts and artists on the part of a church-related writer must be the result of official morality and dogma—as though the church, even the Roman church, were in any period monolithic, and as though ecclesiastics were not as much part of their culture as anyone else. The Trévoux reviewer's comment, springing from a *secular* assumption about the relative value of theory and practice, points the way toward a more thoughtful and scholarly evaluation of ecclesiastical writers' comments on the arts in all periods.

Because Menestrier, and later Le Jay, are fundamentally concerned with the issue of expressive movement, they often discuss the actions of ballet characters in generally descriptive terms that suggest pantomime. William Carroll, S.J., in his unpublished paper "The Jesuit Impresario," suggests that in the case of Le Jay, at least, the absence of technical dance terminology in his treatise could perhaps be attributed to its being written in Latin, at a time when the contemporary dance vocabulary was French. Even if this accounted for the absence of technical dance terms from Le Jay's work, however, it would not explain the relative absence of dance terms from Menestrier's French treatise. Both of these Jesuit theoretician-producers wrote as they did, not to indicate that their ballets were heavily mimed, but to emphasize their concern as classical aestheticians for expressive movement. Le Jay's words clarify the issue:

> The gestures and motions, moreover, that express more felicitously the subject and approach more closely to nature give more pleasure and demonstrate a more perfect example of art. Accordingly, if you wish to dance the winds, your dancing should be light and headlong, marked with frequent whirls and spins that might imitate eddies of winds. If you represent Vulcan and the Cyclops, [your dancing] should be repeatedly broken up with interruptions and little pauses such as are felt between the blows of the hammer on the anvil. If you present country people, they should beat the ground with a heavy and slow step and use boorish and clumsy movements that the unsophistication of the country brings forth. If you show sorrow on the stage, the dancer should proceed with slow paces; let him at one time raise his

---

[22] *Memoires de Trévoux*, February 1750, 520.

head and hands to the sky; at another let him fold and wring his hands and fix his eyes on the ground; then let him open and unfold his arms; let him be seen to call upon gods and men to share his grief. But if on the other hand you are representing happiness, the dancer should be swift and agile, propelling his feet with repeated leaps, so that he scarcely seems to touch the ground, snapping his fingers, and jumping lightly with his whole body. If you bring forth crazy people or drunks, their movements and carriage should be strange, without order and disturbed, so that they will express mental disturbance. *But let us abstain from things that which pertain more to the dance instructor than to the poet.*[23] [emphasis added]

It is when Menestrier analyzes the quantitative parts of a ballet that we are finally on the threshold of the ballet master's domain. We leave the rarified atmosphere of the ancients and can almost hear the violins and see the dancers practicing their *jetés* and contretemps. These quantitative parts are the ballet's structural elements, the scaffolding on which the expressive images are displayed. The author identifies them as the beginning, or *overture;* the middle section, divided into *entrées;* and the end, the *grand ballet,* which is usually called the *ballet général* in the college-ballet programs.[24] These divisions, he is careful to tell us, correspond to Aristotle's *principium, medium,* and *finis,* in tragedy and epic poetry.[25]

In summary, although Menestrier disagrees with some of the other seventeenth- and eighteenth-century theoreticians on a few points of practice, he stands solidly with most of them in his aesthetic and philosophical position. This suggests that the ballets he and his successors created at Louis-le-Grand were rooted in the same theory and produced by means of the same practices and processes as the ballets seen at court and in the public theaters of Paris. Noverre published his *Letters on Dancing and Ballets* in 1760, the year before the last ballet on the rue Saint-Jacques. The opening of the first letter underlines the shared concerns of Jesuit and non-Jesuit producers:

Poetry, painting and dancing, Sir, are, or should be, no other than a faithful likeness of beautiful nature. It is owing to their accuracy of representation that the works of men like Corneille and Racine, Raphael and Michelangelo, have been handed down to posterity, after having obtained (what is rare enough) the commendation of their own age. Why can we not add to the names of these great men those of the ballet masters who made themselves so celebrated in their day? . . .

---

[23] Le Jay, *De choreis dramaticis,* 822.

[24] Menestrier, *Ballets anciens et modernes,* 257f.

[25] Idem., "Remarques pour la conduite," 55.

A ballet is a picture, or rather a series of pictures connected one with the other by the plot which provides the theme of the ballet; the stage is, as it were, the canvas on which the composer expresses his ideas; the choice of the music, scenery and costumes are his colours; the composer is the painter. If nature have endowed him with that passionate enthusiasm which is the soul of all the imitative arts, will not immortality be assured him?[26]

The Ballets, the Greek Chorus, and the Counter-Reformation

In the preface to his tragedy *Sephœbus Myrsa*, acted at Louis-le-Grand in February 1712, with intermedes called *Morceaux chantés* (Sung fragments), Charles Porée, S.J., wrote, "We warn the public that the acts of this tragedy are separated by French poetry, written for singing, which recalls exactly the choruses of ancient tragedy."[27] These intervals separating the acts of the tragedy were a baroque reincarnation of the ancient Greek chorus. In Greek theater, the chorus sang and danced as it commented on the action of the tragedy.

At Louis-le-Grand this classical theatrical convention was the source of the three kinds of intermedes that developed. Gradually, intermedes that were primarily danced became identified with the August commencement ceremonies. Those that were mostly sung took place in the late winter or early spring, during Carnival season.

Musical productions, especially those that were complete operas, like the 1688 *David et Jonathas*, could also include their own danced intermedes. According to Menestrier, primarily musical shows could be interrupted for entrées of ballet, and most musical productions had three acts plus two ballet intervals.[28] *Récits en musique*, or musical intermedes, were usually more closely related to their dramas than were the ballets, although there was not necessarily any relation between one *récit* and another. The intermedes for *Joseph vendu par ses frères*, probably from the tragedy's March 1698 performance, demonstrate the way these *récits en musique* worked. Musical intermedes did not always have their own titles, as the ballets did. The intermedes for *Joseph vendu* are called simply "Intermèdes chantez à la tragédie de *Joseph vendu par ses frères*" (Intermedes sung at the tragedy of Joseph

---

[26] Jean Georges Noverre, *Letters on Dancing and Ballets*, trans. Cyril W. Beaumont (St. Petersburg: 1803; reprint ed., Brooklyn, N.Y.: Dance Horizons, 1966), 9f.

[27] Lowe, "Répresentations en musique," 24 (translation mine).

[28] Menestrier, *Ballets anciens et modernes*, 207; 265, 268f.

sold by his brothers). As in the ballets, mythological characters appeared, but in conjunction with characters from the accompanying drama. The characters from the drama who appeared in the *récits* were often shown in situations analogous to those in the main piece. In the first musical intermede for *Joseph vendu*, the Shepherds of Israel sing of the untroubled pleasures of rural solitude (scene 1), and Envy and a chorus of Furies plot to ruin their idyll (scene 2). In the second intermede Joseph sings the "Plainte de Joseph dans la cisterne" (Joseph's lamentation in the cistern). He is there because of the hatred and rage inspired in his brothers by Envy and the Furies. In the third intermede a chorus of Israelites mourn Joseph's fate (scene 1); they are joined by the Spirit of Israel, who tells them that all will yet be well (scene 2). It is not clear how these three intermedes were placed in relation to the tragedy's five acts, but one function of all intermedes, including ballet, was to follow the grave denouement of the tragedy with a happy ending.[29] *Joseph vendu* most likely ended with the Spirit of Israel foretelling good fortune.

From 1685 to at least 1688, these February and March *récits en musique* became full-scale operas, comparable to those of Lully and his successors at the Royal Academy of Music. It was necessary for the Jesuits' socially highly placed students to be knowledgeable about this ultrafashionable art form—in the same way that it was necessary for them to be able to dance in ballets at Versailles and other great houses.

The best-known of these operas, and the only one whose score survives, is *David et Jonathas,* composed by Marc-Antoine Charpentier and performed in February 1688 with the tragedy *Saul.* After 1688 early-spring tragedies with musical intermedes continued, but not often on the same operatic scale. On the basis of Lowe's repertory list, the only later opera of which we are certain was *Isaac,* by La Chapelle, performed in May 1734 and called *tragédie en musique,* and again in 1754, when it was called *tragédie-opéra.*

Like secular operas, the college operas included dance. The score of *David et Jonathas* includes music for the baroque-theater dances of the period, including chaconnes, gavottes, and gigues, which were performed during the opera in "five ballets."[30] This could mean either that the opera, intermedes for a Latin tragedy, itself had ballet intermedes, or—what is more likely, given the usual structure of baroque opera—that dance was part of the fabric of the opera's acts.

---

[29] Purkis, "Quelques observations," page reference missing.

[30] William Carroll, S.J., private correspondence with Judith Rock, 1981.

Intermedes could have intermedes of their own. The ballet *Jason*, 1701, intermedes for the tragedy *Daniel*, had its own *récits en musique*. This extravaganza of theater forms was produced to celebrate Philip of Anjou's acquisition of the throne of Spain, and the grand occasion at least partly explains the extra set of intermedes. But it is a case of occasion coinciding with the resources of a highly developed and versatile dramatic and lyric theater. If the term *ballet melé de récits de musique* (ballet mixed with musical narrative), which is how *Jason* was described in its program, can be taken to mean, more or less, a ballet with its own intermedes, then at least two earlier ballets also had intervals of music and singing. These were *Orphée* (Orpheus) in 1690 and *Comus* in 1695. According to Menestrier, it was not unusual for a ballet to have musical intermedes.[31]

In ballets with their own musical intervals, the placement of tragedy, ballet, and *récit* sections in relation to each other is a matter of conjecture. One possibility, taking *Jason* as an example and taking into account Ernest Boysse's assertion that the *récits* served to some degree as a program for the ballet's sections, is as follows: *Récits*, Prologue, followed by *Tragedy*, Act I, *Récits*, part 1, *Ballet*, part 1, and so on in this order through *Tragedy*, Act V.[32] The last act of the tragedy would be followed first by the finale of the *récits*, called a *ballet général*, and then by the grander finale of the ballet itself, also called a *ballet général*.

Whatever lesser role dance played in the primarily musical intermede forms, as full-blown ballet accompanying Latin tragedy, it became and remained the favorite baroque manifestation of the Greek chorus on the Louis-le-Grand stage from the 1660s until the Jesuits fell from favor in 1762.[33] The subjects of the Louis-le-Grand ballets were related, at least obliquely, to the subjects of the tragedies with which they were paired. Each of the tragedy's five acts was followed by one of the four parts of the *ballet d'attache* (the term used for a ballet attached to a tragedy), with the grand finale, or *ballet général*, danced after the fifth act. A *ballet d'attache* shared the tragedy's theme but not its characters. A ballet and its tragedy helped to explain each other. The ballet put some element or dimension of the play into mythological and allegorical dress and transposed it to some extent into the contemporary world. In this transposition, the ballet was often, as *Jason* was, related to a political or social occasion or event.

---

[31] Menestrier, *Ballets anciens et modernes*, 207.

[32] Boysse, *Le Théâtre des jésuites*, 227.

[33] Purkis, "Quelques observations," 198.

Their bringing some element of the tragedy into the contemporary world did not mean, though, that the ballets were what we would call "realistic." Instead, some phenomenon or happening, clothed in classical and allegorical imagery, was presented as part of human experience.

In the ballet-tragedy "marriage," the tragedy is the icon of orthodox Christianity, the edifice of the strict classical aesthetic, and the tool for teaching Latin rhetoric. The ballet, however, is the "real world" gorgeously veiled in layers of allegory. Though many of its characters are gods and ideas, they are there to embody ordinary human feeling and experience. They worry about money, make war, go to parties, consult astrologers, go hunting; they do what people in seventeenth- and eighteenth-century France did.

For example, the 1699 tragedy *Joseph établi vice-roy d'Egypte* (Joseph appointed viceroy of Egypt), about the rise of the biblical Joseph to a position of power because of his skill at interpreting Pharaoh's dreams, was accompanied by a ballet called *Les Songes* (Dreams), by ballet master Louis Pécour and composer André Campra. In the overture, Sleep (the father of dreams) and Night introduce Morpheus, Icelus, and Phantasus into the world. The first part of the ballet is built around the idea that the different "humors" cause different kinds of dreams. Mythological figures appear in each of this part's four entrées to illustrate each "humor" and its characteristic dreams. Achilles, representing the "bilious" temperament, dreams of the murdered Patroclus and plans vengeance. Orestes, the "melancholic," has nightmares after the murder of his mother. The young heroes of Carthage, to whom the goddess Juno sends pleasant dreams, embody the "sanguine" temperament. The "phlegmatic" Alcyone holds a celebration on the seashore in honor of Neptune, to ensure the safe return from the sea of her husband, Ceyx; but in the midst of it, he appears to her in a dream, drowned.

Les Songes' second part is about the dreams people in different occupations have. Again, the characters are mythological. In the first entrée, about the dreams of financiers, Bacchus thanks Midas for a party in his honor, showing him all the gods in a dream. Each god offers protection, and Midas chooses Plutus, god of riches. The second entrée shows a poet dreaming of being welcomed by the poets of ancient Greece. In the third entrée, Hippolyte, the hunter, dreams of a hunting horn calling him to the forest. Hercules, representing soldiers, in the fourth entrée dreams of success in battle.

The influence of the passions on dreams is the subject of the third part of *Les Songes*. Ajax, obsessed with his failure to vanquish Achilles, sees his hated enemies everywhere in his dreams, and fights even with harmless shepherds and their flocks. Orpheus dreams of the lost Eurydice, but when he fails to call her back to him, his love turns to fury. Bellerophon, about to attack the Chimera, dreams of Pallas, who tells him how to succeed in his exploit. The Gauls, fighting the Greeks, see the shades of ancient Greek heroes in their dreams and are so frightened that they use their weapons on themselves.

The last part of the ballet is about superstition and its influence on dreams. The deceits of dreams as sources of help, healing, knowledge of the future, and religious solace are the subjects of the four entrées. These, all set in the ancient world, are meant as contemporary warnings against astrology, superstitious medicine, frivolous morality, and false religion. In the closing *ballet général*, Truth, by means of Light, triumphs over the vanity of dreams. In other words, God's truth is superior to any phantasms of the human imagination.

A ballet's theoretical function, through its thematically unified subject, was to embellish and expand the moral of the Latin drama, as *Les Songes* did for the tragedy about Joseph. Presumably, at least one moral of that tragedy attributed Joseph's rise in the world to God, rather than to a magical ability to interpret Pharaoh's dreams. And so, in the ballet dreams in general are debunked as a source of power.

Most of the ballets are, to our eyes, moral rather than religious, never based on biblical stories and never presenting specifically Christian figures. This was in accord with the *bienséance* or propriety of the period. Although Old Testament stories were appropriated for the tragedies and given New Testament implications, the New Testament itself was not used on the Jesuit-college stage.[34] Menestrier, describing how to costume Faith and Religion as ballet characters, reveals the probable reason for the omission of New Testament stories and characters. He says that Faith and Religion must not carry a chalice or a cross, because it is not appropriate to put the things of the altar on the stage.[35] The New Testament would have fallen under the rubric of "things of the altar." Faith and Religion appear in the ballets, not as devotional symbols, but as ideas assumed to be part of every orthodox Catholic's moral universe.

---

[34] The one possible exception to this is suggested by the title of a comedy played in 1740 at Louis-le-Grand: *Les Talents inutiles* (The useless talents).

[35] Menestrier, *Ballets anciens et modernes*, 256.

It would not have occurred to most Parisian Catholics to separate the concepts of morality, orthodoxy, and devotion. The absence from the ballets of overtly Christian references was the result of propriety and piety, not an endorsement of a general morality or religious pluralism. On the contrary, the Jesuit stage was perhaps one of the last remnants of Christendom in its assumption of orthodox Catholic Christianity as the universal norm.

In creating a religious theater founded on the classical aesthetic, the Jesuits, in a curious way, annexed the classical world as a mission field. On their Counter-Reformation stage, they converted the ancient authors and their culture into "the heralds of Christ."[36] The meeting of classical and biblical characters on the Jesuit stage was more than the theatrical result of their Christian-humanist educational system, their concessions to the fashions of the secular theater, and their desire to be au courant with the visual-art world, whose painters regularly translated Christian subjects into classical terms. In their theater the Jesuits were engaged in the Counter-Reformation enterprise of converting the world to orthodox Catholicism, carrying it backward into time as well as out into the world of the present.

The Jesuits at Louis-le-Grand used the ancient world as a screen on which to project their version of the Christian revelation. The Christian story that was reflected back to their audiences not only gained the sophisticated and cultured thinkers of Greece and Rome as characters and participants, it also put on the classical imagery so familiar and congenial to the Jesuits' audience. Far from being a case of the uneasy meeting of sacred and secular, the mixing of biblical and classical figures on their Paris stage was not unlike what the Jesuits were doing in their missions in China. Patiently learning Chinese and introducing Chinese cultural elements into worship, they attempted to make the new faith congenial to the people of China— and especially to educated Chinese. On the rue Saint-Jacques, they attempted to make a newly reformed Catholicism congenial to upper-class Paris, whose visual and literary imagery—and therefore self-image—was rooted in a version of classical antiquity.

The classical figures were transformed into "the heralds of Christ" with an authority and certainty—one can only say a missionary zeal—that in some measure nonpluses a reader possessed of a modern sense of history. Two early Christmas pastorales, produced

---

[36] A. Douarche, *L'Université de Paris et les jésuites des XVI et XVII siècles* (Paris, 1888), 153.

between 1641 and 1671 in the province of Champagne, illustrate the close interweaving, almost the seamlessness, with which the Jesuits combined the classical and biblical worlds on their stage. In *Magni panis inauguratio*, shepherds, devotees of the great god Pan, hear the angels' announcement of the birth of Christ and become the shepherds of Bethlehem, worshipping at the cradle of the *pain de vie*, the "bread of life." This play on words turns on the literal meaning of the Hebrew *beit lechem*, "house of bread," and on the similar pronunciation in French of "Pan" and "pain." In *Parnassus ex prophano sacer*, the Muses meet together on a Judean mountain to discuss the coming birth of Christ and to debate the respective merits of sacred and profane Latin poetry.[37]

In both of these examples, besides the grandeur of Pan and the Muses, we find rustic characters and rural settings. These pastoral elements, borrowed in part from the Arcadian movement, represent a trend that continued during the second half of the century and that became characteristic of the French Jesuits' knitting together of sacred and classical characters and situations. The Arcadians were an intensely earnest literary circle, begun in 1690 by sophisticates from the Roman salon of the exiled Swedish queen Christina; members were required to own at least a quarter of an acre of land in Greece, to take Greek pastoral names, like Thyrsis and Meliboeus, and to compose only literary idylls.[38] Though its home was in Italy, the Arcadian craze also had its parallels in France. It was part of the artistic and social trend toward a rustic—though becomingly laundered—sweetness and simplicity. (Queen Marie-Antoinette, pretending to be a dairymaid at Versailles, is probably its best-known devotee.) The grand and the bizarre, though still part of theater, and especially part of the ballet, with its machinery and effects, began to share the stage with the pastoral in Louis-le-Grand's musical intermedes and in many of its ballet entrées. These idyllic settings met the fashionable Arcadian criteria, seemed appropriate for the shepherds and peasants of the Bible, and supported the conceit of carefully ordered country simplicity that so attracted the Parisian upper classes and court.

A look at the lyrics from the intermedes for *Joseph vendu* gives the extraordinary flavor of the triple-layered world—classical modulated into Arcadian, biblical, and French baroque—created in this

---

[37] Jacques Hennequin, "Théâtre et société dans les pièces de collège au XVII siècle, 1641–1671," in *Dramaturgie et société, Nancy 14021 avril 1967*, vol. 1 ed. Jean Jacquot (1968), 458.

[38] Ibid., 68.

landscape. The first intermede, sung by the Shepherds of Israel,
begins thus:

> We celebrate the sweetness of our solitude;
> the woods and valleys that charm us!
> Sorrow and uneasiness never come to alarm us.
> In this refuge we are happy, all is tranquil,
> everything responds to our wishes.

> We hear nothing in this grove but the music of
>   water;
> and if the birds add their voices,
> it is only to tell the Echoes
> that in this refuge we are happy, all is tranquil,
> everything responds to our wishes.[39]

A second Shepherd adds,

> One never sees trickling tears,
> except the dew Aurora spills,
> which makes a thousand brilliant flowers bloom.[40]

Two others sing,

> Far from here are cruel pains,
> far from here are sad sighs;
> here only the amiable Zephyrs are allowed
> to make a sweet noise,
> as they tell their innocent desires to the new flowers.[41]

Another Shepherd sings exultantly,

---

[39] *Intermèdes chantez à la tragédie de Joseph vendu par ses frères,* Jesuit
Archives, Chantilly, France: "Celebrons les douceurs de nostre solitude; /
Que ces bois, ces Vallons ont de quoy nous charmer? / Le chagrin et l'inquie-
tude / N'y viennent point nous allarmer. / Dans cet azyle nous sommes
heureuse; / Tout est tranquille, tout repond à nos voeux.

"On n'entend point dans ce brocage / D'autre bruit que celuy des eaux; / Si
les Oyseaux y melent leur ramage, / C'est pour faire dire aux Echoes: / Dans
cet azyle nous sommes heureuse; / Tout est tranquille, tout repond à nos
voeux."

[40] Ibid.: "On ne voit point couler de pleurs, / Que ceux que répand
l'Aurore, / Quand elle fait èclore / Mille brillantes fleures."

[41] Ibid.: "Loin d'icy les peines cruelles, / Loin d'icy les tristes soupirs: /
Il n'est permis qu'aux aimables Zèphirs / D'aller par un doux bruit porter aux
fleures nouvelles / Leurs innocents désirs."

> For us Nature renews herself every year,
> and Spring paves the woods and fields with
>   green.[42]

And a third,

> Ceres and Pomona together
> shower their precious gifts on us,
> and in the autumn,
> Bacchus offers us the sweetness of his liquor.[43]

A Shepherd addresses the sun, which may be the sun as it was revered in the ancient world, the sun as an emblem of Christ, the sun as the symbol of the French King, or all three together:

> O Thou, who bringest light to every clime,
> on your arduous journey through the universe,
> O daystar, do you see in magnificent palaces
> pleasures as perfect as those of our countryside?[44]

Three Shepherds pray,

> O God, who reigns over our beautiful days, spite
>   Envy,
> let nothing in such a peaceful life trouble our
>   hearts.[45]

But God does not hear them. In the next scene, a personification of the sin of Envy and a Chorus of classical Furies plot to destroy the Shepherds' idyll. Their evil actions, which take place offstage, are followed, as we saw in the earlier description of these intermedes, by "Joseph's Lament in the Cistern." In the course of his recitative, he attributes his woes to "implacable envy," presumably his brothers' envy of him. Joseph in the well is as ambiguous—or, rather, allegorical—a figure as the sun whom the Shepherd addresses. Joseph resonates in this layered world as the hero suffering under the

---

[42] Ibid.: "Pour nous la Nature / Se renouvelle tous les ans; / Et le Printemps / Pave de verdure / Les Bois et les Champs."

[43] Ibid.: "Cerès d'accord avec Pomone / Prodigue en ces lieux / Ses dons précieux; / Et dans l'Automne, / Bacchus de sa liqueur / Nous offre la douceur."

[44] Ibid.: "O toy, qui portes la lumière / En tant de climats divers; / En parcourant de l'Universe / La pénible et longue carrière, / Astre du jour, dans ces Palais / Ou regne la magnificence, / Vois tu des plaisirs si parfaits, / Que ceux qui dans nos champs comblent nostre espérance?"

[45] Ibid.: "O Dieu, qui règles nos beaux jours, / En dépit de l'Envie: / Que d'une si paisible vie / Rien ne trouble le cours."

dictates of the gods, as the type of Christ, whom wickedness has attempted to destroy and who has temporarily disappeared into the underworld, and also as the emblem of Louis, repeatedly (in French eyes) attacked by the envious powers of the rest of Europe.

In the third intermede, a Chorus of Israelites, no longer in the Arcadian paradise of the Shepherds, laments all that has befallen Israel. They cry, "Israel, my beloved country . . . in the young Joseph you have lost everything." It is as though the Savior were dead, as though the Dauphin of France were dead, as though Israel *were* baroque France, where to be in favor is everything, and where the personal power of the monarch means not just prosperity or security, but identity for the nation.

All is not lost, however, because in the next scene the Spirit of Israel appears (reminiscent of the gods' messenger, Mercury, and the angel Gabriel). Telling the Israelites to dry their tears, he announces the destiny of Joseph, whose future power and glory will determine the fate of Israel. The Chorus responds,

> May he be loved; may he be revered:
> may his name be great through all the world,
> may he be the father of Israel,
> may his exploits everywhere be sung.[46]

History—one might almost say salvation history—will continue to unfold with honor. A hero is saved, virtue will triumph, and the glory of the Sun King will yet win the day in Europe.

The theorists and librettists at Louis-le-Grand used the ancient and biblical worlds, the classical baroque aesthetic, and contemporary French concerns to create a dense literary and theatrical style that was *itself* meant to be read as an allegory for the Christian narrative. *The style* itself, and not only individual characters, costumes, and stage designs, communicated the Jesuits' Counter-Reformation worldview to their audience. On the Louis-le-Grand stage, all of time and space was the mission field. Not only the cultures of Aristotle and Joseph but *all* cultures, including Louis XIV's and Louis XV's, were cast as heralds and followers of Christ.

In this theatrical world, a ballet served in many ways to *balance* its tragedy. The thematic sympathy of a tragedy with its *ballet d'attache* was very important to the Jesuit dramatists and librettists.

---

[46] Ibid.: "Qu'il soit aimé; qu'on le rèvére; / Que son grand Nom vole en tous lieux; / Que d'Israel il soit le Père, / Et qu'on chante par tout ses exploits glorieux."

But for the spectator, the subject relationship was perhaps the least important element in the ballet-tragedy connection. The ballet whirled the grave concerns of the tragic drama into the richly decorated realm of visual allegory. Each character, prop, and costume had as many associative meanings as a court gown had decorations.

In his *L'Autel de Lyon*, Menestrier drew up a list of contrasts between the ballet and verbal theater, which helps us see what else the ballet provided for the tragedy and for the audience between the acts of the tragedy.

1. Tragedy characters are uniformly noble and heroic, while a single ballet can have characters who are fantastic, comic, serious, or historical.

2. Tragedy follows strict rules of time and logic, but a ballet can present things and characters together that are not found together in the natural world: all the hours of the day or all the seasons of the year can dance together at the same time.

3. Episodes in tragedy happen in the same place, that is, within the same stage setting, but ballet scenery changes as often as possible.

4. Tragedy does not use machinery for visual effects; but such effects, created by means of machinery for the purpose of astonishing and delighting the audience, are an indispensable part of ballet.

5. Tragedy turns on the development and consequences of one important decision or action; many different kinds of actions and events are presented in the course of a ballet.

6. Tragedy is about the same few characters through all its acts; in a ballet, the same character rarely appears twice.

7. Tragedy subjects come from the doings of the great and noble; most ballet subjects come from imagination, myth, and the natural world.[47]

This list of contrasts suggests that the key to the hundred-year relationship of Jesuit-college tragedy and its ballet intermedes lies in the issue of contrast itself. The contrast, of course, was not one of aesthetics. The ballet interludes simply emphasized particular elements of the same classical aesthetic and baroque spirit that motivated the tragedy. In its dance technique and style, in its verses and music, and in its stage design, the ballet offered beauty which, like

---

[47] Menestrier, *L'Autel de Lyon consacrée à Louis Auguste* (Lyon: Jean Molin, 1658), 56.

the beauty of the tragedy, was founded on order, proportion, and harmony. The ballet's beauty was the result of truth, because the point of theater dance was the expression of human feeling and the representation of things from the natural world, all by means of the human body, the most perfect—and therefore the most truthful—of nature's efforts.

The most important contrast the ballet made with the tragedy was that it provided a vehicle for a central tenet of the seventeenth-century version of the classical aesthetic: that visual and literary allegory is an essential part of art. The tragedy revealed characters, actions, and events for what they were; illusion was swept away, and the piece most often ended with catastrophe and death. But in the ballet, logical consequence was relatively unimportant and nothing was simply what it seemed. Truth escaped from tragedy's palaces and battles. She donned a fantastic costume and descended on a pile of stage clouds into a world at once more relaxed and more intricate, where symmetry, order, and grandeur were all at the service of riddle and change.

But the Jesuits were educators and spiritual directors as well as theater producers. When the rue Saint-Jacques audience unraveled the ballet's sparkling allegories, they found themselves, their spiritual loyalties and moral choices, at the center.

two · · · · · · · · · · · · · · · · · ·

THE BALLETS BEHIND
THE SCENES

There is no one like the Jesuits
for doing pirouettes.

—M. Despois, *Le Théâtre français sous Louis XIV*

A Jesuit ballet was conceived in the orderly world of aesthetic theory, but it was born in the emotional whirlwind of theatrical production. When a show goes up, theory and practice have to meet. The crucial question is, "Does it work?" A ballet always made some moral point, but it sought to teach by delighting and entertaining its audience.[1] What happened at Louis-le-Grand in pursuit of these Christian-humanist goals of enlightening and entertaining? How often were ballets produced? Who paid for them? Who composed and staged them? Who danced in them and what did the dancing look like?

The Production Schedule

The annual tragedy and ballet were produced because the *Ratio* directed that the senior class in rhetoric should act a Latin play for their fellow students as part of the commencement prize giving, the grand occasion of the school year.[2] From this modest academic decision, an increasingly elaborate production calendar evolved between the 1660s and the 1750s.

In most years, the performing spaces at Louis-le-Grand hosted a variety of theater forms. Performances during Carnival season (a traditional time for court ballet and other theater) and in August

---

[1] Menestrier, *Ballets anciens et modernes*, 291.

[2] William Carroll, S.J., "The Jesuit Playwright" (unpublished paper), 11.

remained the pattern until 1696, when a June show was added. In most years after 1695, there were between three and five—and occasionally six—theater events at the college. This schedule continued until 1752; after this date the archives reflect at least two presentations each year until the end of the decade. In 1759, 1760, and 1761, the only productions of which there are records were the tragedies with their ballets in late July or early August.

Besides these regular occasions in the school calendar, the Jesuits at Louis-le-Grand also produced quasi-theatrical celebrations for special events, such as the birth or death of an important person or the monarch's recovery from an illness. For example, on August 11, 1721, five days after the annual tragedy and ballet, the college joined all of Paris in celebrating the young Louis XV's recovery from an illness. The Jesuit salute to this occasion included specially composed songs, music, fireworks, and allegorical decorations around the college courtyard. A song which has survived from this fête tells us that there were fireworks and free wine for "the people" all over the city, that the Jesuits' students played games, and that the wealthy among them gave dinners and had music in their rooms. The song begins, "Among the new celebrations admired in Paris, Louis's college put on one of the most beautiful."[3]

One student, the Duke of Tremouille, a relative of the convalescent king, wrote a poem about all the trouble he went to in honor of his kinsman. He built a fireworks display with his coat of arms on top; on either side he put two barrels of wine, dispensed by servers in satyr costumes. He addressed Louis in his poem,

> Powder [meaning gunpowder for fireworks] is very
>   rare at present,
> a thousand times more so than silver or gold:
> To make fire joyous and noisy enough
> I have run all over Paris looking for it!
> "Waterspouts," "sheaves," "suns,"
> I have found very few;
> And I am very tired out from my promenade;
> So, Louis! please don't get sick again![4]

---

[3] *Chanson sur les réjouissances faites au Collège de Louis-le-Grand, le lundy 11 aoust 1721 au sujet de l'heureux retour de la santé du Roy,* Jesuit archives, Chantilly: "Parmi les Fêtes nouvelles / Qu'on admira dans Paris, / Le Collège de Louis / En fit une des plus belles. / Les vive le Roy repetez, / Retentissoient de tous cotez."

[4] *Le Mercure,* August 11, 1721, 355.

In the same article in which Tremouille's poem was quoted, *Le Nouveau Mercure* summed up the Louis-le-Grand celebrations. The report began with the news that André Campra, music master at the college, had given half a dozen concerts in churches recently, and that his *Te Deum* was chanted in the college as part of that day's festivities in honor of the King. Then it described the fireworks in the "grand courtyard," which was completely illuminated in spite of being what the *Mercure* called "vast." In addition, the entire façade of the college on the rue Saint-Jacques was lit, as were the windows of "many young gentlemen"—like the Duke of Tremouille.

These extra celebrations at Louis-le-Grand included elements of theater, and especially of ballet: sumptuous decoration and spectacle, exotic costume, songs, music, and verses. Long before baroque ballet became the vogue in Paris, the Jesuits were creating spectacular public and religious events for their colleges and for towns. Individual members of the Society also served various aristocrats as "masters of ceremonies." Menestrier apparently began his career as an organizer of fêtes, tournaments, and theatrical displays at the Court of Savoy. In the production of these court extravaganzas, the director combined decoration, special effects, music, dance, costume, song, and speech. Menestrier and others brought this expertise to the college ballets, the ballet being the theater form in which this much diversity could flourish without violating the rules of the classical aesthetic.

By the early eighteenth century, frequent productions of drama, music, and dance were well established at the college. But the archives are incomplete. How many productions were there for which we have no records or whose records must be sought in other places? And were Jesuit ballets sometimes performed at court—or vice versa?

For example, there is a certain amount of suggestive confusion around the college ballet of 1661. In two of his letters for February 1661, Loret mentions the court ballet, *L'Impatience* (Impatience).[5] Lowe, who has compiled the most complete repertory list for Louis-le-Grand, has not found a record of the name of that year's August ballet; but Philidor, who preserved some of the Jesuit-ballet scores, gives *L'Impatience* as that year's title.[6] Since Beauchamps was the King's dancing master and creator of court ballets and also ballet

---

[5] Loret, *Muze historique*, Letter 8, February 19, 1661; Letter 9, February 26, 1661.

[6] I found this reference in a French library, but unfortunately have lost my notes giving the details of the citation.

master at the college,[7] the sharing of ballets (though no doubt with censorship of the romantic parts) by the King and the Jesuits does not seem unlikely.

To sum up the college's dance production schedule, most years after 1657 saw a full-blown summer ballet in addition to the dancing which was part of opera, musical intermedes, special events, and—perhaps—comedy (if the Jesuits followed the example of their former student Molière and included dance within the fabric of the play). Exceptions to this pattern occurred in 1683, when Queen Maria Teresa died, and in 1694, a year of war and bad harvests. The year 1694 must have been terrible indeed, because in 1709, a nightmare year of war, sickness, famine, and an empty national treasury, the Jesuits presented not only the annual tragedy and ballet in August but a tragedy with musical intermedes in February, a tragedy in March, and a heroic drama with musical intermedes in June. All of this when the country was so destitute that "the King himself had to have his silver furnishings, his gold plate, and even his throne melted into bullion."[8] François de Dainville, S.J., is certainly correct when he states that by the eighteenth century, theater dominated the lives of the students at Louis-le-Grand.[9]

The Budget

But who paid the bills? Baroque ballet was one of the most expensive theater forms, because its obligatory diversity and lavish production required an endless amount of paraphernalia. When Cardinal Mazarin, astute producer of politically effective ballets during the Fronde uprising, was trying to renovate the Louvre palace in the late 1650s, he calculated that he could realize an extra three hundred thousand livres a year toward his project by temporarily abolishing the court ballet. And so he did.[10]

The college ballets constantly taxed the Jesuits' financial ingenuity. A 1721 letter testifies both to the problem of financing the ballets at a provincial college and to the stratagems resorted to in order to pay the bills:

---

[7] Wendy Hilton, *Dance of Court and Theatre: The French Noble Style, 1690-1725* (Princeton Book Company, 1981), 25.

[8] Maurois, *History of France*, 226.

[9] François de Dainville, S.J., *L'Education des jésuites* (Paris: Minuit, 1978), 478.

[10] John Russell, *Paris* (New York: Harry N. Abrams, 1983), 81.

You will be well-advised to cut the ballet from the college pieces. The Jesuits want it, but it raises the budget by multiplying roles. Seven or eight tragedy roles are not enough, and parents find the sum a little steep; the only thing to do is to get the town to pay. For myself, if I had a voice in the chapter, I would gladly shorten the spectacle. A Father Talon, who used to teach rhetoric in Paris [at Louis-le-Grand], once, in a like case, needed a lot of actors to cover expenses. He pressed parents to consent to the students giving ballets; the mothers agreed, if their sons could be the king. He promised them all that their sons would be "the king" and kept his word by putting on the stage a ballet about all the kings of Japan.[11]

The writer may be referring to the ballet that accompanied the August 1721 tragedy, *Theocaris, Martyr of Japan;* in any case, the letter points to one aspect of the Jesuits' financing of their ballets and plays. The students who acted and danced in them were to some extent responsible for meeting the budget. An eighteenth-century student's college bill from the Jesuit school at Clermont/Ferrand includes the following theater expenses:

For the roles of the tragedy: 24 livres

For the pastorale, given to the "régent" of rhetoric: 10 livres 43

For dancing in the ballet: 6 livres

For the expenses of the piece given at Carnival: 4 livres[12]

Charging students for the privilege of performing, a practice familiar from court ballet, was also done at Louis-le-Grand, royal and other patronage notwithstanding. The students paid a fee, which was actually a share of production expenses, for acting in the tragedy and dancing in the ballet. This meant that, although the ballet raised the cost of theater production, it also provided additional income because it used additional students.

Noble students with starring roles contributed more heavily to production costs than did their lesser schoolfellows, and they also picked up the bill for the lunch accompanying the performance. In addition to contributing to the ballet budget in these ways, the student performers provided or paid for their own costumes; this was no small item of expense, since most dancers played multiple roles during a ballet, and the same costume was rarely allowed to appear twice during a production. The Jansenists periodically accused the Jesuits of making extra money by renting out their theater costumes, of which they must have had an enormous number by the eighteenth

---

[11] François de Dainville, S.J., "Décoration théâtrale dans les collèges de jésuites," *Revue d'histoire du théâtre* 4 (1951): 372 (translation mine).

[12] Ibid., 371.

century. However, at Louis-le-Grand, even with all this student subsidy, the ballet can hardly have been self-supporting. In addition to the grand production scale expected of the Jesuit ballet in Paris, professional dancers were often brought in from the Opéra, and were presumably paid for their work.

Of course, performing groups have always sought to cover at least part of their costs through ticket sales. There is sharp disagreement among researchers on whether, when, and to what segment of the audience the Jesuits charged admission to their theater. The evidence on this point is, so far, contradictory.

According to Dainville, the financial archives of many provincial towns include contributions to the local Jesuit theater, items like "10 livres for the theater of the comedy, for the decoration" (359). It is not clear whether the city of Paris contributed to the Jesuits' productions, either before or after the King became the college's patron in 1682. The monarch, however, did underwrite the ballet, though to what degree is not certain.

Aubin Bourgoin refers to "the enormous expense" of the ballets, and tells us that at some colleges, like La Flèche, the prefect had a special fund to meet theater expenses, and that one of his duties was raising funds to keep this theater account solvent.[13] Between 1617 and 1682 the Paris college was particularly fortunate in the results of its fund raising. They received new gifts from benefactors nearly every year. By 1746 Louis-le-Grand had an income of 44,294 livres, which, even taking into account the inroads of inflation, made it the richest French college.[14] This income provided domestic and scholastic necessities for the Jesuits and their students. However, the opinion of contemporaries was that there was "no luxury" at Louis-le-Grand, neither extra servants, mounted equerries, nor pieces of art, other than those given by benefactors. Strict economy was practiced, so much so that some felt the fathers could almost be accused of "stinginess."[15] But even this stringent domestic economy on what was considered a large income was not enough to protect the college from financial difficulty. Detailing France's economic vagaries during the period, Dupont-Ferrier elegantly sums up the Jesuits' economic

---

[13] Aubin Bourgoin, *Histoire des représentations théâtrales dans les lycées et collèges* (La Roche-sur-Lyon: 1897), 17f.

[14] Dupont-Ferrier, *Vie quotidienne d'un collège*, 93.

[15] Ibid., 93f.: "Aucun luxe: ni serviteurs étrangers, ni écuries montées, ni objets d'art, en dehors de ceux qu'offraient de généreuses amitiés. Une economie stricte. Si bien qu'on ne manquait pas d'accuser les Pères de ladrerie."

problems by saying that they were like many great nobles: they saw the King, spoke with his ministers, and had debts.[16]

How are we to understand the Jesuits' lavish outlay of time and money on ballet production in the light of these somewhat contradictory financial realities? First of all, they did not regard the ballet as a frivolous or extra activity, to be dispensed with when the budget was tight. Second, they preferred grand public events to domestic comfort. Many writers on French court life of the seventeenth and earlier eighteenth centuries mention the surprising degree of personal discomfort with which even royalty lived at home. Palaces were built for *gloire*, for display, not for coziness and domestic ease. Likewise, the Jesuits and their students at Louis-le-Grand apparently saw nothing odd about financing the ballet while living in a probably similar degree of discomfort and austerity. In these centuries, public display was nearly always valued over personal convenience.

In the arts, and especially in the performing arts, finances are—and apparently always were—a problem. Financing the college theater was a constant worry, exacerbated in some years by war and an empty national treasury. Nevertheless, drama was staged at the college no matter how dire France's situation, and the ballet was produced in all but one desperate year. This fine disregard for the state of the budget by the theatrical directors drew repeated protests from Jesuit superiors—and sometimes from the Louis-le-Grand professors themselves. Jouvancy wrote scathingly about the enthusiasm of his younger colleagues for spending money on productions which, in his opinion, did not always merit the outlay:

> The prudence of young professors leaves something to be desired. They imagine they have staged an excellent tragedy when the decors are magnificent, the costumes covered with gold, and the music delicious: what can magnificent trappings do for a skinny horse?[17]

The Libretto

Molière said that he invented his comedy-ballet form because there were only a few good dancers available, and they needed time to change costumes between ballet entrées. Instead of putting the dancing in intermedes, where groups of danced entrées followed each other quickly, he scattered dances throughout the play, so the danc-

---

[16] Ibid.: "En somme, notre collège avait ce point de ressemblance avec les grands seigneurs du temps: il voyait le roi, parlait aux ministres et avait des dettes" (95).

[17] Dainville, "Décoration théâtrale," 371 (translation mine).

ers could change clothes between one appearance and the next.[18] The creative process, so mysterious and impressive, is usually shaped, to a larger degree than we care to acknowledge, by just such prosaic elements.

A ballet at Louis-le-Grand was created by a member of the faculty, usually a professor of rhetoric, like Le Jay, who wrote the libretto for *L'Espérance* (Hope) in 1709. The librettist, or "inventor" of the ballet, needed to be a person of parts. According to Menestrier, the composer of ballets must know music, poetry, geometry, natural philosophy, and rhetoric in order to preserve true cadences, observe movement, and express the quality of things, actions, and feelings.[19]

This polymath began by choosing a subject. Menestrier's principal rule on this point was that the subject must be ingenious and pleasing. An ingenious subject lent itself to a well-constructed libretto and "natural" ballet entrées. By "natural" he meant that each entrée must be about something really associated with the subject. The ballet subject was judged pleasing when it allowed a good mix of comic and serious characters and events, of myth and history, and of reality and fantasy.[20]

Menestrier advised the librettist to remember that all subjects are wholes made up of parts. So, when Le Jay chose "hope" as his subject in 1709, he then had to decide upon and order its parts. This ordering was begun by identifying a mythological foundation for the subject and by basing the ballet's "plot" on an ancient writer. The mythological framework and ancient source for a ballet became the allegorical veil for its references to current events and morality.

L'Espérance, for example, contained a lively thread of *actualité*, or current events. (*Actualité*, suggested by Carroll as the term for this dimension of the ballets, is the word used today for the French evening television news.) The year 1709 was beset by war, plague, and famine, and people urgently needed the counsel of hope. The story of Pandora's disastrous box, at the bottom of which hope was found, was the perfect allegory for this *actualité*. When Le Jay wrote his treatise on dance sixteen years later, he stated that ballet *must* be cast in the form of allegory because "dance lies in the realm of imitation."[21] Because its function is to imitate, it must appear to be *like* something from myth, history, or imagination.

---

[18] Hilton, *Dance of Court and Theatre*, 25.

[19] Menestrier, "Remarques pour la conduite," 50.

[20] Menestrier, *Ballets anciens et modernes*, 52f.

[21] Gabriel Le Jay, "De choreis dramaticis," chap. 5.

Hope accompanied the tragedy *Joseph agnoscens fratres* (Joseph recognizing his brothers), also by Le Jay. In the biblical story, Joseph, sold into slavery in Egypt, has risen to the position of steward to Pharaoh, and his brothers come to Egypt during a famine in Israel to buy grain from him. Like the French, they are suffering from the evils of Pandora's box, and have nothing left but hope. As Jouvancy directed in the *Bibliotheca rhetorum* in 1728, each part of the ballet was meant to reinforce the feelings stirred up by the preceding act of the tragedy, and to prepare the audience for the action of the next act, while also "filling out the time with wholesome diversion."[22]

With these points of contact between his tragedy and his ballet subject established and these orientations for his *actualité* and his allegory chosen, Le Jay divided his subject into parts and entrées, which were to the ballet what acts and scenes were to the tragedy. The maximum number of parts allowable to a ballet was five; the total number was decided on the basis of the subject's requirement. Le Jay decided on four parts, representing the four aspects of French life where hope was most needed: agriculture, commerce, the arts, and war.

Each part was then given several entrées. The usual number was between four and six. *L'Espérance* has three entrées in each part, perhaps because there was little money in the production budget. Many of the entrées of a ballet were created especially for it. But old entrées were also often used, refurbished with new dances and contemporary *actualité*. This practice led Menestrier to grumble about stock ballet characters, wishing that games, zephyrs, amours, Scythians, Libyans, foreigners in general, Cyclopes, Silvains, and shepherds would not show up on the stage quite so often.[23]

Although Menestrier felt that a ballet attached to a tragedy did not need an overture, the Jesuit ballets had overtures by at least the 1680s. The overture presented the subject by sung or spoken verse. In his "De choreis dramaticis," Le Jay wrote that because silent communication has limits, song and speech introduce the ballet's plot, explain to the audience what the dancing, costumes, and settings cannot explain, and rest the visual and movement senses by appealing to the hearing and intellect. The overture section also set a tone of grandeur for the piece, presenting the ballet's title character accompanied by a suite of followers. Stage machines were often used in this section, because they helped to create an atmosphere of marvels, and piqued the audience's excitement and expectations.

---

[22] William Carroll, S.J., "The Jesuit Impresario" (unpublished paper), 11.

[23] Menestrier, *Ballets anciens et modernes*, 301.

In *L'Espérance*'s overture section, Pandora opens her box, and its evils (who are her suite of followers) escape into the world. Stage machinery may have been used, as the libretto tells us that the evils make themselves felt "in the air, on the ground, and on the seas."[24] However, there is a note in the margin of the libretto that apologizes for the lack of splendor in that year's ballet, owing to the difficult financial situation; so it may be that machinery and special effects were kept to a minimum. The ballet's title character, Hope, is presented at the end of Pandora's second speech, after the escape of the evils. She says, "Be consoled, mortals; Hope remains with you."[25]

The libretto continues with a paragraph explaining the "division of the ballet," or the way it has been shaped into its four parts. The action of each part is about the promises the central character, Hope, makes to that part's presiding god or goddess. These promises are related to the subject of "hope" in that they are real things people in France were hoping for as they suffered the ravages of Pandora's evils in 1709. They are, in that sense, "natural" elaborations of the subject and will ensure "natural" entrées in the ballet.

In the first part, an allegory about the state of French agriculture, Hope promises Ceres, the earth goddess, that abundance will succeed famine. Ceres bewails her frozen and desolate empire in the first entrée. In the second, Bacchus, Flore, Pomone, and Vertumne mourn that there is only water to drink and that nothing is growing—neither flowers, trees, nor foodstuffs. After their speeches, they dance. In the third entrée, the people of the countryside make a sacrifice to Hope, with songs, an instrumental "symphony," and three dances: "the pleading shepherds," "the frightened shepherds," and "the joyous shepherds." Hope promises that abundance will return, and the entrée ends with a dance of all the rustic divinities.

Plutus, god of riches, presides over the second part of the ballet; Hope promises him that prosperity and ease will return to France. In the first entrée, Harpies chase him and he hides. In the second, Games and Pleasures (for which people will pay in prosperity) search for him to help him return to "business." But greedy old men (those who profit from war) keep him captive. Hope proclaims that she alone will avenge Plutus, and in the next entrée she brings in

---

[24] *L'Espérance*, Yf 2571, 2572 (Bibliothèque nationale, Paris), Overture entrée: "Pandore ouvre la Boete fatale. Aussitost la Sterilité, les Maladies, l'Oisivité, la Discorde, la Guerre et mille autres Monstres se font sentir dans l'air sur la terre, et sur les mers."

[25] Ibid.: "Consolez-vous, Mortels, l'Espérance vous reste."

a troupe of Mexicans bearing gold ingots (the wealth of the New World) as his ransom.[26]

The librettist has not indicated dances in this part of the ballet, though there is a great deal of action. It is possible that this was a primarily dramatic and pantomimic section, as there are many speeches and no singing. There are occasional indications in the Jesuit literature on dance that one of the ballet master's responsibilities was the arrangement of pantomime sequences for the ballets. It is also possible that the ballet master added to the number of dances requested by the librettist.

Apollo, protector of the arts, is the god who presides over the ballet's third part. Hope has promised that she will restore the arts, which are languishing in the rain of disasters. In the first entrée, Terpsichore, goddess of dance, brings the other arts in her "suite." She addresses them thus: "Dance, Music, and Choruses, give the Theater its glamor. . . . Make a pleasing blend of the comic and the serious . . . on this august day make a new effort to show what you can do."[27] She finishes her speech with a dance "mixing the comic and the serious." But her dance is interrupted by the sound of warlike music, and she complains that Mars, the god of war, is ruining the arts. In the second entrée, painters, architects, and a comic peasant leave their work and follow Mars because they cannot make a living. The third entrée shows Parnassus, home of the arts, in disarray. Apollo laments that the Muses sing only sad songs and the Poets throw away their laurel crowns and tear up their poems. His song is followed by an ensemble of poets dancing their despair. But Hope encourages them all, and they return to their normal occupations.

The last part, under the auspices of Peace, the deity for whom everyone longs, draws together all the warring people, whose struggle has so deranged France's national life. Mercury, the messenger of Jupiter (who is an allegory for Louis XIV), calls all the combatants together. But Discord creeps among them again and tries to destroy what Mercury—and Jupiter—have created. In the second entrée, the people, wanting harmony, take up arms against Discord. But she is triumphant, holding Peace captive. Hope reassures everyone that, though Discord is making a final effort, they will soon have Peace.

---

[26] Ibid., part 1, second entrée: "Mais esperons que quelque Dieu propice s'interessant pour les humains, de ces Usurpateurs punira l'injustice."

[27] Ibid., part 3, first entrée: "C'est à la Danse, à la Musique, C'est à l'agrement de mes Choeurs Que le Théâtre doit ce qu'il a de douceurs. . . . Donnez un mélange agréable Du Comique et du Sérieux. . . . Montrez par un nouvel effort, Dans cet auguste jour ce que vous sçavez faire."

Then Peace appears, seated on a cloud and singing that she has set Hope to reign in her place until she returns to the earth.

In the closing *ballet général*, everyone pays homage to Hope, the regent of Peace, who has delivered all from the evils of Pandora's box. *Ballet finales*, also referred to by Menestrier as *grands ballets*, were composed entirely of dance and music. They had more dancers than any single entrée, and longer and more complex dances. Usually all or most of those who had danced during the ballet reappeared in the *ballet général*, though not, except for the title character, in their former roles. The finale had, to some extent, its own theme, so that it was like a coda to the four or five parts of the ballet. It therefore demanded new characters, costumes, and setting.

Having divided his scenario into the overture, parts, entrées, and *ballet général*, and laid out the action to take place in each, the librettist then wrote the spoken verse for the ballet. This was theoretically considered the *least* important task, partly because the verses were in French rather than Latin.

Once the poetry was written, the librettist's solitary work was done. He had created the scaffolding for the five aspects of a ballet's creation: idea, characters, characterization, harmony, and decoration.[28] In the collaborative style inherited from court ballet, he now became the project director, overseeing the work of a group of other specialists as the theatrical details of his structure were fleshed out. Le Jay specified that the librettist was responsible for helping the ballet master and dancers interpret the libretto and for coordinating music, scenery, costumes, and stage machinery to give the production a "unity of tone."[29]

The collaboration with major and minor theater artists that the Jesuit librettist initiated and oversaw was the source of much of the grandeur and originality of ballet in the Jesuit theater. The librettist began immediately to work with "the technicians," as the ballet master and musical composer were called. The ballet master translated the libretto's ideas and situations into dances and also into occasional pantomimic sequences, where the action called for them. The composer, in collaboration with both the ballet master (who was also a musician) and the librettist, wrote or scored the music—for the overture, dances, and other points where music was needed to carry the action along—and also wrote the lyrics of the ballet's songs.

---

[28] Menestrier, *Ballets anciens et modernes*, 143.

[29] Carroll, "Jesuit Impresario," 4f.

In the Jesuit ballets, as in the court ballets, the dance entrées and pieces of music were sometimes parceled out among several ballet masters and composers. This may have been in response to any number of practical constraints, such as available rehearsal time, the schedules of various artists, specialty of styles, and so forth. For example, in 1711 the dances in *Apollon législateur* (Apollo the law-maker) were by two ballet masters, Joseph Blondy and Pécour. In 1718 the music for the third and fourth entrée (of which part, we are not told) of *L'Art de vivre heureux* (The art of living happily) was by André Campra. On some occasions, the professional dancers who appeared as guest artists composed their own dances.

The librettist-director also collaborated with costume designers and designers of sets and machinery. These artists are not named in the Jesuit programs, but because the visual elements and stage effects of ballet were so important to its success, the Jesuits must have taken the same care in choosing them as they did in choosing their ballet masters.

In addition to his work with set designers, the author of the piece was expected to direct the construction of the scenery. Then as now, theater directing in any of the performing arts was a hands-on affair. Franz Lang, who was playwright and director at the Jesuit theater in Munich (one of the largest theaters in western Europe) and the author of the eighteenth-century Jesuit handbook on acting, warned his colleagues that they needed *personal* experience as both actors and stagehands.

> If some directors think that manual work is beneath their dignity, or if they think they can direct a play from an armchair, let them say good-bye to the stage and pound a chair in a classroom where they may receive more applause than from playgoers.[30]

In 1686 the August tragedy and, apparently, the ballet were by Jouvancy. A letter from the Jesuit Talon to the Prince of Condé, written from Louis-le-Grand and dated August 6, 1686 (the day before that year's prize-giving performance), describes the nearly around the clock efforts of the director to complete the scenery and attend to other production details:

> From four o'clock in the morning to nine in the evening, we live in the Tower of Babel here, where, on my life, I have never heard such an uproar; the day had scarcely appeared this morning, when, having a need to leave my room, I found little Father Jouvancy, in his little jerkin and cap, followed by ten or twelve big rascals, all in their night-

---

[30] Carroll, "Jesuit Playwright," 17.

shirts, going to assault various corners of the theater and give the first alarms of their clatter.[31]

One of the reasons the University of Paris eventually banned school theater from its program was the amount of preparation time needed for productions. Carroll states that the annual August tragedy and ballet were rehearsed for a full year.[32] Dupont-Ferrier suggests that three months or so was the usual rehearsal time for a major show.[33] That this was adequate time for the preparation of a full-scale baroque ballet is suggested by a paragraph in the August 1721 *Nouveau Mercure*, which informed readers that a court ballet, to be given "after All Saints Day," was in the process of preparation.

Three months to create and rehearse a five-act Latin tragedy and a complete ballet cannot have meant a leisurely production period. Though the study of Latin was a major part of the students' curriculum and though expert ballet masters staged the ballets, all of the actors and many of the dancers were children and teenagers with limited experience and varying degrees of talent. The rehearsal period for a show that, in its finished state, could be anything from three to six hours in length could cause a nearly complete cessation of studies.[34] But the preparation time was usually seen as a legitimate part of the students' training in rhetoric and dance, as well as being a productive investment in public relations. However, not all the public reaction was favorable. The Jansenists periodically complained because some rehearsals took place on the Opéra stage—which those pietists saw as a spiritually dangerous place.[35]

---

[31] Dupont-Ferrier, *Vie quotidienne d'un collège*, 299f.: "Nous sommes ici des les quatre heures du matin jusqu'a neuf heures du soir, dans la tour de Babel, ou, de ma vie, je n'ay ouy un si grand tintamare; et a peine le jour a-t-il paru, ce matin, qu'ayant été contraint de sortir de ma chambre, le petit P. Jouvency, avec son petit justaucorps et son bonnet enfancé dans sa teste, suivy de dix or douze grands coquins, tous en canessons et en chemise, s'en alloient donner l'assaut a quelques coings du théâtre et donner les premieres alarmes de leurs charivaris."

[32] Carroll, "Jesuit Impresario," 13.

[33] Dupont-Ferrier, *Vie quotidienne d'un collège*, 298.

[34] In his *Recherches sur les théâtres de France* (1735), Pierre François de Beauchamps states that the interminable length of a tragedy and its intermedes led to the eighteenth-century vogue for shorter theater pieces, such as the one-act tragedy.

[35] Raymond LeBègue, "Les Ballets des jésuites," *Revue de cours et conférences* 37, no. 2 (1936): 138.

Beyond the specific shape that the librettist-director gave to a ballet, how did the structure of the Jesuit ballets change over time? The best sources for studying the elaboration of the ballet's form are the libretti and programs that have survived. The Jesuit college, like other colleges, had been using programs for its ballets since the 1650s. The custom of giving out programs to theater audiences originated in the baroque-college practice of giving programs to the audience at public displays of rhetorical skill. "Programme" is defined in at least one seventeenth-century dictionary as "a college term."[36] Programs and libretti do not give identical information about the ballets. The libretti tell us more about basic structure, action, and characters. Programs, especially the later ones, often contain the ballet's spoken and sung poetry, the names of the dancers in relation to the roles they played, descriptions of dances as solos, duets, trios, and the like, and the name of the ballet master. Unfortunately, it is not always possible to consult both the libretto and the program for every ballet. The elaboration of the structural elements of the ballets becomes fairly clear if, using available programs and libretti, we compare the structure and details of several ballets taken from different parts of our hundred-year period.

According to the program of *Le Destin* (Fate), danced in 1669, the ballet had four parts, each with six entrées. It had a cast of eight students and, apparently, no guest performers. The librettist's name is not listed, but one program names Beauchamps as ballet master and composer. The libretto of *Comus*, performed in 1695, stated that the ballet had five acts (rather then "parts"), whose number of entrées varied between five and seven. Le Jay was the author, but we do not know who created the dances and the music. The student cast numbered fifteen; no guest artists are mentioned. *L'Espérance* (1709) had a musical overture and an overture entrée, four parts with three entrées each, and a closing *ballet général*. The libretto includes the verses and songs which were part of the entrées. The author again was Le Jay, the dances were by Pécour, and La Chapelle wrote the music. We do not know the number of student dancers, but there were at least four guest dancers from the Opéra. In 1749, *Les Héros de roman* (The heroes of fiction) was given with the August tragedy. The ballet program states that there were a musical overture and three overture entrées, four parts with three entrées each, and a *ballet général*. There is no indication that the entrées included speeches or songs; but it is likely that they did, since it was still the fashion in the mid-eighteenth

---

[36] A. Furetiere, *Dictionaire universel* (The Hague and Rotterdam, 1701), s.v. "programme."

century for ballets to mix dancing, singing, and speaking. The dances in *Les Héros* were by Louis Dupré; the program does not tell who wrote the libretto or composed the music. The twenty-five students who performed in this ballet were outnumbered nearly two to one by the forty-nine Opéra professionals with whom they shared the stage.

At least four changes in the ballets' structure emerge from this comparison of four ballets created between 1669 and 1749. First, the productions became longer. In spite of Menestrier's statement that when a ballet comprises the intermedes for a tragedy, it does not need an overture, many of the Jesuit ballets attached to tragedies did have overtures and overture entrées.[37] The addition of overture, overture entrées, and a long *ballet général* contributed to the visual spectacle of the performance and provided more opportunities for dancing. The second noticeable change is in the increased importance of speaking and singing in the ballets, especially during the first thirty years or so of the eighteenth century. Third, the cast increased dramatically: from the eight dancers of *Le Destin* to the seventy-four who appeared in *Les Héros*. And fourth, as the ballets became more elaborate and the dancers and ballet master became the real stars of the August productions, they are more frequently and more fully acknowledged in the programs.

One key to understanding the structure of a Louis-le-Grand ballet is its relation to the school's prize-giving ceremony. Eyewitness accounts of the event sometimes say that the prizes were given out "after the piece," which means after the *ballet général*, which followed the solemn fifth act of the tragedy and made a celebratory finish to the action. Often, between 1640 and 1674, when the ballet was less elaborate, the academic prizes were given out before or in the absence of the *ballet général*, and the prize giving itself made the happy ending to the tragedy. Apollo distributed laurel crowns and books to the young winners and called on the Muses to sing the praises of the donor of the prizes. In this period, at the Jesuit college there were various benefactors to be praised, but from 1682 the donor was the King.

Prize giving could also be part of the *ballet général*, in which case the distribution itself became an interval within the finale. A third option was to make the giving of the prizes part of the idea and action of the ballet. A very early instance of this choice was at Caen in 1628, when the ballet theme was youth at various ages trying to defeat ignorance and the other enemies of learning. The victors were rewarded for their triumphs, as Apollo distributed prizes after each of

---

[37] Menestrier, *Ballets anciens et modernes*, 265.

the ballet's parts.[38] A similar structure was devised at Louis-le-Grand over a hundred years later, when *Curiosité* (Curiosity) was given in 1737. "Good" and "bad" aspects of curiosity were presented, and the students who had done well because of their "good" curiosity were rewarded.

It is important to remember that in spite of all its theatrical glitter, the ballet, along with the tragedy, was created to be the setting for this prize-giving ceremony. The lavish production values of the Louis-le-Grand stage were, on one level at least, meant to be a tribute to the royal donor of the academic prizes, to honor outstanding students and their families, and to call attention to the excellence, taste, and social position of the college.

The Ballet Masters

To please the King and enhance the college ballets, the Jesuits commissioned spectacular dances from their ballet masters, dances worthy of the splendid decor, costumes sparkling with jewels, and the astonishing stage machinery gracing their theater.[39] In the same spirit in which they invited Molière's actors to rehearse their students in declamation, the faculty of Louis-le-Grand guaranteed that the dances for their ballets would be spectacular by employing the most accomplished dancing masters in France to create them.[40] While three of these ballet masters—Beauchamps, Pécour, and Dupré—worked for the Jesuits, they were also directors of the Royal Academy, which later became the Paris Opéra.

There had been dancing masters in the French Jesuit colleges since at least 1604. In that year, at the college in Lille, several "players of instruments," paid by the town, came to the college four or five times a week to teach dancing to the students and to play at rehearsals for an upcoming February performance.[41] Between 1600 and 1638 dancing masters seem to have been hired on a piecework basis, preparing the students to perform in the annual prize giving, for royal visits to the college or the town, at the consecration of a new church, and on regular Church-festival days. In the second half of the century, as the ballets became an increasingly important part of the

---

[38] Purkis, "Quelques observations," page reference missing.

[39] McGowan, *L'Art de ballet*, 224.

[40] Dainville, "Décoration théâtrale," 370.

[41] Ibid., 208.

college theater, ballet masters began to appear in college records as regular employees.[42]

Beauchamps, the first regular ballet master at the Paris college of whom we know, was a supremely gifted dance professional, accomplished musician and composer, second director of the Royal Academy of Dancing, composer of the King's ballets, and Louis XIV's personal dancing teacher. Beauchamps came from a long line of "ménetriers" or dancing masters-fiddlers; the words were synonymous, since a dancing master also had to be an accomplished violinist. Conversely, musicians were often dancers. Jean Baptiste Lully, the great Italian-turned-French violinist who became the autocrat of seventeenth-century French music, was also a dancer with professional technique.

In order to be recognized as a dancing master in the seventeenth and eighteenth centuries, a boy began his six-year training period when he was about eight years old. (Women do not appear to have been officially recognized as professional teachers and choreographers, though they did teach and choreograph, in addition to dancing professionally.) At fourteen, he took demanding examinations under the supervision of the Corporation des Ménetriers, the musicians' guild, which had also been the professional guild of dancing masters since the fifteenth century. If he passed, he became known as a "maître à danser" or "maître de danse." By his late teens, the successful candidate was performing and teaching professionally.[43]

Beauchamps went through this system of training, eventually becoming the director of the new Royal Academy of Dancing's supervising board of thirteen established masters. The Academy had been created by the King on March 30, 1661, as the dancing masters' new guild—a reflection of the increasing importance of the ballet.

Hiring Beauchamps as their ballet master meant that the Louis-le-Grand faculty commissioned choreography from the major figure in seventeenth-century French dance. It was Beauchamps who fixed the five dance positions, still the basis of ballet technique, and who developed the first flexible and usable form of dance notation. Dances notated in his system furnish us with most of our technical information about baroque dance. When one of his collaborators, Raoul

---

[42] Ibid., 209. Ballet masters at Louis-le-Grand from the late 1660s until 1760: Pierre Beauchamps, late 1660s to 1697; Louis Pécour, 1699-1711; Joseph Blondy, 1698-1715; Froment, 1720-1724; de Laval and Malter the elder, in collaboration, 1726-1730; Malter the elder, 1735-1745; Louis Depré the elder, 1748-1750; Rivière, 1755; le Voir, 1758-1760.

[43] Hilton, *Dance of Court and Theatre,* 24f.

Feuillet, more or less pirated the ballet master's system and published it in 1700, the editors of the Jesuits' *Trévoux* journal published a protest on Beauchamps' behalf.[44]

In addition to creating the dances for the majority of the Louis-le-Grand ballets between 1669 and 1697, Beauchamps also composed much of the music and even conducted the orchestra—as he had done for Molière when they collaborated on *Les Fâcheux* (The bores) in 1661.[45] One of the important sources of information about the nature of the ballets on the Paris college stage is the record of their ballet masters' and composers' work in other settings. The collaborations of Beauchamps, for example, with Molière and Lully, the principal dramatist and the principal musician of the period, suggest that his work for the Jesuit stage was probably in a similar style. The dancing in the ballets at Louis-le-Grand was "cut from the same cloth" as the dancing in Molière's comedy-ballets and the dancing in Lully's opera-ballets.

Because Beauchamps was for nearly thirty years the dancing master for the rue Saint-Jacques ballets, it is more than likely that at least some of the dances from those ballets were notated. The Jesuits themselves, interested in new scientific systems in all areas of knowledge, were aware of and interested in Beauchamps's system of writing dance, as is evident from their journal's several references to Feuillet's book. The sharing of ballet entrées among colleges and sometimes reusing them at Louis-le-Grand also point to the practicality of preserving the dances in notation. Even if the dancers themselves could not read the notation, Beauchamps could, and would thereby have saved himself work by occasionally reusing dances and their music. We do not know exactly when learning to read Beauchamps's notation became a normal part of the training of baroque dancers; but the English dancing master Kellom Tomlinson, in his 1735 *Art of Dancing,* uses the notation, and asserts that learning to play musical instruments by ear and to "dance without book" are bad practices; he offers to teach young dancing masters "the art of dancing and writing by characters."[46]

Unfortunately, none of this supposed notation for the Jesuit ballets has survived. Unless it exists in some forgotten archive or in some undiscovered box in a Paris cellar, it probably met the same fate as did the contents of many Jesuit libraries when the order was

---

[44] Christout, *Ballet de cour,* 180.

[45] Astier, "Pierre Beauchamps and the *Ballets de Collège,*" *Dance Chronicle* 6 1983): 142-44.

[46] Hilton, *Dance of Court and Theatre,* 44.

suppressed in 1773. Civic authorities confiscated whole collections of books and papers. Innumerable music manuscripts were lost, burned, or, as happened at the German College in Rome, sold to butchers and fish peddlers as wrapping paper.[47]

The Dancers and Their Vocabulary

When Beauchamps and his successors chose dancers, amateur or professional, what qualities did they look for? How could a ballet master tell if a young student would be worth the time and trouble it took to teach him the style, the vocabulary, and the thousand subtleties of performing? Michel de Pure recommended that the ballet master look first for someone with a strong constitution. The prospective dancer must also have the time, inclination, and discipline to submit to constant practice. In addition, there must be evidence of a good ear for music, physical grace, a lively facial expression, a subtle intelligence, and the quick observation and responsiveness that result in versatility.[48] These requirements for a dancer have changed hardly at all over the last three centuries.

The Louis-le-Grand ballets were danced by students from the rhetoric class and often by professionals from the Opéra. There were three student performing groups at Louis-le-Grand: the rhetoric students who acted in the tragedies and danced in the ballets every summer; a second group for the Carnival shows; and a group from the youngest class, who performed in the comedies. According to Carrol, to be admitted to any one of these three troupes was the reward for long months of apprenticeship and preparation (140).

Within the rhetoric troupe, dancers would have been chosen for principal ballet roles on the basis of technical competence and general suitability for the serious or comic nature of the part. Social rank probably also influenced the casting. If two members of the dance "company" had equal technique and presence, it is likely that the one of higher rank was cast in the more important role, as a compliment to his family and the "beau monde" who attended the ballet—and to enhance the school's social prestige. Prize giving probably influenced casting as well. A talented dancer receiving a prize during the afternoon may have been specially featured in the ballet, as an extra reward for good work.

At some Jesuit colleges, a place was apparently found in the cast—if only in the back row of the ensemble—for all the students of

---

[47] Carroll, "Jesuit Playwright," 35.

[48] Ibid., 140.

the class presenting that year's ballet.[49] But at Louis-le-Grand, the performances were not usually seen as opportunities to put every member of a class onstage, regardless of ability. The commencement-day tragedy and ballet, when the college was on display for a theatrically discriminating and socially elite audience, was not a time for indulgent casting. The number of students in ballet cast lists for performances between 1654 and 1749, varies from eight to twenty-six, with fourteen or fifteen being the average number. These small numbers of student performers reflect the selection process that determined student casting.

The names of the students dancing in a ballet were listed at the back of the program, under the heading "Names of the Dancers" or "They Shall Dance in the Ballet." For ballets with *récits*, like *Jason*, 1701, the programs include two separate cast lists: "Reciting Actors" and "Dancing Actors." The heading at the back of the program for *Le Portrait de la nation françoise* (Portrait of the French nation), 1738, may cast light on the problem of what was done with boys who, for whatever reason, needed to be included in the ballet but were not good dancers. That year, the student cast list, which has twenty-three names, is titled "Dancing or Playing a Role in the Ballet." The distinction probably refers to dramatic roles in pantomime entrées. At the bottom of the 1738 cast list are also the names of four students who were recognized for "Speaking the Prologues of the Ballet." Though they are not indicated in the program, these prologues were the spoken "program notes" which sometimes were given as brief but elegant rhetorical pieces before each section of the ballet. This was another way in which members of the rhetoric class who were better at speaking than at dancing could be part of the ballet.

The names of the Opéra dancers were not listed separately at the end of the program, as the students' were, although as time went on, a dancer's name was included under or beside the description of each entrée in which he appeared. It is not clear how often Opéra dancers were included in the cast, but by the end of the seventeenth century, some ballets included more professionals than students. In 1698, in addition to its seventeen student performers, the *Ballet de la Paix* (Ballet of peace) presented eighteen Opéra dancers (including, perhaps, the young Froment who later became ballet master at the college). In 1749 *Les Héros de Roman* (The heroes of romance) had twenty-six students and forty-nine dancers from the Opéra. The ballet programs for 1701, 1706, 1715, 1736, 1738, and 1748 include the names of professional dancers. In 1748 *Nouvelles ecclésiastiques* complained

---

[49] Carroll, "Jesuit Impresario," 8.

that the ballet, *Le Grand Monarque* (The great king) was danced by "the best dancers and jumpers of the Opera" and a very small number of students from the college.[50] Among the Opéra dancers at Louis-le-Grand that year was the renowned Vestris, the mid-eighteenth-century "god of the dance."[51]

Opéra dancers were probably part of the ballets on many occasions, because of the relationship of the college and the Opéra through the ballet masters. In his repertory list, Lowe includes a note from the 1725 ballet program which informed the spectators that "the dances performed by the gentlemen from the Opéra were created by themselves."[52] It is likely that individual star dancers reserved for their own exclusive use at least some of these dances, and that they performed them often in other settings, including the Opéra.[53] In 1755 *La Prosperité* (Prosperity) included an entrée by the celebrated Ruggieri brothers (194).

Joint performances onstage on the part of the Jesuits' students and Opéra professionals are evidence that the technique of the college ballets was the mainstream baroque technique of court ballet and professional theater in its various stages of development. In the seventeenth century a central reason for teaching the students to dance was to fit them to perform creditably in the King's ballets. It was said that the fathers at Louis-le-Grand trained the creators and cast for the ballets at Versailles.[54] In the eighteenth century, professionals trained by the same ballet masters who had coached the Jesuits' students brought the virtuosity of the Opéra to the rue Saint-Jacques, where, in addition to all-professional group pieces and spectacular solos, they shared entrées and group pieces with the Louis-le-Grand students. The Opéra dancers were more accomplished, but they and the students performed the same dance vocabulary.

An examination of parts of the program for *L'Empire de la Sagesse* (Wisdom's empire), 1715, gives a picture of how students and professionals worked together in the ballets.[55] The ballet master was

---

[50] Boysse, *Le Théâtre des jésuites*, 325.

[51] *Le Portrait du Grand Monarque*, Bibliothèque nationale, Yf2790, Ballet General.

[52] Lowe, *Marc-Antoine Charpentier:* "Les danses de Mrs de l'Opera ont été concertées par eux-memes" (189).

[53] Christout, *Ballet de cour*, 164.

[54] Lowe, *Marc-Antoine Charpentier:* "Visiblement, ceux-ci préparent les ordonnateurs et les figurants du corps de ballet de Sa Majesté" (44).

[55] *L'Empire de la Sagesse*, Bibliothèque nationale, Res. Yf 2678.

Blondy, and the cast included nineteen students and thirty Opéra dancers. Among them, these forty-nine dancers played sixty-six different kinds of characters, in solo and group dances. A few of these characters, like Jupiter, Minerva, and the Passions, reappeared. But, except for four of the Passions, played by the same Opéra dancers in the overture entrée and in the *ballet général*, repeat characters were played by different dancers.

The piece began with an overture entrée, continued with four parts, which had three entrées each, and concluded with a *ballet général*. Sanadon, the Jesuit librettist, described the subject of the ballet as the effort to regulate the Passions, or feelings, since the use we make of them creates the happiness or unhappiness of our lives. The four parts of the ballet were about the origins of the Passions, what stirs them up, the effects they produce, and how to keep them from doing harm. The characters who played out this moral scenario were the usual baroque ballet characters, familiar from college and secular stage alike: divinities, personifications, national groups, animals, shepherds, heroes, warriors, and so forth.

The overture entrée began with a solo by the Opéra dancer Gaudrau, as Discord. He was followed by a group of Passions, played by eleven Opéra colleagues. Next, Minerva, goddess of Wisdom and the presiding figure of the ballet, was danced by a student, followed by seven students as Virtues. Finally Mercury (the Opéra soloist Le Blanc) entered, and after him was a group piece for the Beaux Arts, danced by thirteen students and five professionals.

There seem to have been two kinds of solo billing. The first indicated dances by those playing major characters. The second kind of solo, indicated by the words "they will dance alone," is a solo section within a group dance.

The first entrée of the first part of *L'Empire* was danced by five students as Jupiter, Apollo, Mars, Plutus, and Morpheus. After them were the people of the four parts of the world: four students and a professional as Europeans, five students as Africans, four students and a professional as Americans, and one student and four professionals as Asians. There were at least four student solos and one professional solo in the course of the entrée. The five gods were probably danced in the serious or "noble" style, and the national groups may have been comic or "grotesque" dances. For example, the group dance for the Asians may have been similar to that in a 1747 ballet at the Rouen college.

A group of Chinese, whose gravity supports the idea one usually has of their nation, decide to liven up their seriousness with dances allowed by the customs of their country. But their great modesty permits less movement of the feet than of the head, which they rock with all the grace which one would expect.[56]

Besides being entertaining, a mostly stationary character dance like this, emphasizing the upper body, would have made a very effective contrast to the intricate footwork and floor patterns of the serious dances.

The next entrée had an all-Opéra cast, with one solo (Prometheus) and two groups (Elements and Statues) followed by a group dance of Animals, which would have offered a chance for acrobatic comedy.

The third entrée opened with "Warriors," played by "all the actors of the tragedy and the ballet," and therefore possibly a pantomimic section. It is possible that this large group included only students, since only students acted in the tragedies; and while professionals were credited in the entrées in which they appeared, only students were listed at the end of the programs as "acteurs du ballet." However, the dance immediately after the "Warriors" included students as well, which raises the mundane but essential question of how they changed their clothes in time to come back onstage. But this program does not include the speeches or songs that were almost certainly part of the ballet, so there may have been time for a quick change while predominately musical or dramatic action was taking place. As with most period documents about dance, the programs raise nearly as many questions as they answer.

Another of these questions is the nature of the "Mascarade" which closed this part of the ballet. A large group piece, it involved fourteen students and two Opéra dancers. Not identified in terms of its characters like the other groups, it may be an echo of an older form from court ballet, also called a "Mascarade." This was a more or less improvised dance-happening, which was directly influenced by current events and surrounding circumstances.[57] If the Jesuits did use a form of the old Mascarade from time to time, it would have provided yet another element of diversity and contrast within the ballet, as well as an additional vehicle for the ballet's *actualité*.

---

[56] LeBègue, "Les Ballets des jésuites": "Quelques Chinois dont la gravité soutient l'idée qu'on a communement de leur Nation, prennent le parti d'egaier leur Phlegme par des Danses que l'usage de leur Pays ne défend pas. Mais la Modestie qui les dirige permet moins de mouvements a leurs Pies qu'a leur Tête, qu'ils balancent avec toute la grace qu'on peut attendre d'eux" (*L'Imagination*) (324).

[57] Christout, *Ballet du cour*, 158.

The second group of dances in part 2 of *L'Empire* was an all-student entrée, balancing the all-Opéra entrée, which took place at the same point in Part 1. The second part's last entrée was divided between students and professionals. A student Jupiter and his suite of twelve student gods were assailed by the Opéra dancer d'Angeville and his eight Opéra Titans. It is easy to imagine that some competitive show-off dancing was part of this entrée, as the two groups pitched their battle. The student Jupiter blasted the professionals with his thunderbolts in the end.

In the last part of the ballet, we find its only female characters other than Minerva and, presumably, some of the Beaux Arts (like Terpsichore). A student Diana and her suite of Nymphs, eleven students and two professionals, were enticed by a mixed group of Cupids—five students and three Opéra dancers. This was followed by another all-Opéra entrée of vigorous athleticism, as Jason and his companions were set upon by a troupe of warriors. Jason distracted the invaders by throwing a golden apple among them—a visual touch full of choreographic possibilities, as the apple could be thrown from dancer to dancer.

The third entrée was fairly evenly divided between professionals and students, and the *ballet général*, though it used all the student dancers as Virtues and Young Heroes, was clearly meant to display the Opéra performers. Blondy, the ballet master, entered in a chariot and danced as Minerva. Twelve dancers from the Opéra were enchained Passions, d'Angeville was Diogenes, who emerged with his lantern, searching for "reasonable men," and there were three Opéra solos, by de Can, Paris, and Boizot. Diogenes' search for "reasonable men" may have been related to the prize giving. According to the program, he examined those around him in the light of his lantern, and then, "recognizing all of them as such, he puts down his lantern and marks his joy," that is, he danced the long virtuoso solo which traditionally closed a ballet.[58]

The Jesuit practice of presenting student and professional dancers together on their stage was sometimes deplored by contemporary as well as later writers. Jansenists and others protested allowing the "excommunicated" Opéra dancers to fraternize with the Jesuits' wellborn and impressionable students.[59] The complicated

---

[58] Ibid.: "Diogène . . . vient la lanterne à la main chercher des hommes raisonnables, et les reconoissant tous pour tels, il met bas sa lanterne, et marque sa joie."

[59] Félix Hémon, "La Comédie chez les jésuites," *Revue politique littéraire*

issue of the church's attitude toward theater professionals in France in this period needs to be reexamined. On the Jesuit stage, the practice of professionals and nonprofessionals performing together was an artistic issue and not a religious one. It was a continuation of the later-seventeenth-century court-ballet custom of staging productions with a mixed cast of amateurs and professionals. In court ballets, and especially in the final *ballet général,* professionals, male and female courtiers, and even bourgeois amateurs appeared together.

Dance-history scholars sometimes mistake social issues for theology. During Louis XIV's reign, virtually every dance aficionado in Paris was eager to be known as "a regular dancer in the King's ballets."[60] As technical standards improved, the key to that distinction was not name or rank, but competence as a dancer (164). The King, who performed in court ballets for eighteen years, and the Jesuits, with their network of theaters all over Europe, had the greatest respect for theatrical skill. They did not assume that professional dancers were dangerously sinful persons, or that dancing for an audience was impious or socially degrading to the well-born and well-trained amateur.

An important thread in disentangling twentieth-century misunderstandings of baroque church-theater relationships is the distinction drawn between professional dancing and professional acting. This distinction has not always been preserved in accounts of the church's attitude toward the theater; it is often difficult to know whether period documents refer to dramatic actors or professional dancers, as both are sometimes called simply "actors." The reason for the social distinction between actors and dancers was the court ballet, the traditional art, preserve, and pastime of the nobility since the sixteenth century and the source from which professional dancers had been born. Professional actors, on the other hand, could claim no such lineage. The great emphasis on acting and tragedy at Louis-le-Grand was in the service of baroque classicism and the teaching of public speaking, and was, in the minds of its directors and actors, far more distant from professional drama than the college ballet was from professional dance.

"Rhetoric" or the art of communication, was thought essential to the social presentation of self. To act in the college tragedy was an exercise in the verbal clarity and public self-confidence needed to claim—and retain—one's social position. The student actor learned to

---

22 (November 29, 1879): 532.

    [60] Christout, *Ballet de cour:* [Ils était] "soucieux de se parer du titre de 'danseur ordinaire des ballets du roi.' " (17).

assume the verbal elegance, biblical morality, and classical severity of the tragedy as the ground and context of his public and—his teachers hoped—personal life. Students were trained as actors in order to learn the philosophical, historical, and moral perspective of the plays in which they appeared, and not for any vocational purpose. The art of acting was appropriated for didactic ends. When Molière, a Louis-le-Grand student, decided to use his experience vocationally, his teachers were no doubt dismayed, though they later respected and made use of his expertise. With dance, the situation was quite different. Dancing, both social and theatrical, was considered a necessary upper- and middle-class skill (insofar as there was a "middle" class). It was valued for its own sake as well as for the social presence and grace it gave. The Louis-le-Grand directors taught their students to dance so that they could be competent participants in court and other ballets. "Great nobles, who would have scorned to declaim three verses of Corneille, hesitated not at all to mount the Opéra stage alongside its professional dancers."[61]

However, as amateurs became more competent dance performers, there was concern in some quarters about the *social* consequences of this professionalism. If a wellborn young person decided to become a true professional at the Opéra, what would become of the family property? In this period in France, it was only a minority of Catholics, including the Jansenists, who rejected art and artists, theater and performers, on religious grounds.

The French actor, Laval, suggested that the excommunication of dramatic actors was a ploy of aristocratic families (most of whom were well connected ecclesiastically as well as socially), aimed at keeping their children off the professional stage by threatening them with the loss of their inheritance. Legally, an excommunicated child had also to be disinherited.[62]

That the negative attitude of the French church toward actors was largely the result of social rather than theological conservatism is also suggested by comparing the French view of theatrical professionalism with that of the far more theologically scrupulous Italian and Spanish churches. When the Italian comedians opened in Paris in 1716, as Aghion reports, their record keeper wrote in the troupe's account book, "In the name of God, the Virgin Mary, and St. Francis of Paul, and the souls in purgatory, we have opened May 18, 1716,

---

[61] Ibid.: "De grands seigneurs qui dédaigneraient de déclamer trois vers de Corneille, n'hésiteront pas a monter parfois sur la scène de l'Opéra auprès des artistes attachés a ce théâtre" (165).

[62] Max Aghion, *Le Théâtre à Paris au XVIIIème siècle* (Paris: 1926), 408.

with "The Happy Surprise" (407). In the same period, the Pope gave his official protection to Spanish comedians. Finally, the Italian actors in France received the sacrament freely, making it necessary to base an explanation for the French church's hostility toward dramatic actors on social rather than ecclesiastical issues (408). In 1669, in a partial attempt to address these concerns and to further distinguish between actors and dancers, the King (the symbol of the Catholic faith in France) issued an official decree that one did *not* degrade oneself by performing in public as a dancer (165).

When these dancers—student and professional, noble and bourgeois—performed on the rue Saint-Jacques stage, what did their dancing look like? What did they actually do? The technique that Beauchamps codified was the descendant of Renaissance dance, as twentieth-century ballet is the descendant of the dance of Beauchamps's time.

Renaissance dance used a vocabulary in which the feet and legs were mostly parallel. The action of the ankle was more important than that of the knee and hip, since large jumps were not a prominent part of the technique, except in some male solos. Arm movements were minimal and not an important part of the overall design. The design itself was oriented toward the patterns dancers made on the floor as they moved, and toward the shapes created by groups of dancers together, especially when viewed from above. Sometimes the names of personages being honored in the Renaissance ballet were spelled out by the dancers in formation—exactly as marching bands do today during the halftime of football games.

The clothing of the sixteenth century influenced the dancing, as clothing always does. Shoes were flat. Breeches, cloaks, and floor-length skirts were made of stiff, heavy fabrics. Sleeves were constructed so as to make raising the arms above the shoulder nearly impossible, and undergarments were formidable. Men wore swords, and men and women both wore hats, ruffs, and jewelry.

During the earlier seventeenth century, the Renaissance vocabulary and style underwent slow change, as did fashion. There is no notation from this period: our information about the technique comes from libretti, treatises on dance, eyewitness accounts of performances, engravings of dancers and theaters, and other indirect evidence. In 1623 a French dancing master, de Lauze, published his *Apologie de la danse*. Steps cannot be reconstructed from his descriptions, but he makes it clear that at that time the foundations for the technique of the later part of the century were being laid. The dance which he says is in "the new style" is the courante, which was Louis XIV's favorite dance and which remained the foundation for dancing lessons for over a hundred years.[63]

Though the specifics of the earlier-seventeenth-century dance vocabulary are in many ways a matter of conjecture, we know that from the 1640s to the 1670s, innovations were taking place in court ballet and its technique. Some understanding of the court ballet that Louis XIV inherited and perfected is necessary for an understanding of Jesuit ballet, since the Jesuits were said to preserve in their theater the style and grandeur of Louis's court ballets. Between the 1640s and the 1670s, the period that encompassed the King's personal appearances as a theatrical dancer at court (1651–1669), court ballet reached its apogee. Christout identifies this peak with the production of the *Ballet de Flore*, the setting for Louis XIV's last performance, in 1669.[64] After this, the court ballet declined and eventually disappeared, as professional dancers took over the stages of Europe and the groundswell of political revolution began to build. The court ballet's longest echo was preserved (though with changes) on the Louis-le-Grand stage.

The mid-seventeenth-century flowering of court ballet was the result of the stage design of Vigarani and Torelli, Lully's innovations in music and use of dance in his operas, and the development of professional dancers by Louis's support of the ballet and through the work of Beauchamps.[65] As a result of the work and patronage of these men, there were at least four innovations in the production of court ballet. A new sense of organization emerged in the handling of themes, space, and movement. Music became more dramatic, and the suite of dances became fashionable. Stage machinery and effects reached new heights of development. And dance moved somewhat away from the "figure" or design-on-the-floor orientation of the Renaissance, to become more proscenium-oriented in response to the new way in which theaters were being built.

Because spaces for theater dance were now raised, with a fixed "front" from which the audience viewed the proceedings, *steps*, as distinct from figures, became more important. As steps became more inventive and difficult, the requirements for a dancer—even for a court dancer of noble birth—grew stricter. This was the period when Molière complained that there were only a few well-trained dancers. Because theatrical technique was becoming more complex and more distinct from social dance, only those with a natural elegance or

---

[63] Hilton, *Dance of Court and Theatre*, 45.

[64] Christout, *Ballet de cour*, 155.

[65] Ibid., 185.

presence, and with enough time to give to technical study, could measure up to the small but growing number of professionals who also danced in the court productions.

Technical innovations were moving the vocabulary toward the baroque technique that would be recorded in Feuillet's dance collection of 1700. A moderate amount of turn-out (the rotation at the hip socket which displays the inner leg and whole foot rather than the front of the leg and foot) was increasingly used. The leg was stretched, and the arms, now more shaped and held, became important in the overall design created by the dancer's body.[66]

In the 1660s, when Beauchamps became the director of the Royal Academy of Dancing and the ballet master for the Jesuit college, these changes were in progress and the baroque vocabulary that he eventually codified and notated was emerging. The technique notated in Feuillet's book, published in 1700, is the summation and full statement of the technique with which Beauchamps was working during his thirty years as the seminal dancing master in Europe.

As steps assumed a new importance in the technique, most ballet masters and critics called for the preservation of expression. De Pure, writing in 1668, described the effect at which the dancer aimed. The head, the shoulders, the arms, the hands of the dancer must speak; which means that the dance does not consist only in exceptional dexterity of the feet and accurate timing, but in a rigorous agreement of steps with the dramatic situation and the role the dancer is playing. Without this "rigorous agreement," the dance becomes

> nothing but a convulsion on the part of the dancing master and the dancer, a grotesquerie without spirit or design . . . risky jumps which mean nothing and have no more sense than those who do them and invent them.[67]

His statement tells us that the tension between the expressive dance and the pure dance, or dance as virtuosic display, continued to grow as the court ballet reached its peak of popularity. The expressive dance, which became the "action ballet" espoused by Noverre in his late-eighteenth-century program of reform, was favored, but the pure dance was also used in some entrées, and especially in the closing *ballet général*. This use of dance to display form, line, and movement continued on the Jesuit stage in the long technical displays by the star

---

[66] Ibid., 163.

[67] Ibid.: "n'est q'une convulsion du maistre et du danseur, qu'une bizarrerie sans esprit et sans dessein . . . et que des saut périlleux, qui ne signifient rien et qui n'ont plus de sens que celuy qui les a fiats et inventez" (139).

professional, or by the ballet master, that usually closed the *ballet général*.

But de Pure's statement tells us, too, that virtuoso jumps and exceptional dexterity in the footwork were becoming a normal part of what the dancer did. It also tells us that the technique placed new stress on a harmonious design of head, shoulders, arms, and hands to accompany and embellish the activity of the feet and legs. These two elements—precise and brilliant footwork and harmonious and expressive use of head, arms, and hands to make a complete design with the body—are two cardinal characteristics of baroque dance technique as it has come down to us from the work of Beauchamps and Feuillet, and their successors.

From the 1660s, when ballet began to be the centerpiece of the Jesuit theater, the technique consisted of set steps, variously combined, and complimentary *port de bras,* or arm movements. Turn-out increased to a comfortable ninety degrees or so, and the number of aerial steps in the vocabulary grew.[68]

The decade of the 1690s, from which some notation has survived, is the first point at which the dance vocabulary can be definitely described. The technical demands, especially on male dancers performing in the serious or "noble" style, were impressive. Male solos were full of cabrioles (jumps during which the legs are beaten together one or more times while the body is in the air) and multiple pirouettes. The more difficult of these turns are supported on one *demi-pointe,* the metatarsals of one foot. (There are also baroque pirouettes which are half turns supported on the *demi-pointes* of both feet.) These virtuosic displays were meant to be accomplished with apparent ease and relaxation. The classical aesthetic and the period sense of decorum decreed that the dancer not show unseemly effort, no matter how difficult the steps.

Most members of any ballet audience in this period were themselves dancers. Ballroom technique was only a little less complex than theatrical technique and shared the same vocabulary. A ballet audience would have appreciated what they were seeing not only visually but with a very active kinesthetic sense, since they would have known in their own bodies how most of the movements felt.

The baroque technique in the noble or serious style, which was the vocabulary of the serious entrées of the Jesuit ballets, is based on "sinking" and "rising"—that is, on bending the knees and then straightening them and rising onto the toes. ("Toes" is misleading

---

[68] Ibid., 164.

here; the word does not refer to the blocked toe-shoe of the nine-teenth-century ballerina, but to the half-toe or *demi-pointe* position of the foot, commonly called "standing on tiptoe.") Shoes or the lack of them are always important to the technique of a dance style. Later seventeenth- and eighteenth-century dancers wore leather shoes with small heels. The heel accentuates the calf muscle, making the turned-out leg more shapely, and also facilitates bending the knee. But it makes jumping more difficult, especially the jumps from a straight-leg position—sometimes embellished with beats—which are also part of baroque technique. The dancer of our own day who puts on heeled shoes and attempts, with baroque ease and decorum, to accomplish these beaten jumps from a straight leg, appreciates very quickly the technical accomplishments of Beauchamps, Pécour, and others like them. The precise and brilliant footwork and small flickering jumps that are known in contemporary ballet technique as *petit allegro* come from baroque-theater dance.

The torso is entirely upright and centered in this technique, as it was in Renaissance dance. This element of the style is partly the result of clothing and partly a response to the tenets of good breed-ing. Seventeenth- and eighteenth-century clothing, especially theatri-cal costume, was less cumbersome and more flexible than clothing had been in the sixteenth century. But both men and women wore boned corsets and heavy fabrics, and women or those playing female roles wore stiffly constructed petticoats and frames called panniers to hold out the wide skirts. Skirts were shorter for theatrical costume than for street wear, showing the action of foot and ankle.

Classical ballet has inherited its relentlessly upright carriage from this corseted position of the center body. A wellbred person simply did not lounge, sag, slump, lean or stand hip-shot, at least not in public. Similarly, too much tilting of the head, shrugging of the shoulders, and so on, was considered affected. The expressiveness of the head, shoulders, arms, and hands in baroque technique comes, not from emotional gestures and poses meant to convey what we think of as "self-expression," but from a relaxed and harmonious use of these parts of the body to create a pleasing and symmetrical physi-cal design, which subtly communicates feeling.

The head can turn gently from side to side to complement the movement of the rest of the body, and the gaze is allowed to drop to the floor only for expressive purposes. The arms are *always* curved, with the curve beginning at the shoulder and traveling through the elbow and wrist. The hands are soft with curved fingers, but are never limp or forgotten. The arm is moved as a unit from the elbow, with the hand passing through the center line of the body, always creating a round design in space. As the hand moves through this path in space, it never rises above the level of the shoulder.

There are many complexities involved in mastering the arm movements of baroque dance, but this brief description gives a sense of the very different styles of baroque and classical ballet *port de bras.* Classical-ballet arm movements are from the shoulder, with the arms often raised above the head, and sometimes stretched straight at the elbow in large jumps. One reason for the great difference in the *port de bras* of the two techniques is the difference in the size of the leg movements. Baroque technique has none of the high extension of the legs which is so essential to contemporary classical ballet; in baroque dance the legs are not usually carried higher than a forty-five degree angle at the hip. Because arm movements in both techniques are meant to complete and complement the design created within the body by the legs and feet, the size of the leg gestures determines the size of the *port de bras.*

Feuillet's *Chorégraphie* contains a forty-page section on the baroque-step vocabulary. Each page has an average of twelve diagrams showing how to execute various steps. The total vocabulary, however, is not as large as a first glance at the book leads one to believe. Feuillet has notated every possible variation of every step, for both the left and right foot, and in every possible direction. There are, for example, ninety-four ways of doing a *pas de bourrée*, a movement composed of three steps. It can be done to the front, back, or side; it can begin in one direction and end in another, and it can be done turning, and with beats. These variations are possible for any of the eleven basic steps that Feuillet notates and explains in his section on *pas*. These eleven steps, the building blocks of baroque-dance technique, in the order of their mention by Feuillet, are *temps de courante, demi-coupé, coupé, pas de bourrée, jeté, contretemps, chassée, pas de sissone, pirouette, cabriole* and *demi-cabriole,* and *entre-chat* and *demi entre-chat*. Most of these terms for dance steps are still used in the classical-ballet vocabulary, but the modern movements to which they refer are, for the most part, quite different from their baroque counterparts. The *pas de bourée, jeté,* and *entre-chat* of contemporary ballet retain the closest resemblance to the baroque steps from which they are derived.

This technique was the heart of baroque-theater dance and was used in what was called the "noble" style, which was derived from court dance, both social and theatrical. But, as we have seen, Jesuit ballets also had some pantomimic entrées, which were half-acted and half-danced. There were dancers whose specialty was the creation of pantomime; Lully, who included a great deal of pantomime in his operas, regularly called on the talents of one particular ballet master, Louis Hilaire d'Olivet, to create those sections of his shows.[69] The pantomime was more directly emotional and dramatic than the movements of baroque technique (though the basic baroque vocabulary could be part of the action). These mimed entrées were also sometimes acrobatic. At court, professional acrobats were employed to jump, tumble, and build human pyramids. The athleticism suggested by some of the entrées in the Jesuit ballets would have lent itself especially well to this freewheeling acrobatic pantomime—and would also have provided ballet roles for boys physically unsuited to the noble style of dancing.

In addition to the noble style and pantomime, there was also a character style of baroque dance. This was reserved for comic characters, who were to the rest of the ballet what Falstaff or Bottom are to Shakespeare's plays. The most complete exposition of this strand of baroque technique is Gregorio Lambranzi's *New and Curious School of Theatrical Dancing*, published at Nuremberg in 1716. Lambranzi was a Venetian dancing master of the late seventeenth and early eighteenth centuries. His book consists of engravings of ballet entrées, each with a dance melody printed above, and a verbal sketch of the dance underneath. The entrées vary from mild comedy to acrobatic slapstick. Many take their point from grotesque costumes. One duet, for example, is for two dancers dressed so that each appears to be only a leg, with its foot emerging from an enormous pantaloon. Many of the entrées are for "peasants," and there are numerous comic duets for a man and a woman.

The step vocabulary was that of the noble style, but with comic embellishments and exaggerations. For example, the steps are often performed with the legs turned in instead of turned out. In his book Feuillet follows his drawings and description of Beauchamps's five positions of the feet with what he calls the five "false" positions; that is, the same five positions with the legs rotated inward instead of outward. These were sometimes used in "grotesque" or comic dancing.

Two examples from Lambranzi's book give a sense of this grotesque or character style and the kind of ballet entrées in which it was used. Plate 4 shows a peasant in front of rustic cottages. His arms and hands are held awkwardly, and his body is bent to one side from the hips. The description under the engraving reads:

> This plate represents the first peasant step. It is then done the opposite way with the other foot, and succeeded by *contretemps* and *pas de*

---

[69] Hilton, *Dance of Court and Theatre*, 29.

rigaudon, with a drawing to and fro of the arms, knees and legs, but in divers manners in peasant style.[70]

There are several dances for Scaramouch, one of the standard Commedia dell'Arte characters. Plate 26 shows an entrée for three Scaramouches.

Scaramouch enters with two baskets, each containing a smaller Scaramouch, which he sets down. When he has danced the whole of the air once, the small Scaramouches open the baskets, which greatly surprises him. They jump out, kick him from behind and push him to the ground. Then they dance the whole of the air themselves. Afterwards Scaramouch, having got up, catches first one then the other, and forces them back into their baskets. This ends the first half of the air. During the second half he takes up the baskets and exits with long strides.[71]

When Pécour took over Beauchamps's position at the Royal Academy in 1687 and at Louis-le-Grand around 1699, he continued to work in the retiring master's style. Pécour had choreographed for court ballets until 1692. As a dancer, he had inherited many of Beauchamps's ballet roles; and when notated collections of dances for both theater and ballroom began to appear in the early eighteenth century, they included many of Pécour's pieces. Approximately three hundred and fifty dances have survived in Feuillet notation, most of them from the period between 1700 and 1725. Of these at least one hundred and fifteen are by Pécour. That so many of Pécour's dances were notated suggests that the dances he created as ballet master at Louis-le-Grand may also have been notated. It is possible that some of the dances by Pécour which appear in the existing collections were used on the rue Saint-Jacques stage, but no indisputable notation from Pécour's ballets for the Jesuits has survived.

As with Beauchamps's collaborations with Lully and Molière, Pécour's work with the composer André Campra is another source that helps us to speculate about his work for the Jesuits. Pécour and Campra created two of the most famous and successful baroque opera-ballets, *L'Europe galante* in 1697, and *Les Festes vénitiennes* in 1710. In 1699, the year Pécour took over as ballet master at Louis-le-Grand, they collaborated on the ballet *Les Songes* for the Jesuits. We can assume that their collaboration at the Jesuit college was marked by the same style and made use of the same dance and music vocab-

---

[70] Gregorio Lambranzi, *New and Curious School of Theatrical Dancing,* trans. Cyril Beaumont (Nuremberg, 1716; reprinted New York: Dance Horizons, 1966), 19.

[71] Ibid., 23.

ularies as their work together at the Opéra. After 1699 there were at least three years during which both Pécour and Campra were employed by the Jesuits—though *Les Songes* was apparently the only Louis-le-Grand ballet that they created together. However, it may be that the presence of both artists at the college meant that the *récits en musique* composed by Campra for performances in May and December 1700 and February 1704 also included dance.

In any case, with Pécour we arrive at the period when our knowledge of baroque technique on the Jesuit stage can be deduced from documented evidence: the notation contained in Feuillet's 1700 book on Beauchamps's system and in other collections of notated dances, many of which were choreographed by Pécour himself. He and the ballet masters who succeeded him at Louis-le-Grand were working with the fully developed baroque technique, which the college stage shared with the Opéra and other professional stages. While they were training the Jesuits' students, these artists were also training the next generations of professional dancers and directing the shape of European social dancing through the published collections of their choreographies.

The Ballet Music

The baroque Jesuits were not known for their music, as some orders were, like the Oratorians. When the Society was founded, Ignatius forbade his followers to chant the divine office or keep musical instruments in their houses.[72] These rules came from his sense of the order's priorities, rather than from any antipathy toward music. On the contrary, Ignatius took great personal delight in liturgical music. In accord with the founder's spirit, if not with his stated priorities, music had a place in the Jesuit colleges by the early seventeenth century. The character of this musical activity varied from college to college; at Louis-le-Grand, music seems to have been valued more as an adjunct of ballet and other lyric theater than as a separate art.

Menestrier wrote that "the concerts, symphony, and ballets are concerned with the sound and agreement of instruments, the design made by the body, and its figured movements."[73] The relationship between a baroque dance and its music is an intimate one, and the

---

[72] Rudolf Wittkower and Irma B. Jaffe, ed., *Baroque Art: The Jesuit Contribution* (New York: Fordham University Press, 1972), 111.

[73] Menestrier, *Représentations en musique*, 167(?) (translation mine).

music for the Louis-le-Grand ballets is an important clue to what the ballets looked like. Fortunately, a few ballet scores have survived.

In 1690 the sometime composer Philidor compiled a group of ballet scores, calling them "Ballets des jésuites, composées par Messieurs Beauchant, Desmatins, et Collasse" (Jesuit ballets composed by Beauchant [Beauchamps], Desmatins, and Collasse). The handwritten manuscript is confusing in that it exists in slightly different versions and, though called "Jesuit Ballets," includes ballets from the College of Harcourt, and one which may have been performed by the Comédie-Italienne. Nevertheless, it is the only authenticated primary musical resource for the seventeenth-century Jesuit ballets, and demonstrates the musical expertise that dancing masters like Beauchamps were expected to possess. (The score for *Les Arts florissantes*, in the seventh volume of Charpentier's *Melanges*, is thought to be the score used for the 1685 *Ballet des arts* at Louis-le-Grand, but this is not certain.)[74] So far, no music for the eighteenth-century ballets has come to light.

The second ballet score in the collection has been identified as the music for *La France victorieuse sous Louis le Grand*, first danced at the college in 1680. The version of the scores considered here, Res. 516 from the Bibliothèque du Conservatoire, lists this ballet simply as a "Ballet des jésuites par M. Beauchamp." The score contains thirty-eight separate pieces of music.

It opens with a fifty-five measure overture and continues with a twenty-four measure prologue, taken with a repeat. This musical prologue is an unusual element: there is no musical prologue in the other Philidor scores, nor is a musical prologue indicated in most libretti. During this prologue, Apollo appears on Parnassus surrounded by Poets. He sings and they respond as a chorus. Their singing is followed by a series of dances, interspersed with singing by Apollo and his suite.

The next piece of music is a twenty-measure Sarabande—probably an expressive Sarabande "a l'Espagnole." The Sarabande, one of the ten dance forms most commonly found in Lully's ballets and operas between 1673 and 1687, was characterized by Tomlinson as less grave than the Courante, but slower than the Passacaille and Chaconne.[75] It was commonly a solo entrée for either a man or a woman, danced sometimes with castanets to emphasize its Spanish flavor.

---

[74] Lowe, *Marc-Antoine Charpentier*, 52.

[75] Hilton, *Dance of Court and Theatre*, 37, 263.

Next are three dances of undesignated form, for Statues, Old Women, and Pickpockets. The Statues' dance appears to be a Loure, Gigue, or Forlane; these are similar double-meter dances, with six beats to the measure and of varying speed. The dance for the Old Women was in triple meter, and probably very slow; it may have been the somewhat old-fashioned Courante. A brisk Rigadoon or Bourée may have served the Pickpockets; their dance has four beats to the measure and was probably quick and light, in keeping with their shifty trade.

A long two-hundred-and-sixty-two-measure Chaconne follows. Often found in the closing *ballet général* on both secular and college stages, the lively and intricate triple-meter Chaconne provided ample scope for technical displays. Though Chaconnes were choreographed for large groups as well as for solo dancers, no group choreography has survived in notation. Of the ten scores included in Philidor's collection, five end with a Chaconne; and of those five, one concludes with a series of three Chaconnes, probably for a medley of virtuoso solos interspersed with group dancing by all those appearing in the ballet. Often used on the Paris college stage, the Chaconne was less associated with expression than some of the other forms, representing something of a concession to the "pure dance."

The next identified dance form is the very popular Minuet, here in a twenty-four measure Minuet for the Muses, which may have served as the opening for part 2. The character who enters following this dance is Apollo, and the Muses were probably his "suite." The Minuet became and remained very popular during the period of the Louis-le-Grand ballets. As reconstructed from period notation, this dance form moves fairly quickly, and is not the languid business sometimes seen in romantic representations. It has a triple meter and small precise footwork, including momentary balances in the course of its step pattern. Choreographed for duets and groups, its quickly changing floor patterns make it visually effective onstage.

After ten dances identified by the name of the character or characters who danced in them (such as Apollo, The Spirit of Parnassus, The Rejoicing People) rather than by the name of a dance form, there is another Minuet, danced by a group of Dryads. A Canarie, the fastest of the double-meter dances, follows it as part of the same musical "suite." The third piece in the suite, rhythmically and melodically similar to the Canarie, is called simply "Air"; it was probably a song or a sung section of the Canarie.

Singing during the ballets, sometimes by the dancers themselves, was another practice carried over from court ballet. In 1622 a spectacle for Louis XIII and Anne of Austria given at the Jesuit college in Lyon, began with Merlin predicting the downfall of Philip Augustus. His words were then acted out by six soldiers doing "pyrrhiques," or warlike dances, and the soldiers stopped in the middle of their performance to sing.[76] A hundred years later, the practice was still current on the Jesuit stage. The *Nouveau Mercure* for August 1720 printed a song called "Pont Neuf," from that year's ballet at Louis-le-Grand, *L'Industrie* (Work). Mixing song and dance in this way was part of the conceptual revival of the ancient Greek chorus, which had been a singing and dancing group.

At the beginning of Louis XIV's reign, during his minority, lyric and choreographic music were generally separate genres. But this changed as court ballet and opera ballet continued to develop within the context of baroque taste and the classical aesthetic. There were many threads of influence shaping this growth, including the rivalry between those who favored French musical forms and those who preferred the Italian. The Jesuits followed the lead of Lully, who, though he was Italian, came to stand for the French style.[77] More than any other single composer, Lully created a French opera style by fusing elements from the ballet and the classical tragedy, to make what he called *tragédie-lyrique*. The Jesuits also produced this opera form at Louis-le-Grand, especially at the end of the seventeenth century, calling it *tragédie en musique*. To create a distinctively French recitative style, Lully turned to the declamation used by actors, which was related to academic rhetorical speaking. Once again, the threads of rhetoric, acting, dancing, and music were intertwined. The drawing together of these threads was characteristic of both secular and Jesuit theater.

Dance forms often were accompanied by lyrics during the hundred years of the Louis-le-Grand ballet. In the Philidor score there were sung "dances of character" as well as sung figured dances, like the Sarabande and, perhaps, the Canarie. It was probably not the dancers who sang—at least not while dancing—because of the breathing difficulties involved in adequately doing both things at once. De Pure stated that there were three reasons for including songs in the ballets. They allowed the dancers to catch their breath, they pleased the audience's ear, and they verbally clarified the onstage action. Even if they did not sing while they danced, many baroque dancers sang well, one result of the musical requirements and training for a dancer; and some gained a reputation for their voice as well as for their dancing.

---

[76] McGowan, *L'Art de ballet du cour*, 217.

[77] Lowe, "Représentations en musique," 30.

To return to the *La France* score, the "Air" is followed by a twenty-one measure double-meter solo for Religion. As in the rest of the score, there are no directions for tempi, but this was probably one of the grave and slow dances, perhaps a Gavotte. This relatively slow dance is surprisingly full of jumps; the basic gavotte step is a *contre-temps*, which includes a spring from one foot landing on the same foot, and a *pas assemblée*, which is another spring bringing the two feet together. After Religion's solo comes a Bourrée, a quick double-meter dance.

All but one of the remaining dances are titled by the characters who performed them. The Furies' dance is a twenty-five measure flurry of sixteenth notes, which gives a sense of swirling agitation even on the page. It is followed by a solo for Rumor, a group piece for Frosts and Winds, and a dance for a group of Frenchmen. Then there is another Bourée, a duet for Mercury and Prudence, a solo for Mars, and a group piece for French Heroes.

Next is a twenty-three-measure dance for Spaniards, which appears to be a Sarabande. Spanish entrées were very fashionable in French ballet and opera during the seventeenth century, and the Jesuit college apparently joined in this vogue. As the point of the entrée was to emphasize its characters' nationality, the dance was probably done "a l'Espagnole," with the performers playing castanets as they danced. (This feat is in itself a testimony to the musicality and rhythmic skill of baroque dancers.) Four dances conclude the ballet's score: a group piece for The Germans and The Dutch, a group piece for Young Gentlemen, a solo for Zoroaster, and an ensemble for The Enchanters.

How do the dance forms found in this Jesuit-ballet score compare with the dance forms Lully was using on the secular stage at the same time? Hilton gives the Menuet, Gavotte, Bourrée, Sarabande, Canarie, Gigue, and Chaconne as the most frequently found dance forms in Lully's opera-ballets between 1673 and 1687.[78] In this 1680 Louis-le-Grand score, the named dance forms are the Menuet, Bourrée, Sarabande, Canarie, and Chaconne. The presence of many of the same dance forms in Lully's work and at Louis-le-Grand is another indication that the Jesuit ballets shared the style and vocabulary of noncollege productions and reflected the same trends in theatrical fashion. The close association between the Jesuit college and the Opéra, and among the personnel who worked for both, also had other repercussions on the rue Saint-Jacques. After he became director of the Royal Academy of Music in 1672, Lully obtained from the

---

[78] Hilton, *Dance of Court and Theatre*, 37.

King a virtual monopoly on musical productions in Paris. No other theater in Paris could produce a completely sung work without Lully's written permission.[79] By 1673 productions outside the Royal Academy could use no more than eight musicians, including two singers. The Jesuits had already felt the pressure of Lully's official restraints. Since his appointment as royal superintendent of music in 1661, the Jesuits had had to obtain his permission each time they produced a piece of theater that included music.[80] That the Jesuits were able to obtain Lully's consent for their full-scale ballets and operas—using large numbers of personnel from Lully's own theater—testifies to the enormous influence of Jesuits like La Chaise, who was the king's confessor, and others (90).

One probable reason why Marc-Antoine Charpentier accepted the invitation to compose for the Louis-le-Grand stage was that working under Jesuit auspices allowed him to elude Lully's restrictions. In addition to other work in Paris, including the post of music master at the church attached to the Jesuit Professed House on the rue Saint-Antoine, he had been working with the Comédie-Française, which was endlessly harassed by the autocratic Italian. On the rue Saint-Jacques, Charpentier would not only escape the worst of that situation, but would also have at his disposal musical and scenic resources that were better than those at the Comédie.[81]

Of eighteen composers known to have worked in the Louis-le-Grand theater, at least thirteen composed ballet music. They were Beauchamps, Desmatins, Collasse, Campra, Abeille, La Chapelle, Royer Chéron, Denys, Duché, Allouette, Chochereau, and Le Maire. If the score for the *Ballet des Arts* is indeed the same score as that for *Les Arts florissantes*, Charpentier also belongs on this list. Some of these composers, notably Charpentier and Campra, also composed music for other college productions. Charpentier created at least three major lyric tragedies, or operas, for the Jesuit school: *Jephté* (1686), *Celse martyr* (1687), and *David et Jonathas* (1688). Lowe, whose study of opera at the Jesuit college is an important source of information about music at Louis-le-Grand, believes that there were probably also operas by Charpentier in 1689 and 1690.[82] Many, if not all, of these musicians were composing and performing in other theatrical and religious settings around Paris during their tenure at Louis-le-Grand,

---

[79] Ibid., 27.

[80] Lowe, *Marc-Antoine Charpentier*, 89f.

[81] Ibid., 54.

[82] Ibid., 52.

as reports in gazettes like the *Mercure* and the lists of theatrical events compiled by Beauchamps, Lavallière, and the Parfaicts attest.

However, many of the college-ballet programs do not list composers. Early in the period, composing music for dance was considered a somewhat lowly musical task—though surprisingly large numbers of people seem to have done it, including Louis XIII.[83] The music was meant to serve the dance, and a baroque dance and its music are usually inseparable. Another reason may be that the Jesuits themselves composed music for their theater and may have felt that acknowledgement was either unsuitable or unnecessary. Librettists also were not usually named in the ballet programs, but we know many of them because they were sometimes mentioned in gazette articles about the ballets, and because literary records were kept within the order (and preserved in Sommervogel's *Bibliography*). It may be that in-house music was more often used in the provinces, where other artistic resources were limited, rather than in an urban college like Louis-le-Grand, which had a theatrical reputation to maintain and could call on the talents of the best-known French composers of the day. In any case, none of the Jesuit-composed music was published, except, like the "Pont Neuf" song, occasionally in gazettes. In 1618 the Jesuits' superior general wrote to the music director of the college in Belgium that he could not allow publication of the Jesuits' music, "not even under a pseudonym," the use of which was common in these centuries. The art of music, he felt, was "not at all in keeping with our profession."[84] (Fortunately, as the century progressed, his opinion was not shared by large numbers of his brothers.)[85]

Who were the interpreters who played and sang the music composed for the Louis-le-Grand ballets? And on what did the instrumentalists play? To answer the second question first, the score for the 1689 ballet *Sigalion* indicates trumpets, violins, hautbois, and bassoons. Other instruments, including drums, were probably used also. As for the musicians and singers, for the most part we do not know their names. We do know that singers and instrumentalists as well as dancers were imported from the Opéra for the ballets. For example, in 1735 the famous tenor Pierre Jéliotte appeared in the August performance at the college.[86]

---

[83] Christout, *Ballet de cour*, 13, 32 n. 15.

[84] Carroll, "Jesuit Playwright," 35.

[85] Hennequin, "Théâtre et société": "Enfin plus s'avance le siècle, plus on voit la musique prendre d'importance, se meler aux ballets, et les 'récits' a l'action elle-meme. L'opéra de college n'est pas loin" (460).

[86] Dupont-Ferrier, *Vie quotidienne d'un collège*, 293?.

If Menestrier's advice was followed, the orchestra of Opéra players, sometimes conducted by the ballet master, performed in costume. He suggested dressing the players as tritons, sirens, fauns, satyrs, Moors, nymphs, shepherds—or whatever accorded with the ballet's subject.[87] Not only were the musicians subjected to the constraints of costume, they were perhaps used as part of the decor and scenic effects, as they had been in court ballet. Menestrier enthusiastically recounts seeing musicians dressed as the Muses and crowned with oak leaves, playing under a giant oak tree and, in another ballet, riding on a "chariot" as sea divinities (211f.). In the annals of court ballets, there are accounts of musicians and their instruments in trees, in the caves of stage-machinery mountains, and descending on machines from the ceiling.

The professional personnel involved with the Louis-le-Grand ballets seem to have been a closely knit network of artists who collaborated with each other in the major theaters of Paris, as well as at the Jesuit college. This means that no picture of dance at Louis-le-Grand is complete without the acknowledgement that because they commissioned work from professional ballet masters, dancers, musicians, and designers, the Jesuits were patrons as well as producers of baroque dance.

Some of the artists in this network were, like Beauchamps and his nephew, Blondy, related by blood, while others were related as teachers and students, like Beauchamps and Pécour. Collegial relationships, like that of Lully and his secretary-student, Collasse, or Molière and Beauchamps, or Marchand and Rameau, connected the Jesuit productions with seminal artists of the period who influenced the Jesuit theater but did not themselves work in it. It is with good reason that Lowe has asked, "Must we not believe that some days the Opéra had an authentic branch at Louis-le-Grand?"[88]

---

[87] Menestrier, *Des Ballets anciens et modernes*, 208.

[88] Lowe, *Marc-Antoine Charpentier"*: "Ne doit-on pas croire que certains jours l'Opéra avait réellement une succursale a Louis-le-Grand?" (85).

three · · · · · · · · · · · · · · · · · ·

THE BALLETS ONSTAGE

It's always the same thing: three parts of the world, three mountains,
three lions, three lynxes, three soldiers, four rivers, four forests,
Discord everywhere, and Religion, for no particular reason, suddenly
descending on a cloud to settle everything.

— Claude François Menestrier, *Des Ballets anciens et modernes*

The Jesuits used, adapted to, and supported contemporary art styles in much the same way they incorporated native customs and beliefs into their mission work.[1] In the seventeenth and eighteenth centuries, allegory was the cornerstone of both ballet and the visual arts. Ballet librettists and painters were often rhetoricians. The sixteenth-century Dutch painter Jacob de Backer was a member of the Antwerp Chamber of Rhetoricians; painting itself was called "the pulpit of the brush."[2] Le Brun, court painter to Louis XIV, lectured on theories of expression, and Poussin used the same terms to describe the goals of painting that were used to describe the goals of rhetoric. Rhetorician and painter both turned to Cicero, who had said that the great orator instructs, delights, and moves.[3]

Visual Allegory and the Ballets

All the arts in this period are so intertwined that they are like the allegorical image of the snake holding its tail in its mouth: the longer each art is studied on its own, the more difficult it becomes to say where one begins and another leaves off. But the art of the the-

---

[1] Wittkower and Jaffe, *Baroque Art,* 2.

[2] John B. Knipping, *Iconography of the Counter-Reformation in the Netherlands* (Nieuwkoop, Netherlands: B. de Graaf, 1974), 1:45.

[3] Germain Bazin, *The Baroque: Principles, Styles, Modes, Themes,* trans. Pat Wardroper (Greenwich, Conn.: New York Graphic Society, 1968), 40.

ater served as a frame of reference for the other arts in this theatrical age. There is an anonymous painting of Bernini's sculpture *The Ecstasy of St. Teresa,* displayed in the Cornaro Chapel in the Church of Santa Maria della Vittoria in Rome. On either side of the figure of St. Teresa, which is presented on a stagelike platform, members of the Cornaro family, donors of the painting, sit in theater boxes watching the action, chatting and commenting as though they were at the ballet. As Bazin states, in the baroque centuries "the visual language of all the arts is dominated by that of the theater" (66).

A revealing image for a discussion of visual allegory in the rue Saint-Jacques ballets is Rubens's painting "The Triumph of the Catholic Faith," completed sometime between 1626 and 1631, now in the Louvre. This painting, which conveys the mood of its time so well, has been called the "apotheosis of the Counter-Reformation."[4] What is so striking about "The Triumph," as about baroque visual art—and staging—in general, is its warm, lively, crowded sensuality. Solid flesh overflows its classical draperies in human and angelic figures alike. The viewer is swept along in a crowd of enthusiastic, well-fed people.

This is a different world from that of medieval symbolism. The Platonic system of ideals still operates, but now joyously incarnate rather than straining upward toward some future and unseen life. John Knipping describes what now began to happen in the old system of visual allegory.

> The platonic way of thinking, which in the medieval mind had also been the carrier of abstract but real ideas, encountered here the spirit of the age, which was so strongly inclined towards the concrete. What the thinking individual sees before him in its mere generality must now be expressed by images clad in very clear and palpable forms. *The allegorical figure had to lose its hieratic immobility.* . . . Everyday life acquires its own value and hallowing. Man embraces earth with enchantment and this earth reveals itself with an always gentle ripeness. The splendors of future glory which radiated over the image of medieval man's life, paled before the young and ever changing brilliancy of the present delight in which Christianity and Antiquity, spiritual and sensuous life, natural and supernatural seemed almost playfully to interpenetrate each other. [emphasis added] (13)

Newly clothed in Counter-Reformation optimism, the old symbolic figures romped through the baroque imagination.

Two strains in seventeenth- and eighteenth-century French art played a part in the ballets. These are sometimes called "classical"

---

[4] Knipping, *Iconography,* 13.

and "baroque." (The "rococo" style, which appeared toward the end of our period, seems not to have become a part of ballet design at Louis-le-Grand.) The two styles with which we are concerned can also be seen as baroque art that tends toward the quiet and controlled rendering of images, and baroque art that, like Rubens's "Triumph," tends toward the ecstatic and voluptuous. France, unlike Italy and Germany, remained closer to the Netherlands in its artistic preferences—that is, more "classical." Nevertheless, there was a distinct strain of voluptuousness, especially in theater art; and both strains, wherever they were found—in the theater, easel painting, sculpture, or architectural decoration—swarmed with allegory.

Intricately related visual and verbal allegory was literally everywhere in Europe in the baroque centuries. Educated Parisians encountered it every day in books in their libraries, in statues in the parks, in the exterior and interior decoration of townhouses and public buildings, in the theater, and in public celebrations. Perceiving and deciphering it was a skill, a spiritual exercise, a pastime, and irrefutable evidence of breeding, taste, and education.[5] Even devotional works, including some editions of Ignatius's *Spiritual Exercises,* were illustrated with classical baroque allegories.[6] These condensed incarnational messages, which the new age so enthusiastically received and multiplied, were a legacy from the Renaissance. In 1579, when Francesco de' Medici married Bianca Capello, the Florentine Neo-Platonic Academy worked for a year to create symbolic material for the decorators, poets, and musicians to use in mounting celebrations of the occasion.[7]

---

[5] I recently had an experience that gives a small taste of the way in which baroque Parisians must have encountered these casual allegories. Walking in San Francisco, I passed a shop window in which were displayed four wooden female figures wearing classical draperies. One was crowned with roses, one carried a sheaf of wheat, one was garlanded with vine leaves, and one held a flame. Without stopping to think, I said to myself, "Oh, there are the four seasons." Spring wore the roses, Summer carried a token of the nearing harvest, Autumn was wrapped in the fruits of the vintage, and Winter carried life-giving fire. All of them also no doubt carried other layers of reference, most of which I, unlike a seventeenth-century Parisian, could not read: Spring is also Persephone, Summer is also Ceres, for example. The fire of Winter probably had some reference to the winter solstice and the new light of spring. And so on. This experience must have been multiplied many times over for the educated seventeenth- or eighteenth-century inhabitant of Paris.

[6] Knipping, *Iconography*, 1:21.

[7] Bazin, *The Baroque*, 47.

Architecture, as well as painting, poetry, rhetoric, and theater, could be a forest of allegory. An especially good example in Austria is the baroque monastery at Melk, which was built as a sacred triangle. In the hall, Hercules, emblem of princes, symbolizes "excellence in the human sphere." In the library, Hercules Christianus, a symbol of Christ used since the Renaissance, proclaims that human excellence comes from Christian perfection, which princes must possess. In the church, Peter and Paul, martyr-apostles, are the two athletes of the faith who in themselves constitute the Christian Pillars of Hercules.[8]

This building is a good example of the hidden complexity of baroque allegory, including the allegory contained in the ballets. As most of us would probably miss most of the Melk allegory, we also no doubt miss most of the ballet allegory in studying the libretti and programs. A long process of immersion in this way of seeing and understanding is necessary before the images begin not only to emerge but to emerge in relation to each other. The symbols were meant to be read as intricate statements, long and complex as beautifully turned sentences in a rhetorical display. In the Melk example we probably would not immediately see the sacred triangle, itself a reference to much mystical thought and literature. Missing the subtlety of the relationship among the three spaces, we would be more inclined to feel that it simply "makes sense" to put structures having to do with human nature, learning, and worship in relation to each other, as symbols of life, and of life in a religious community. But we would almost certainly miss the political references to the "prince," and the relationship of Hercules in the hall to Peter and Paul in the church.

Architectural allegory was placed clearly within another allegory: nature as the setting for human apotheosis. In Catholic theology, the apotheosis of the man Jesus took place in relation to the created world, as does the salvation of the individual's soul. In the baroque era, the social apotheosis of the human being—the attainment of *gloire*—took place in the world of the five senses. In the same way, a building, especially a building like Versailles, which was an allegorical monument to the apotheosis of a monarchy, was carefully placed in its natural setting. Versailles in its gardens, which lay in turn in an open and gentle countryside, was an allegory of the monarch at the heart of his realm. The astonishing fact that it was open to the public underlines the essential theatricality of baroque allegory and the very fuzzy line drawn between art and life. Ordinary people, often an important part of the audience for upper-class displays

---

[8] Bazin, *The Baroque*, 42f.

(displays never without some political allusion), were invited to the "show." If they could not read all the subtleties, they understood the main drift of the "performance" and saw themselves literally and figuratively "placed" in relation to it. Twentieth-century grandeur, such as it is, takes place behind guarded doors, electric fences, and police lines. During the reign of Louis XIV, penultimate age of grandeur, anyone—any man, that is—could watch the King eat his dinner. All that was necessary was the clothing of a "gentleman"—which meant a sword and a plumed hat, both of which could be rented cheaply from the palace concierge. When Louis walked in the gardens, they were so full of "the people," as well as of courtiers, that a way had to be cleared in front of him, so that he could move about.[9]

A building alone, apart from its inhabitants, could present an allegorical drama, and contests were held in which rhetoricians tried to read the allegories contained in the structure and decoration of new buildings. When the Town Hall was opened in Amsterdam in 1665, local rhetoricians gathered to vie with each other in explaining the allegorical riddles hidden in the gods and animals decorating it.[10]

Allegory was taught systematically in the Jesuit colleges and various formal exercises prepared the novice for the gymnastics of its interpretation. On December 17, 1686, Le Jay was in charge of a display of enigmas at Louis-le-Grand. The subject was "The Triumph of Religion" (which had also been the subject of the August ballet in 1681). The point was to celebrate the King's "destruction of heresy"; the Edict of Nantes had been revoked the year before and the repression of Protestantism was intense.

Le Jay published his enigmas early in 1687. In the preface, dedicated to the King, he wrote as follows:

> Sire, suffer me, by these feeble symbols to represent to Your Majesty what is perhaps the greatest achievement of your reign to date: the reestablishment and triumph of Religion, which by your piety and zeal you have today raised to that pinnacle of grandeur from which the trouble of Heresy in these last centuries has dragged it. . . . Ought not one to tell, and retell in a hundred different ways, how by the sole force of your Edicts and the gentleness of a fatherly goodness you have, in less than a year, returned to the Church more than a million Heretics, destroyed more than sixteen hundred Impious monuments, and exterminated a dangerous Party in France. . . . I have only tried to represent by Inscriptions and natural Symbols the means by which Your Majesty has done this: [I will be] overjoyed if the painting

---

[9] Ibid., 37.

[10] Knipping, *Iconography*, 1:13.

I have done can catch Your Majesty's eye for a moment, and in so doing mark the profound respect with which I am, Sire . . .[11]

What were Le Jay's "feeble symbols" like? Visual designs, they were part of a complex verbal and conceptual structure established in a rhetorical panegyric of the King delivered by Quartier, a Jesuit. The room where he spoke was decorated so that it was "proportioned to the design of the discourse" (11). The designs for the allegorical decorations were executed by the younger Corneille, of the Royal Academy of Painting, who was also a theatrical designer in Paris. The entrance to the room represented an Arch of Triumph. On top of it, Religion, in a chariot drawn by two white horses, held aloft a chalice topped by the Host. A dove hovered over her head. Louis stood on the "ground" beside her, dressed as a young Hercules; he held a scepter to show that Justice and her Edicts were the only arms he needed to destroy Heresy, which was represented by the seven-headed hydra sprawling dead at the King's feet, with the wheels of Religion's chariot about to roll over it. On either side of the Arch were busts of Henri IV and Louis XIII, who began the attack on Protestantism. A cartouche over the doorway of the Arch represented the revocation of the Edict of Nantes by showing the destruction of the Protestant church at Charenton.

Once the viewer was inside the room, the first of the many "devices" to meet the eye was a stand on which hung an eight-sided diagram of the solar system, with the sun in the center, surrounded by the planetary spheres, each with its astrological sign. It was a double reference to the Sun King and the theories of Copernicus. The Latin motto over it read, "From there he spreads his light over all the world."[12]

Around the room in a frieze ran a motto praising Louis as defender of the faith in France and other countries. A portrait of the King rested on a dais, attended on either side by Piety and Wisdom, with Happiness hovering overhead. From the other end of the room, a portrait of Religion looked straight at the portrait of the King, to show that he had given her back her peace. In the midst of all these allegorical constructions, a rhetorical display was given and the "devices" interpreted.

Dainville states the relation of these sorts of allegorical displays at Louis-le-Grand to the college theater.

---

[11] Gabriel Le Jay, *Le Triomphe de la Religion sous Louis-le-Grand* (Paris: Gabriel Martin, 1687); translation mine.

[12] Ibid.: "De là dans tout le monde il répand sa lumière" (124).

This pleasure in allegory, and the agility which found so many ways through its forest of symbols, prepared the spectator, both student and adult, to find the keys of the college theater productions. This is what explains the silence of so many programs, especially the Parisian programs.[13]

By "silence," Dainville means the fact that most Parisian ballet programs do not make any attempt to explain the allegories contained in the production. The assumption was that the educated audience would be able to decipher them on its own, and that part of its pleasure in the show would come from doing so.

The Jesuits' pleasure in these creations, in their theater as well as in other settings, highlights the relationship of their theater to their theology, and also their conflict with the Jansenists. The crux of the conflict was the human relationship to the created world. In the 1730s, the Jesuits provided the money for the Stairway of the Five Senses, at Bom Jesus do Monte, in the Portuguese town of Braga. The Stairway stands within an allegorical garden, whose terraces contain the stations of the cross and fountains dedicated to the gods of Olympus, some of whom also represent planets. The fountain for the crowning Chapel of the Resurrection is built around Hercules the Christ Bearer. Halfway through the stations is the Stairway, beginning with a fountain in which water pours from the stylistically depicted five wounds of Christ. On the staircase are Old Testament figures, originally attended by classical gods and heroes, who were later removed by an Inquisition. In the most stark contrast imaginable to this garden riot of symbolic orthodoxy and mythology are the words of the Jansenist Port-Royal convent's superior, Angélique Arnauld. She said, "I love all that is ugly; art is nothing but lies and vanity. Whosoever gives to the senses takes away from God."[14]

The Costumes

For those who chose the Jesuit direction in theology and art, several handbooks helped in playing the game of allegory. These circulated around Europe in numerous editions and languages, and were used by educators, designers, painters, sculptors, and theater artists. Most of these books were compiled in the sixteenth century and, modified over time, carried Renaissance allegory into the art of

---

[13] François de Dainville, S.J., "Allégorie et actualité sur les tréteaux des jésuites," in *Dramaturgie et société Nancy, April 14–21, 1967*, ed., Jean Jacquot (Paris, 1968), I:439; translation mine.

[14] Bazin, *The Baroque*, 36.

the baroque centuries. Some books depended on verbal tags and mottoes for communication, or on poems that accompanied the visual figures. Others attempted to communicate as much as possible through the figures themselves.

The best-known of these books, and the most influential for theater design, was Cesare Ripa's *Iconologia*, first published at Rome in 1593. Translated into several European languages and illustrated at different times by different artists, the *Iconologia* was a collection of allegorical personifications; it was especially useful to ballet designers and painters, because it communicated through visual rather than verbal allegories. As Menestrier, who apparently used it, said, allegorical costumes were found equally in ballet and painting.[15] Among its French editions were those of 1644, 1677, 1681, and 1698. Though he based some of his costume ideas on Ripa, Menestrier did not wholeheartedly endorse the *Iconologia*'s approach. He grumbles that

> [o]ne should avoid the monstrous figures with beasts' heads on human bodies, or serpents' tails, with which Cesar Ripa has infected painting . . . and with which he has filled his *Iconologie*, which are not at all proper to the beautiful and grand designs within which one treats heroic subjects. These monsters are nevertheless suffered in ballets as well as in great works of painting. They are very appropriate to the grotesque.[16]

Nonetheless, Ripa's book, both directly and as a shaper of common allegorical conceits, was one of Menestrier's sources. A comparison of five ballet characters described by the Jesuit with their corresponding figures in Ripa's book shows how some of these characters were translated to the stage. An initial difference between Ripa's personifications and Menestrier's figures, which would have been true in all seventeenth-century and most eighteenth-century ballet, is that where Ripa's allegories are often dressed in vaguely classical draperies, most ballet characters would have worn clothing whose style and shape followed the fashions of the day. (Exceptions to this rule were the soldiers costumed *a l'antique*, in Greek or Roman style tunics, armor, and helmets.)

---

[15] Menestrier, *Des Ballets anciens et modernes*, 228.

[16] Ibid.: "Il faut seulement éviter les figures monstrueuses de têtes de bêtes sur des corps humains, de Jambes a plis de serpens, dont Cesar Ripa a infecté la peinture, par les bizarreries ridicules, dont il a rempli son Iconologie, et qui ne sont nullement propres a ces beaux et grands desseins ou l'on traite des sujets heroiques. Ces personnages monstrueux se souffriroient plutost dans les Ballets que dans les grands ouvrages de peinture. Ils sont aussi fort propres aux grotesques" (149f.).

Fortune was a frequent ballet character. Ripa presented her as a female figure, because "Fortuna" is grammatically feminine, as are most of the Latin nouns for the allegorical concepts.[17] It is likely that the Jesuits and other ballet producers cast her as feminine for the same reason. Ripa shows her nude and blindfolded, carrying a scepter topped with a wheel in one hand, and in the other a cornucopia, from which cascade crowns, a bishop's miter, coins, jewels, and the Roman fasces, symbol of power. Menestrier costumes her in fabric woven so that it appears to change color as the light strikes it; her costume is decorated with scepters, crowns, and weapons as symbols of power—whether as designs drawn on the fabric or objects attached to it is not clear. Like Ripa's figure, she is blindfolded and carries a wheel.

An important thing to notice about Ripa's visual allegories is that they have a suite of attendant characters, whether present in the drawing or suggested in the accompanying verse with its classical or biblical reference. So from each of Ripa's plates, a complete ballet entrée could be made, since in the ballets, personifications have suites of attendants, who by their presence complete the meaning of the allegory. In Ripa's plate for Fortune, Commerce (dressed like Mercury), Poverty, and Time surround the main figure, together with a peasant and an eager young boy.

Night, another favorite ballet character, is presented by Ripa as a barefoot woman, dressed in dark colors, kindling fire. Over her head are stars and a crescent moon. Menestrier's Night wears a black costume covered with stars, and on her head is a crescent moon.

Ripa does not have a single image for Love, but includes two aspects of love containing elements of Menestrier's costume suggestions for that character. One is Enforced Love and the other is Lewdness. Both images include a Cupid, with his blindfold, bow, and quiver. In Enforced Love, Cupid, who has dropped a flaming torch and holds an hourglass, is the central figure. Behind him, Potiphar's wife pursues Joseph. In Lewdness a beautiful woman reclines on a bed with goats' legs, fondling the Cupid figure, who holds his bow and an arrow. At her feet is a goat, symbol of lust, and behind her a classical king amuses himself in his harem. The recommended ballet costume for Love is rose-colored, covered with flaming hearts. The dancer has veiled eyes, a bow in his hand, and a quiver on his back. In this instance, Menestrier chooses Cupid as the personification rather than the female figure.

---

[17] Knipping, *Iconography*, 1:15.

Enmity, as depicted by Ripa, is very close to Menestrier's costume for Hate. Enmity is a woman wearing a black robe decorated with red flames. She holds an eel, and beside her a dog and a cat regard each other balefully. Behind her, Hamilcar and Hannibal swear before a tripod's smoke and flame to be Rome's enemies. The smoke and flame of the tripod and the colors of Enmity's costume signify that this feeling is a mixture of rage and melancholy. Menestrier's Hate wears fire-colored garments and carries a flaming, smoking torch of black wax. There is black on her costume as well to show that hatred includes sadness.

In the *Iconologia,* Faith is a woman dressed in white, for purity; she wears a helmet, because her mind is protected against false doctrine, and reads a book, which represents the Bible. She holds a heart bearing a lighted candle, because the light of faith comes from the heart as well as the brain, and beside her a cherub holds a large cross and a chalice with the Host. Behind her an angel prevents Abraham from sacrificing Isaac. Menestrier's Faith wears white and holds a book. However, her eyes are veiled, to show submission to mystery, and she wears a crown like Constantine's instead of a helmet. She is not accompanied by cross or chalice, because it was "improper" to put sacramental symbols on the stage.[18]

In the visual allegories of the painting and ballet of this period, not only was each figure associated with particular attributes—as Hercules was with princely strength—but each also carried additional references. The Sun meant "sight"; Bacchus and Ceres signaled "a taste for good cheer"; Apollo indicated "an ear for poetry and music"; Pomone and Flore symbolized "the scent of fruit and flowers"; Venus with four Cupids was read as "touch"; Proteus was the allegory for "skill"; Esculapeius attended by Exercise, Rest, and Joy meant "health." So in a ballet entrée about health, Esculapeius would enter with his suite: Diana and her Nymphs for "exercise"; Night and Sleep for "rest"; and Momus for "joy."[19]

Many writers called both ballet and painting "mute poetry," because each physically "expressed the soul." Menestrier follows Plutarch in saying that a ballet is a painting which speaks by its movement and by its characters (138). Ballet characters' costumes are an essential part of the communication (138f.). Commenting on the

---

[18] Menestrier's characters are described on pp. 255–57 of *Des Ballets anciens et modernes*. The figures are found on plates 152, 16, 45, 70, 156, and 84 of *Iconologia*, ed. Edward A. Maser (Hertel, 1758–60; reprinted by Dover Publications, 1971).

[19] Menestrier, *Des Ballets anciens et modernes*, 151f.

costuming for his ballet *Les Songes* (Dreams), Le Jay directed that its characters should be dressed "with a view to the greater magnificence of the performance."[20] Magnificence was a cardinal requirement for ballet costumes on the Jesuit stage as much as at court or at the Opéra. Rich fabrics contributed to the splendor. Cloth of gold, cloth of silver, brocade, satin, velvet, silk gauze, lace, embroidered muslin, real and imitation pearls, and precious stones were used. Hairdressing and head ornaments were lavish, with a profusion of turbans, plumes, flowers, jewels, crowns, wigs, and various additions of false hair. Dancers wore heeled shoes with ribbon bows or short boots with heels. Some ballet designs show dancers wearing what looks like a version of the antique sandal. Masks were at least sometimes worn, and props held in the hand or attached to the costume completed the ensemble.

Although costume designers were not named in the programs, a ballet needed more costumes than any other theater form, because costumes were, to such a large degree, its "voice."[21] The 1698 *Ballet de la Paix* (Ballet of peace) at Louis-le-Grand had two hundred and three of these splendid creations.[22] As in the court ballets, some of these were the same costume produced five or ten times over for a group of dancers, since the costumes for each entrée were similar in design. Menestrier stipulates that in order to keep the audience in suspense, costumes should be as varied as possible, and that if the same or similar ones must be used, the interval between them should be as long as possible. However, all the dancers in a single entrée should be dressed in the same color and fashion, if this is feasible.[23] College costumes were probably reused, since many ballets had similar entrées and characters that, like Fortune, Love, Hate, and the other common allegorical figures, were costumed according to unchanging visual and rhetorical convention, following the *Iconologia* and other sources.

Neither historical accuracy, everyday reality, nor geographical authenticity was attempted in the costumes for court ballet, and the same was apparently true on the Jesuit stage. A court-ballet chef, for example, would wear white taffeta or gauze instead of a dirty cotton apron.[24] What the costume *did* have to do was help the audience

---

[20] Le Jay, "De choreis dramaticis," 814. The quotation is taken from an unpublished translation by John Rundin.

[21] Menestrier, *Des Ballets anciens et modernes*, 212.

[22] Dupont-Ferrier, *La Vie quotidienne d'un collège*, 300.

[23] Menestrier, *Des Ballets anciens et modernes*, 253.

[24] Christout, *Ballet de cour*, 28.

identify the character beyond the shadow of a doubt. This is a curious paradox about these allegorical ballets: the audience took great pleasure in unraveling layers of complex meaning from the visual and verbal images, but "open-endedness" in the modern sense was not a part of the aesthetic. A character had to be identifiable in order to provide a starting point for reading the allegory. This was so important that Lang felt it was better to be comically obvious than to risk ambiguity. "It may help at times if the characters carry signs with large-lettered identifications."[25]

Besides ensuring recognition of the characters, costumes could, as Menestrier pointed out, sometimes make up for mediocre dancers. If a poor dancer were given an astonishing costume, the audience would watch it instead of the dancing.

Costume also had to facilitate, or at least refrain from hindering, movement. Though dancers were sometimes encased in the shells and furs of animals, the costume usually allowed a reasonable amount of physical freedom. There were even "tights" that were worn by professional acrobats for tumbling entrées of goblins and fools. It may be that the three students at the Rodez college, who in 1757 shocked the ballet audience by appearing to be nude, were wearing tights.[26] But baroque dancers must often have balked at the weight and awkwardness of costumes and props. De Pure irritably directs that the costumer must make the dancers wear what suits the ballet, and not what appeases their vanity.[27] Male characters often wore a very short skirtlike costume which left the legs free and visible, and which is said to be the origin of the modern ballet tutu. Female roles were costumed differently, depending on whether they were played by a man or a woman. Men playing female characters wore skirts to the knee, garlands of flowers and ribbons around their calves (to make them appear more slender), and yokes of muslin or lace where the décolletage would have been, to hide their hairy chests. On the public stage, female dancers wore calf-length skirts which left the feet and ankles visible.

In 1727 Lang published a wardrobe catalogue called *Imagines symbolicæ*. Its author intended it for "producers with a low budget and a lively imagination," and described costumes from *A* for "acidie" to *Z* for "zephyr."[28] Lang alludes to the allegory books when he directs

---

[25] Carroll, "Jesuit Playwright," 20.

[26] LeBègue, "Ballets des jésuites," 138.

[27] Christout, *Ballet de cour*, 141.

[28] Carroll, "Jesuit Playwright," 19.

that classical art shows how to dress the Muses, gods, seasons, planets, and signs of the Zodiac. *Imagines* is especially interesting for the glimpse it give us of the relationship between ballet costumes and props. Lang mounts Concupiscence on a crocodile and makes him stroke a partridge while he rides. A sycophantic courtier is draped in clinging strands of ivy, carries a barometer, and kicks a deflated globe of the world. Sloth leads a tortoise, has a stringless bow over his back, and lazily fans himself. Meekness carries a lamb and leads an elephant. Curiosity is wrapped in a cloak embroidered with frogs and ears. Gossip's hair is festooned with chirping tree crickets; and History rides on the back of Saturn (Father Time, who carries a scythe) and looks backward over his shoulder, ready to use his quill and paper to write down what he sees. Marriage drags a ball and chain, wears a halter around his neck, has a water snake coiled around his legs, and carries a basket of love apples (tomatoes) in his hand (20). Streams and rivers carry urns, Painting a brush and pallet, Architecture a level, Fishermen nets and hooks, Masons a trowel and hammer, Time a scythe and an hourglass, Love a bow, Religion a palm branch, Winds bunches of feathers, Indians drums, Savages clubs, Hate a smoking torch, and Furies torches and snakes.

Because the ballet was a "mute comedy," the props carried by the dancers were essential parts of their costumes. The dancers, however, often thought otherwise. Menestrier complains that it was getting harder and harder to make the dancers carry—and dance with—their characters' proper symbols. (This reluctance is hardly surprising; he expected Time, for example, to dance with a chiming clock on his head.) Like a good historian, Menestrier reminds himself that it was just as bad in Saint Augustine's time. The saint complained about the pass things had come to in the theater: Someone had to go out onto the stage and shout out what and who the dancers were supposed to be.[29]

Menestrier confirms that most characters were part of the educated public's common iconography, recognizable because they were always dressed in a similar way. Mercury, for example, had wings, a cape, and his caduceus. Apollo was never without his lyre and laurel crown. National groups had their characteristic dress: Moors sported tight curls and earrings and Americans wore feathers. Towns wore their coats of arms.

Dressing personified ideas and purely imaginary characters presented the greatest challenge to the designer. Some of Menestrier's ideas for the more imaginary and abstract characters must have

---

[29] Ibid., 147f.

translated into beautiful costumes. For the Future, he suggests an indeterminate color, covered with floating gauze, because the future is unknown.[30] Fate wears blue, covered with stars and mirrors (because one searches for one's destiny in astrology and magic mirrors), is crowned with stars, and carries a wand.[31] The Horizon's costume is half black and half white, to signify the difference in light between two hemispheres (150). If we imagine his Four Seasons dancing together in a ballet entrée, the satisfying visual rhythm created by the contrast between the costumes becomes apparent. If these characters were in the same entrée, they could not wear the same color; but the style of the costumes would be the same, and a "base" color might be used. Spring is in green, covered with flowers, wearing a crown of roses. Summer wears golden brown, the color of harvest, with a crown of wheat ears on her head and a scythe in her hand. Autumn is dressed in olive green or drab brown, carries a cornucopia of fruit, and wears a wreath of vine leaves. Winter is a slow-moving old man in white fur, with a long beard (254f.).

The "low characters" in a ballet provided a different challenge to the costumer. Rollicking peasants and buffoons were dressed in pieces of different-colored fabric and often hung with small bells—like jesters in motley. Comic characters sometimes offered the challenge of turning human beings into Lanterns, Bottles, Fat Poultry, Monkeys, Lobsters, Ninepins, and Trees (145f.).

We can assume that dancers in the Jesuit theater sometimes wore masks, as did other baroque dancers. Menestrier depicts the Sun and Moon in rayed masks of gold or silver (255). Occasionally *Nouvelles ecclésiastiques* railed against the Jesuit students for the "deceitful" practice of wearing masks in their theater performances. Though the Jesuit writers on dance rarely mention them, it is difficult to believe that masks were unusual in the Louis-le-Grand ballets, since they were worn at the Opéra and in court ballets during much of this period. But there also seems to have been a social and religious distrust of the idea of the mask, especially among pietists, who equated it with lies and deceit. Because the point of the baroque arts was the "expression of the soul" through physical media, to conceal "the soul" made a stronger impression than it possibly could today. At Louis-le-Grand in 1675 and in 1731, a ballet entrée in *La Mode*

[30] Menestrier, "Remarques pour le conduite," 55.

[31] Menestrier, *Des Ballets anciens et modernes*, 255f.

(Fashion) called for Indians who had painted their faces so that, as the program said, "no one could read the movements of their soul."[32]

Made of leather, parchment, or papier mâché, court-ballet masks helped to stylize characters. The faces of savages were sunburned, those of Furies were twisted and red, those of Rivers aged and venerable, those of Nymphs fresh and young, and those of comic characters exaggerated or caricatured. Children who played dwarfs wore enormous false heads. One reason for these masks, apart from emphasizing the characterization of a role, was that a dancer played several parts during a ballet, and the masks helped each character appear different from those who had gone before.[33] For a comic or bizarre effect, masks were also sometimes worn on the back of the head, the elbows, and knees.

Menestrier's description of the costume and suite of The World in a ballet entrée makes a graphic sketch of the way character, costume, suite of attendants, and action worked together in the ballet allegories. The World was dressed in a map, with France on his heart, Germany on his belly, Italy on one leg, Spain on an arm, and Australia or *terra incognita* on his rump. Carried by Atlas and Hercules, he wore Mt. Olympus on his head; he was sick because he had been overfed by Ceres, the goddess of fruitfulness, and Bacchus, god of wine. Mars, the god of war, thought bleeding him might effect a cure, but his doctors, Apollo and Esculapeius, ordered a restorative diet—forty days of Lent.[34]

The Stage

Some Jesuit stages, like that of the Vienna college, were as lavish as the best-endowed royal opera house. Built for the Jesuits in 1650 by Emperor Ferdinand III, the Jesuit theater at Vienna was a three-thousand-seat house with a separate practice stage.[35] Louis-le-Grand, however, in spite of its location in one of the theater capitals of Europe and its status as a "grand collège," did not have an indoor theater on anything like this scale. There is very little visual record of the Paris college theater, and what there is shows stage design for the tragedy rather than the ballet. (According to McGowan, visual records that show details of seventeenth-century French ballet staging are rare in general.)

---

[32] LeBègue, "Ballets des jésuites," 324.

[33] Christout, *Ballet de cour,* 168f.

[34] Menestrier, *Des Ballets anciens et modernes,* 144f.

[35] Carroll, "Jesuit Playwright," 17.

By the 1630s, a well-equipped theater needed "nether regions" under the stage, side spaces for machinery, and a sturdy floor for vigorous dances. Light could come from the front of the stage, or from the back or sides, though side-lighting was particularly important—as it still is for dance. Directors insisted that the light be neither bright enough to show how the stage effects were done, nor dim enough to hide them! A front curtain, capable of being raised and lowered, was also considered necessary.[36]

By the late seventeenth century, the productions at Louis-le-Grand seem to have had all of these accoutrements; though we know least about the lighting arrangements. The college had three separate theaters. Only one seems to have been a permanent indoor theater, while the other two were outdoor constructions put up each year for the comedy and the ballet. The largest of the three had a one-hundred-and-two-foot proscenium, was thirty feet deep, and forty-eight feet high.[37] If this was the indoor Salle Ordinaire des Pièces, its size would reflect the importance of Louis-le-Grand and its theatrical activities; Dainville says that the usual size of these indoor halls was about eighty by twenty-four feet.[38] Descriptions of performances and scraps of information about the theater and the stage support speculations that the Louis-le-Grand theatrical arrangements, permanent and temporary, were commodious.

The theater for the August ballet was put up every year in the large entrance courtyard and was almost square. Outdoor theaters were not uncommon during this period; Versailles had one, as did some country houses. Two of the walls from the baroque courtyard were still standing in 1921; in 1984, it was apparent that the courtyard had been altered and was much smaller than in the period of the ballets.

The stage was against the rhetoric classroom at the far end of the space, and the classroom, probably by means of its long windows, served as the backstage area. Platforms for the audience (some of whom also sat on the stage, as they did in the public theaters in Paris) ran around the other three sides of the court. The college windows served as box seats. As a protection from uncertain weather, an immense canvas awning covered the whole courtyard; unfortunately, it was a better protection from the sun than from the rain.

---

[36] Christout, *Ballet de cour*, 22.

[37] Hémon, "Comédie chez les jésuites," 531.

[38] François de Dainville, S.J., "Lieux de théâtre et salles des actions dans les collèges des jésuites de l'ancienne France," *Revue d'histoire du théâtre* 1 (1950): 189.

Loret mentions rain at the 1656 and 1657 shows, saying that he ran for cover to save his new hat.[39]

Though the stage and the theater were temporary, they were luxuriously so. In 1651 the stage and its scenery were on public view for four days after the performance, and the *Gazette de France* reported that as many people came just to look at the constructions as had come to the performance.[40] However, either the arrangements were not always so impressive or French staging was less impressive to foreign visitors, because in 1662 a Belgian, Daniel Papenbroeck, made a somewhat disparaging entry in his journal after going to the Louis-le-Grand tragedy and ballet.

> This huge construction, rising to many floors, was equal to the width and height of the college itself. It was an elegant structure, little used by the few actors who played on the middle part of the theater. It was occupied by the men and boys in the audience as well as the actors and those who provided other amusement. No use of a drop scene, nor a vault of heaven, nor music was used to quiet the audience.[41]

Though Papenbroeck's comment suggests that there was no front curtain, other sources suggest that, at least by 1674, there was.[42] We do not know exactly what the scene-changing capacity of the Paris college was; but it must have been considerable, since Louis-le-Grand was famous for its ballet, and numerous and elaborate scenic effects were indispensable for that theater form. One piece of indirect evidence for the college having had at least adequate machinery for scenic effects and changes is that its "magasin" for storing scenery and machines was larger than the storage room at the Comédie-Française. But during part of this period, the Comédie was thought to be rather poorly equipped, and the comparison does not necessarily indicate a high degree of mechanical sophistication. Le Jay says that the college had enormous circular machines, fifty meters around, which could accomplish quick scene shifts and provide for multiple exits and entrances of the singers and dancers in the ballets.[43]

In any case, when the ballet performances were reviewed, writers often praised the beauty of the stage design, as did the *Mercure* in 1732 and 1739. Though we do not know very much about the

---

[39] Dupont-Ferrier, *Vie quotidienne d'un collège*, 299.

[40] Ibid., 300.

[41] Dainville, "Décoration théâtrale," 358; unpublished translation by James Empereur, S.J.

[42] Emond, *Histoire du Collège*, 133f.

[43] Lowe, *Marc-Antoine Charpentier*, 72.

designers who worked for the Jesuits, the architects in 1720 were Gherardini and Legrand, the designer in 1732 was the painter Lemaire, and in 1748 the architect Blondel designed the settings, which were executed by the painters Tremblin and Labbé.[44]

In addition to the outside artists and architects who created the mise en scène for the ballets, there were also Jesuit painters and theorists at Louis-le-Grand and elsewhere who created and wrote about stage design. The Italian Jesuit trompe l'oeil painter Andrea Pozzo was one of the most influential perspective theorists of the late seventeenth century. Between 1693 and 1700 he published two volumes of theater plans and stage settings at Rome. However, this work seems to represent an elaboration of current practice rather than technical innovation.[45] Interested in many of the seventeenth- and eighteenth-century scientific discoveries and movements, the Jesuits were also interested in visual perspective. The French Jesuit DuBreuil, at Louis-le-Grand, published *La Perspective pratique* in Paris in the mid-seventeenth century, but his work seems to have been more theoretical than practical—an attempt to interpret classical spatial theories.[46]

In French baroque ballet, decor was less important than either costume or stage machinery; the French were said to excel at costume, the Italians at decor. There is some evidence that ballet design in the Jesuit colleges was influenced by the secular theater. The sets used in 1676 for *L'Alliance de Tolose et des Pyrénées* (The Alliance of Toulouse and the Pyrenees) at the Toulouse college seem to have been based on those done by the Italian designer Torelli for a 1647 *Orpheus*. Torelli's sets had also been used that same year in Paris, at the Marais theater for the *Marriage of Orpheus and Eurydice* and later by Corneille for his *Andromede.*[47]

The ballet, like the tragedy, had conventionalized set types. The three basic set types for tragedy were noble-tragic, consisting of arches of triumph, pyramids, obelisks, and palaces; comic, which usually had an urban square with arcades and shops; and sylvan, which showed countryside or cottages among trees.[48] Menestrier identifies ten set types for lyric theater: celestial (as opposed to sa-

---

[44] Ibid., 70–72.

[45] Per Bjurstrom, "Baroque Theatre and the Jesuits," in *Baroque Art*, ed. Wittkower and Jaffe (New York: Fordham University Press, 1972), 103.

[46] Ibid., 102.

[47] Dainville, "Decoration théatrale," 370.

[48] Christout, *Ballet de cour*, 170f.

cred)—for classical divinities—and military, rustic, maritime, royal, civil, historic, poetic, magic, and academic (146).

One of the only surviving visual representations of a stage at Louis-le-Grand is of the set for the 1759 tragedy *Régulus*.[49] Tragedy usually had only one set, because of its adherence to the classical unities of time, place, and action. There was a ballet that year, as usual, and it would have taken place on the same stage, but with a variety of changing scenes, since it was not bound by the classical unities. An examination of this rare drawing of a Paris college production is useful for understanding the ballet, if only by contrast. Also, some of the ballet set types, the celestial, civil, historic, and royal, would have made use of some of this tragedy set's visual elements.

The first thing that strikes the viewer about this tragedy set is the symmetry of the design. The only asymmetry is in decorative details on the bases of the two downstage columns, and in the sculptures that decorate the next-to-the-top level of the central arch of triumph. Behind the arch are the long sides of palatial buildings flanking a courtyard; through the center of the arch we see the courtyard's farthest side, beyond an exactly centered column or fountain. Side streets run off at the same angles on both sides of the set. (The total effect is a little like the Louvre courtyard or the Place Vendome.) In spite of the careful use of perspective to give a sense of distance, the enormous width of the design contrasts strongly with the comparative shallowness of the useable stage space.

An emphasis on symmetry was characteristic of central strains of thought as well as of much of the art of the baroque centuries. One reason the rococo style in painting and architecture came as such an innovation in the later eighteenth century was that it glorified asymmetry. So far as we know, symmetry remained a staple of Jesuit ballet staging. In the nine pages of dance figures (the arrangement of dancers in space) from the 1667 ballet at the College of Nobles in Parma, which Menestrier includes in his *Des Ballets*, there is no asymmetry at all in the choreographic design.[50] Similarly, much of the notation for eighteenth-century-theater dances gives a visual impression of symmetry on the page, and in many cases the dancer creates a basically symmetrical floor pattern on the stage in the course of the dance.

---

[49] Collège Louis-le-Grand, 86 CAR 141OX, Carnavalet Museum, Paris.

[50] Menestrier, *Des Ballets anciens et modernes*, 179–95.

This appreciation of symmetry—and dislike of its opposite—was, like allegory, characteristic of the period. Theologians, following Abelard and his "mundane egg" theory, surmised that the Creation had originally been smooth and round; irregular coastlines, caves, violent storms, mountains, and the sea were evidence of the effects of human sin.[51] Thomas Burnet's *Sacred Theory of the Earth*, published in Latin in 1681, which propounded these theories, was taken seriously even by many of the French "philosophes" late in the eighteenth century. Burnet's description of the state of things before the Flood is reminiscent of a pastoral scene in a ballet.

> The Face of the Earth before the Deluge was smooth, regular, and uniform, without Mountains, and without a Sea. . . . And the Smoothness of the Earth made the Face of the Heavens so, too; the Air was calm and serene; none of those tumultuary Motions and Conflicts of Vapours, which the Mountains and the Winds cause in ours: 'Twas suited to a golden Age, and to the first innocency of Nature.[52]

An English traveler, John Spence, spoke for this antipathy toward asymmetry and wildness. In 1730, having visited the Alps, he said, "I should like the Alps very much, if it was not for the hills."[53]

The ballet set, according to Le Jay, prepared the audience for the events they were going to see. The setting dictated the characters, in somewhat the same way that an allegorical figure called forth particular associations in the minds of the spectators. For example, says Le Jay, if your set is a seaport, the audience expects to see Neptune or Tritons. If it is Olympus, then you are announcing the gods. If you present forests, gardens, and shadowy bowers, then the divinities of the countryside are about to make an entrance.[54] Sets were so expensive that their availability—and reusability—sometimes influenced the ballet libretto. This partly explains the endless repetition of similar characters and entrées on the Jesuit stage and elsewhere.

The sets themselves posed certain difficulties for dancers, musicians, and actors alike. None of these could, for example, approach too closely to the upstage area; otherwise, they would destroy the illusion of grand scale and distance. This meant that the usable stage space was relatively small, which probably influenced the vogue

---

[51] D. G. Charlton, *New Images of the Natural in France* (Cambridge: Cambridge University Press, 1984), 42.

[52] Ibid., 43.

[53] Ibid., 42.

[54] Dainville, "Decoration théâtrale," 364.

for machinery. Movable mountains, ships, trees, architectural arcades, and so on provided additional space for action and for exits and entrances, as well as an onstage place to wait when not dancing, playing, or speaking.

Both ballet and tragedy sets were decorated with allegorical sculpture. In 1720 the stage for the tragedy and ballet was designed in honor of Louis XV. Besides the obligatory statue of the King, there were Rumor with his trumpet, Mercury, Apollo and his lyre, Tragedy and Comedy, Momus (a male substitute for Terpsichore) dancing to a basque drum, Painting, and Drawing.[55]

One difficulty in knowing what conclusions to draw from surviving descriptions of Louis-le-Grand stage design is that in many instances it is hard to tell whether tragedy or ballet design is being described. Another is that it is unclear to what extent the elaborate tragedy set remained the basic set for the ballet, ornamented and transformed by machines. Dainville suggests that on at least some occasions the ballet took place in the tragedy decor.[56] To what extent the changes accomplished by machinery altered the basic setting remains to be determined; the degree of alteration would depend, of course, on the college's stock of stage machinery.

From Menestrier's description of it, the late-seventeenth-century stage machinery at the Royal Academy offered essentially the same kind of stage effects as that at Louis-le-Grand.[57] Though it was very expensive, machinery was a necessary part of any theater engaged in ballet production. As costly sets dictated reuse, an expensive machine dictated the repetition of the effects it could create. Le Jay, a ballet producer at Louis-le-Grand for more than twenty years, described some of the special effects he and others had created.

> We have seen, in this Paris college courtyard, Orpheus descending to the underworld so realistically that the spectator needs only eyesight to understand what is happening. We have seen the siege of Troy done so that one would believe oneself present at it. We have seen the gods of Olympus besieged by the Titans, mountains piled on mountains, Jupiter throwing thunderbolts, and the Giants crushed by rocks. I will not even speak of a tournament and a cavalry battle, of Polypheme blinded by Ulysses' companions, of Orpheus enticing the stones and rocks by the sounds of his lyre—all of these reaping the ap-

---

[55] Lowe, *Marc-Antoine Charpentier*, 70f.

[56] Dainville, "Decoration théâtrale," 364.

[57] Menestrier, *Des Représentations en musique*, 239.

plause of the audience charmed by the faithful imitation of these real or fantastic events which they found in the dance.[58]

This love of metamorphosis, of the fantastic suddenly revealed, is related to the baroque love of allegory. There seems to have been a pervasive sense that the ordinary existed cheek by jowl with the supernatural, which waited to be revealed in the natural world just as allegorical ballet characters existed to have their deeper meanings plumbed.

The whole conceit is reminiscent of the gorgeously painted chancels and ceilings of many Jesuit churches. The building opens out into the heavens, and angelic and human beings come and go across the breach. Onstage, however, the opening of the heavens was very much incarnate in cumbersome machinery. It could be so noisy that one writer on baroque-theater production, Sabbatini, recommended that someone be planted in the audience to start a fight during scene changes in order to distract the crowd's attention; or, failing that, a trumpet might be blown.[59]

This love of stage machinery was a legacy to the Jesuit theater from court ballet. As groups of dancers masked them, trapdoors opened on hinges to let Furies escape from hell. Hell itself was created by putting dancers between two walls of rippling fabric "flames." Hand-turned cylinders crowned with wave shapes made a rolling sea, over which the silhouettes of ships glided on invisible rails. Dolphins surfaced, spouting powder and silver spangles. Bands of silky ribbon turning on rollers allowed fountains to spout "water." Clouds bearing divinities floated down from the "sky"; sets generally had no ceilings, in order to allow these apparitions. These and other effects were

---

[58] Lowe, *Marc-Antoine Charpentier:* "Nous avons vu, dans cette cour du collège de Paris représénter le personnage d'Orphée descendant aux enfers avec tant de vérité, que le spectateur, pour comprendre l'action n'avait besoin que du seul secours de ses veux. Nous avons vu la ruine de Troie figurée avec une telle vraisemblance que l'on croyait assister a l'événement lui-meme. Nous avons vu les dieux de l'Olympe assiégés par les Titans, les monts entassés sur les monts, Jupiter lançant la foudre et les Géants écrasés sous les rochers. Je ne parlerai point d'un carrousel et d'un combat de cavalerie, de Polypheme aveuglé par les compagnons d'Ulysse, d'Orphée attirant par les sons de sa lyre les pierres et les arbres, qui, tous, recueillirent les applaudissements des spectateurs charmés par l'imitation fidèle qu'ils trouvaient dans la danse de ces événements ou réels ou fabuleux" (72f.).

[59] Christout, *Ballet de cour,* 23.

accomplished with pulleys, revolving platforms, cranks, curtains, and cords.[60]

Menestrier is especially fond of stage machines on which dancers can make spectacular entrances; he describes the first entrée of the court ballet done for Louis XIV's wedding, *Hercule amoreux* (Hercules in love). On either side of the stage was a mountain, and on the rocks of these mountains were seated the fourteen Rivers of France. The Moon descended in a machine representing "the heavens"; on landing, "the heavens" opened, and fifteen dancers, who stood for the fifteen noble families from whom the French royal family had descended, stepped out. The Moon and the Rivers sang and the fifteen ladies danced, after which they returned to their machine and were carried skyward.[61]

Menestrier suggests as machines ships, sea monsters, clouds, eagles, elephants, whales, moving thrones, chariots, fountains, rocks, mountains, dryads emerging from their trees, and statues leaving their niches. Dancers dressed as animals—bears, monkeys, rhinoceroses—were also classed as machines. Of all these possibilities, the best are those that suggest deities and enchantment, because they make the audience expect marvels. Like Sabbatini, though, Menestrier warns that the machinery has to be in good working order, or else the ballet will be turned into a comedy. The Jesuits seem to have heeded his warning; according to the *Dictionnaire de Trévoux*, scene changes were accomplished almost without the audience realizing they were taking place.[62]

It may be that some of the ballet overture music, or the music for the beginning of entrées, was music for machines and not for dancers. When machines are center stage, Menestrier warns, no one will pay attention to the dancers. If the machines made their appearance to music—which also would have helped to mask noise—the dancers would have waited until the first surprise was over to begin their entrées. He also suggests that machines be used at night, if possible, since artificial light cloaks their artifice and enhances the general effect they create.[63] But since the August ballets were in the afternoon and since they manifestly made use of machines, either the machines were in prime working order or the audience tolerantly suspended its disbelief.

---

[60] Ibid.

[61] Menestrier, *Des Ballets anciens et modernes*, 220.

[62] Dainville, "Decoration théâtrale," 367.

[63] Menestrier, *Des Ballets anciens et modernes*, 250.

Some machines, like stage settings, suggested specific characters and entrées. Ships went with winds, Tritons, and rowers. The
chariots of sea divinities were often pulled by sea horses or Sirens.
Caves suggested the retreats of dancing fauns, satyrs, shepherds,
savages, sorcerers, thieves, winds, and animals. Clouds brought
planets, angels, and gods. The Zodiac wheel carried its signs and the
sun. The Milky Way brought the classical heroes back to earth. The
whole sky could be a machine which poured thunder, lightning,
perfumed rain or hail, or a snow of flowers over everything (248).

In the Louis-le-Grand ballets, machinery, sets, costumes, and
conceptual layers of verbal and visual allegory alternately revealed
and hid dancers, characters, meanings, and the stage itself. This
"shape shifting" was in the service of Christian-humanist education,
the classical aesthetic, baroque physicality, and the nation as the
theater of the monarch. As we attempt to enter this world and decipher its messages, we may well feel that we are making our way
through one of Menestrier's recommended stage effects—a raging
"storm of sugar" (248).

The Jesuits and the Dance Vocabulary

It is interesting, in relation to the church-and-theater question,
that the Jesuits themselves seem to have occasionally performed in
the ballets, though perhaps only in the provinces. McGowan, writing
on the early seventeenth century, states that the Jesuits sometimes
danced in their productions,[64] and Raymond LeBègue cites an eighteenth-century report, which he acknowledges as questionable, from
Nouvelles ecclésiastiques. He does not give a date, but says that *Nouvelles* gleefully reported that a young priest, "disguised" (which meant
that he was wearing either a mask or a costume which effectively hid
his identity), "danced successfully" in a ballet at the Rodez college.[65]
While they may not have danced often and perhaps not at all in
major cities, where there was a more diverse audience who must not
be "scandalized," it would not be surprising to find that many of the
Jesuits were accomplished dancers. Many of them came from the
strata of society that produced the dancers for the King's ballets, and
the majority of them had probably received their own education in
the Jesuit system. Although ballet masters were not part of the faculty
of a seminary for priests (as opposed to a college like Louis-le-Grand,
which was for young men going into the lay world), not all of the

---

[64] McGowan, *Art de ballet,* 206.

[65] LeBègue, "Ballets des jésuites," 137.

Jesuits would have entered the order at the same age, and so many would have had somewhat different educational experiences. A perusal of Sommervogel's biographies of baroque Jesuit authors gives the impression that most of them entered the order in their late teens or early twenties. In an order that gave so much time and attention to theatrical production, there would have been many young priests who were attracted to it precisely because within it they could serve their religious vocation and at the same time use their theatrical talents and inclinations. In his handbook on acting in the Jesuit theater, Lang specifically urged that the Jesuit director have personal experience as an actor.

As LeBègue writes, it is difficult to believe that those Jesuits who wrote so extensively on dance theory and aesthetics, created the ballet libretti, worked hand in hand with the dancing masters, and oversaw the staging of the show were not themselves dancers. However, if they were, their allegiance would probably have been to theater dance rather than to social dance. Some of the Jesuits made a great distinction between social and theatrical dancing (135). Those who did so embraced theatrical dance for its expressiveness and for its ability to communicate morality and meaning, but drew away from social dance. The latter was associated with romance and flirtation, and was also seen as the preserve of "pure dance," which those committed to the classical aesthetic generally deplored.

Although when they wrote about dance, the Jesuits usually wrote as theorists and not as technicians, one also finds in their work references to the baroque technical vocabulary and directions to dancers and actors, showing that many of them were on intimate terms with the technical and performance aspects of dance—as they would have had to be in order to oversee the production of ballets. One of the funniest references to dance is in the script of a comedy called *L'Esope au collège* (Aesop at school), written by the Jesuit du Cerceau, one of the best of the eighteenth-century dramatists at Louis-le-Grand. Act 3 contains a dancing lesson.

> Sir, to the right . . . stretch your ham! Make two steps: go on. . . .
> Now we begin to go well; dance your Minuet. The arms, sir, the arms.
> . . . Loosen up that ham, make your steps smaller . . . now we're
> getting the dance a little more refined, turn that shoulder . . . stick out
> your chest. Offer your hand . . . go on. The feet more turned out. Lift
> your head . . . there, hold up your body.
>
> Go forward . . . both hands . . . oh, sir, the timing! Turn quickly
> . . . come back . . . make your bow.[66]

---

[66] De Dainville, *Education des Jésuites:* "M., tenez-vous droit. Etendez le

If action was suited to words, this scene would have been reminiscent of M. Jourdain's dancing lesson in Molière's *Bourgeois gentilhomme*.

Lang, a Jesuit, in his 1727 *De actione scenica*, referred Jesuit directors to the movements of professional dancers in their instruction of young actors. Lang emphasized the necessity of walking with self-possession and grace. He suggested a modified fourth position for standing onstage, and stressed the importance of practicing poses of the hips, knees, shoulders, arms, and hands. He was after "the voiceless eloquence of a disciplined body" that could communicate feelings "with a turn of the head or a flick of the finger."

In his "Remarques pour la conduite des ballets," Menestrier included a description of how theater dance communicates the passions; though it is not about the technical vocabulary, the passage eloquently directs the dancer in wedding feeling to form. As has been stated, Menestrier was centrally concerned with expression, generally considered by his contemporaries to be the pinnacle of dance artistry. He takes as his examples anger, fear, and love.[67]

He tells the dancer that anger is uncontrolled, with violent movements and an irregular cadence. It beats the foot, darts forward, threatens with head and hand, while the dancer's eyes throw out furious glances. Fear moves forward slowly and retreats quickly. It has a trembling and suspenseful bearing, and its arms are awkward. It looks distractedly in all directions as it dances.

Love, he says, shows eagerness, tenderness, and a calm face. The eyes are eloquent, throwing out sparks of fire. New love shows constraint at first and grows bolder with progress, in transports of joy over its good fortune. The dancer must show love in all the colors in which the philosophers have painted it. In his directions to the dancer attempting to show love on the stage, written in 1658, Menestrier follows a dance convention of his time. A standard test for the virtuoso dancer was the performance of a suite of dances on the various stages of love and feelings of the lover. Handel was still following this convention in 1734 when he created the "Terpsichore" prologue to his opera *Il pastor fido*. In this prologue Terpsichore dances all the

---

jarret. Faitez deux pas: allez. . . . Commençons tout de bon; dansez votre menuet. Les bras, M., les bras. . . . Dénouez le jarret, serrez vos pas. . . . Allons une danse un peu fine, effacez cette épaule . . . avancez la poitrine. Donnez la main . . . suivez. Les pieds plus en dehors. Levez la tête . . . la, soutenez votre corps. Avancez . . . les deux mains . . . eh! M., la cadence! Tournez court . . . revenez . . . faites la révérence" (Act 3, sc. 7, 8 [p. 523]).

[67] Menestrier, "Remarques pour la conduite," 53f.

feelings of love, representing "the union of Dance with Music and Emotion."[68]

In his directions for "the union of Dance with Music and Emotion," Menestrier is, as usual, fulminating against the "pure dance"— the "Courante, Gavotte, Minuet, and Sarabande, with no expression whatsoever."[69] But this must not be misinterpreted; he is not against these dance forms and steps, only against their use apart from the expression of feeling. He makes this clear when he qualifies his statement with regard to the Sarabande. "Nevertheless, the Sarabande can be danced in the Spanish fashion."[70]

Menestrier's statements are important for our understanding of an important technical reference by another Jesuit, François Pomey, a contemporary and colleague of Menestrier and a teacher of rhetoric at the Jesuit college in Lyon. In his 1671 *Dictionnaire royal augmenté*, Pomey included a description of "A Sarabande Being Danced." Pomey's description is important for several reasons. First, it is additional evidence for the general Jesuit attitude toward dance and the contemporary dance vocabulary. Second, it is one of the most colorful period documents we have about the performance of the Sarabande. And third, when it is read in the light of Menestrier's dance theory, it clears up yet another twentieth-century misunderstanding between dance historians and church historians.

In February 1986, *Early Music* published a very informative article on rhetoric and the French sarabande, by Patricia Ranum. It is an article to which I am profoundly indebted, but it also includes a misunderstanding of the Jesuit attitude toward and involvement with dance. It seems important to deal with this misunderstanding at some length because, like other issues already mentioned in this chapter, it is symptomatic of the misinformation that too often clouds interdisciplinary research in the area of relations between the church and the arts.

In her discussion of Pomey's description of the Sarabande, Ranum represents the Spanish Inquisition's outlawing of the "lewd and suggestive" Sarabande "a l'Espagnole" as the attitude of "the Church," and assumes that Pomey would have shared the Inquisition's opinion. Whatever his personal theology, Pomey's agreement

---

[68] Program for the performance of the Concert Royal and the New York Baroque Dance Company given at Stanford's Memorial Auditorium, November 30, 1984, Palo Alto, California.

[69] Menestrier, *Des Ballets anciens et modernes:* "Il y a des pas de Courante, de Gavote, de Menuet, et de Sarabande, sans aucune expression" (158f).

[70] Ibid. "sinon que la Sarabande peut se danser a l'Espagnol."

with or submission to the Spanish Inquisition regarding the Sarabande—or much else—is unlikely. The Spanish Inquisition, founded in the late fifteenth century, was, in spite of its broader implications, largely a Spanish national affair—a royal ecclesiastical and political weapon.[71] Theologically, it came from a background of holy war against the Moors, and was decidedly anti-intellectual. As a French Jesuit, and therefore a Christian humanist, Pomey belonged to an order that was influential in intellectual matters and belles lettres, an order whose name was synonymous with higher education in Europe. Its founder had been imprisoned by the Spanish Inquisition, and many of its humanist supporters had suffered not only under the Spanish institution but also under the spirit of the new Roman Inquisition instigated by the exceedingly right-wing Cardinal Caraffa in 1542. Insofar as the Spanish Inquisition had been powerful outside Spain, it had been so in large measure because Spain was the leading national power in Europe, and not because the sovereigns of other countries—struggling in this period to establish a degree of national authority in the churches in their dominions—had submitted to it as "good Catholics." As the Spanish Inquisition had been, so was the new Roman Inquisition geographically limited. According to the historian Owen Chadwick, it was a "dead letter" beyond the Italian border, because the monarchs of other Catholic countries refused to have a new papal court system in their realms, wishing to keep local ecclesiastical matters as much as possible within their own jurisdictions.[72] Similarly, the religious orders, especially the influential and, in many ways, liberal Jesuits in France, did not want an additional legal system to placate. So the likelihood of Pomey, or any other French Jesuit, agreeing with or following either Inquisition on artistic and intellectual matters seems remote.

Pomey would, as a matter of course, have had a professional interest in and probably a great deal of knowledge about the various forms of the Sarabande because of the Jesuit ballets. Like Menestrier, Jouvancy, Le Jay, and Porée, he was a professor of rhetoric, and may have been, like them, involved in producing ballets. Finally, both as a Christian humanist and a literate person of his time and place, he would, to some degree, have espoused the classical aesthetic decreeing that dance be maximally expressive of the human feelings. In spite of its amorous associations, the Spanish Sarabande was exactly this.

---

[71] Owen Chadwick, *The Reformation* (Harmondsworth, England: Penguin Books, 1964), 251.

[72] Ibid., 270.

This side trip into Inquisition history and Pomey's professional setting has attempted to show that, in interdisciplinary research, the student must have a care to investigate the background of "obvious facts"; placed in context, they may turn out to be spurious. Ranum's assumption that a celibate priest would naturally have disapproved of the passionate Spanish Sarabande is a case in point. The relationship of religious history to the arts is always far more complex—and far more lively and interesting—than first appears!

Pomey does not tell us whether the dancer he describes was an amateur or a professional, nor does he name either the performer or the theater in which the dance took place. Whoever he was and wherever he danced, Pomey's description of his performance is such a lyrical evocation of the communicative power of baroque dance that it might be taken as a statement of the ideal. Although this dancer was communicating the passion of romantic love, rarely seen in the Jesuit theater, his perfect marriage of feeling and form was the ideal on the Jesuit stage as much as on the secular one. He might pass for the embodiment of Menestrier's dance theory and aesthetic. Pomey's description is important enough to quote in its entirety.

> At first he danced with a totally charming grace, with a serious and circumspect air, with an equal and slow rhythm, and with such a noble, beautiful, free and easy carriage that he had all the majesty of a king, and inspired as much respect as he gave pleasure. Then, standing taller and more assertively, and raising his arms to half-height and keeping them partly extended, he performed the most beautiful steps ever invented for the dance.
>
> Sometimes he would glide imperceptibly, with no apparent movement of his feet and legs, and seemed to slide rather than step. Sometimes, with the most beautiful timing in the world, he would remain suspended, immobile, and half leaning to the side with one foot in the air; and then, compensating for the rhythmic unit that had gone by, with another more precipitous unit he would almost fly, so rapid was his motion. Sometimes he would advance with little skips, sometimes he would drop back with long steps that, although carefully planned, seemed to be done spontaneously, so well had he cloaked his art in skillful nonchalance. Sometimes, for the pleasure of everyone present, he would turn to the right, and sometimes he would turn to the left; and when he reached the very middle of the empty floor, he would pirouette so quickly that the eye could not follow.
>
> Now and then he would let a whole rhythmic unit go by, moving no more than a statue and then, setting off like an arrow, he would be at the other end of the room before anyone had time to realize that he had departed.
>
> But all this was nothing compared to what was observed when this gallant began to express the emotions of his soul through the motions

of his body, and reveal them in his face, his eyes, his steps, and all his actions. Sometimes he would cast languid and passionate glances throughout a slow and languid rhythmic unit; and then, as though weary of being obliging, he would avert his eyes, as if he wished to hide his passion; and, with a more precipitous motion, would snatch away the gift he had tendered. Now and then he would express anger and spite with an impetuous and turbulent rhythmic unit; and then, evoking a sweeter passion by more moderate motions, he would sigh, swoon, let his eyes wander languidly; and certain sinuous movements of the arms and body, nonchalant, disjointed and passionate, made him appear so admirable and so charming that throughout this enchanting dance he won as many hearts as he attracted spectators.[73]

---

[73] François Pomey, S.J. "Description d'une Sarabande dansée," *Le Grand Dictionnaire royal*, 7th ed. (Cologne and Frankfort, 1740), 25. I have quoted the translation used by Patricia Ranum in her article "Audible Rhetoric and Mute Rhetoric: The Seventeenth-Century French Sarabande," *Early Music*, February 1986, 35.

Figure 1: The Collège de Louis-le-Grand, opened in 1564 as the Collège de Clermont and in 1682 declared a royal foundation

LE
TRIOMPHE
DE
LA RELIGION
OU
L'IDOLATRIE
RUINE'E.

BALLET

*Qui sera dansé au College de Clermont, à la grande
Tragédie de Constantin*

Le VI. jour d'Aoust à midi.

A PARIS,
Chez GABRIEL MARTIN, ruë Saint Jacques, au Soleil d'or.

M. DC. LXXXI.

Figure 2: Printed program for the audience at the ballet *Le Triomphe de la Religion,* presented at the Collège de Clermont on August 6, 1681, the year before it came under royal patronage as the Collège de Louis-le-Grand

LE DESSEIN DU BALLET.

LORSQUE l'Idolatrie regnoit dans le monde , elle se vit tout d'un coup détruite par la victoire que Constantin remporta sur Maxence , & par son entiére conversion au Christianisme. C'est le dessein de ce Ballet, qui sera expliqué par une entrée qui servira comme de prelude aux quatre parties suivantes,

ENTREE

Qui sert comme de prelude au Ballet.

LES demons aiant appris qu'un Heros Chrestien devoit un jour ruiner l'Idolatrie, paroissent sous la forme des Divinitez payennes, & font sortir du fond de l'abysme quatre monstres horribles, la Passion, l'Ignorance, l'Artifice, & la Cruauté , dont ils prétendent se servir pour affermir leur empire.

Figure 3: Printed program for the audience at the ballet *Le Triomphe de la Religion,* presented at the Collège de Clermont on August 6, 1681, the year before it came under royal patronage as the Collège de Louis-le-Grand

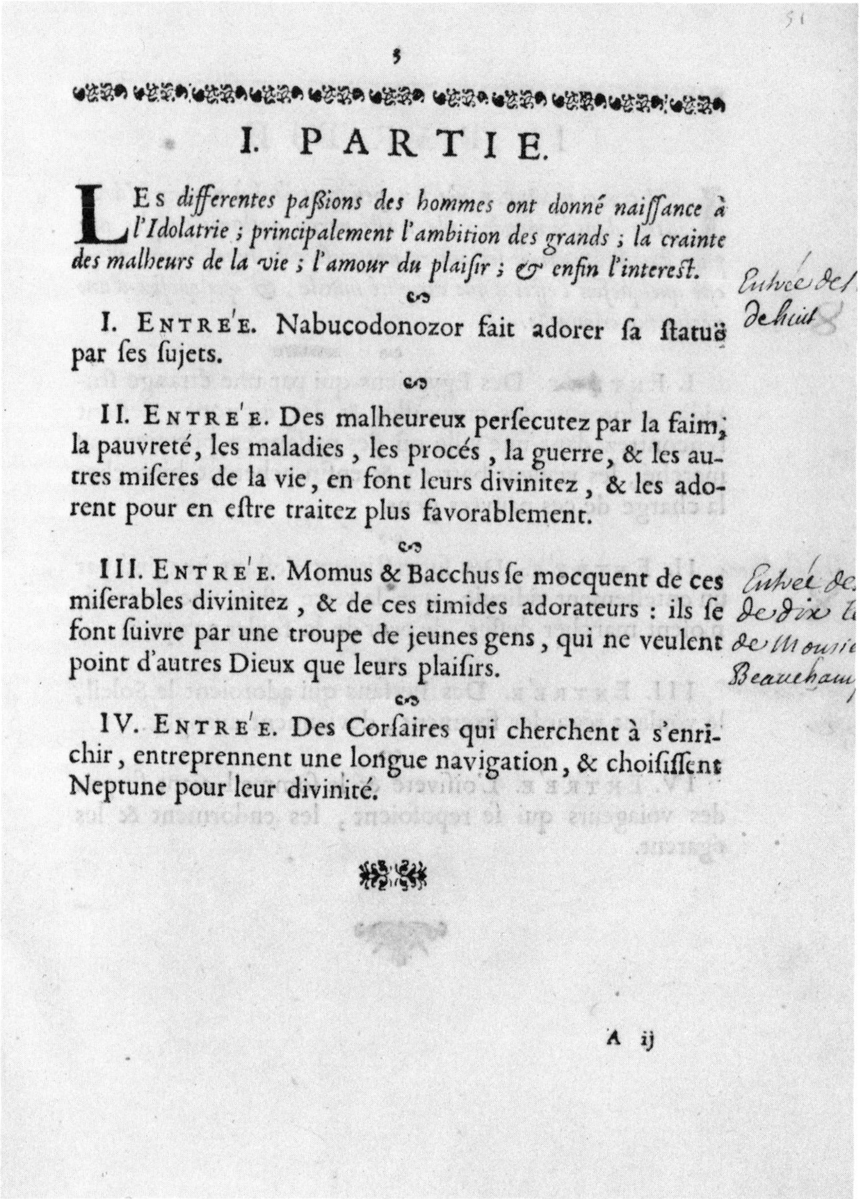

I. PARTIE.

LES *differentes paſſions des hommes ont donné naiſſance à l'Idolatrie ; principalement l'ambition des grands ; la crainte des malheurs de la vie ; l'amour du plaiſir ; & enfin l'intereſt.*

Entrée de l
de huit

I. ENTRE'E. Nabucodonozor fait adorer ſa ſtatuë par ſes ſujets.

II. ENTRE'E. Des malheureux perſecutez par la faim, la pauvreté, les maladies, les procés, la guerre, & les autres miſeres de la vie, en font leurs divinitez, & les adorent pour en eſtre traitez plus favorablement.

III. ENTRE'E. Momus & Bacchus ſe mocquent de ces miſerables divinitez, & de ces timides adorateurs : ils ſe font ſuivre par une troupe de jeunes gens, qui ne veulent point d'autres Dieux que leurs plaiſirs.

Entrée de
de dix
de Mouſie
Beauchamp

IV. ENTRE'E. Des Corſaires qui cherchent à s'enrichir, entreprennent une longue navigation, & choiſiſſent Neptune pour leur divinité.

Figure 4: Printed program for the audience at the ballet *Le Triomphe de la Religion,* presented at the Collège de Clermont on August 6, 1681, the year before it came under royal patronage as the Collège de Louis-le-Grand

II. PARTIE.

L'IGNORANCE n'a pas peu contribué à nourrir l'Idolatrie dans le monde : elle a esté parmi quelques peuples une pure stupidité ; parmi les autres une miserable superstition : elle a esté quelquefois l'effet d'une curiosité inutile, & quelquefois d'une negligence criminelle.

I. ENTRE'E. Des Egyptiens qui par une étrange stupidité adoroient des citroüilles & des oignons, s'estant rencontrez dans une ville où des païsans en portoient au marché, les veulent battre ; & enfin achetent bien cher la charge de ces pauvres gens.

II. ENTRE'E. Des superstitieux s'estant imaginé par un entestement ridicule, que la terre estoit une divinité, n'osent marcher dessus, de peur de la fouler aux pieds.

III. ENTRE'E. Des Persans qui adoroient le Soleil, le voulant regarder fixement, deviennent aveugles.

IV. ENTRE'E. L'oisiveté & le sommeil aiant surpris des voiageurs qui se reposoient, les endorment & les égarent.

Figure 5: Printed program for the audience at the ballet *Le Triomphe de la Religion,* presented at the Collège de Clermont on August 6, 1681, the year before it came under royal patronage as the Collège de Louis-le-Grand

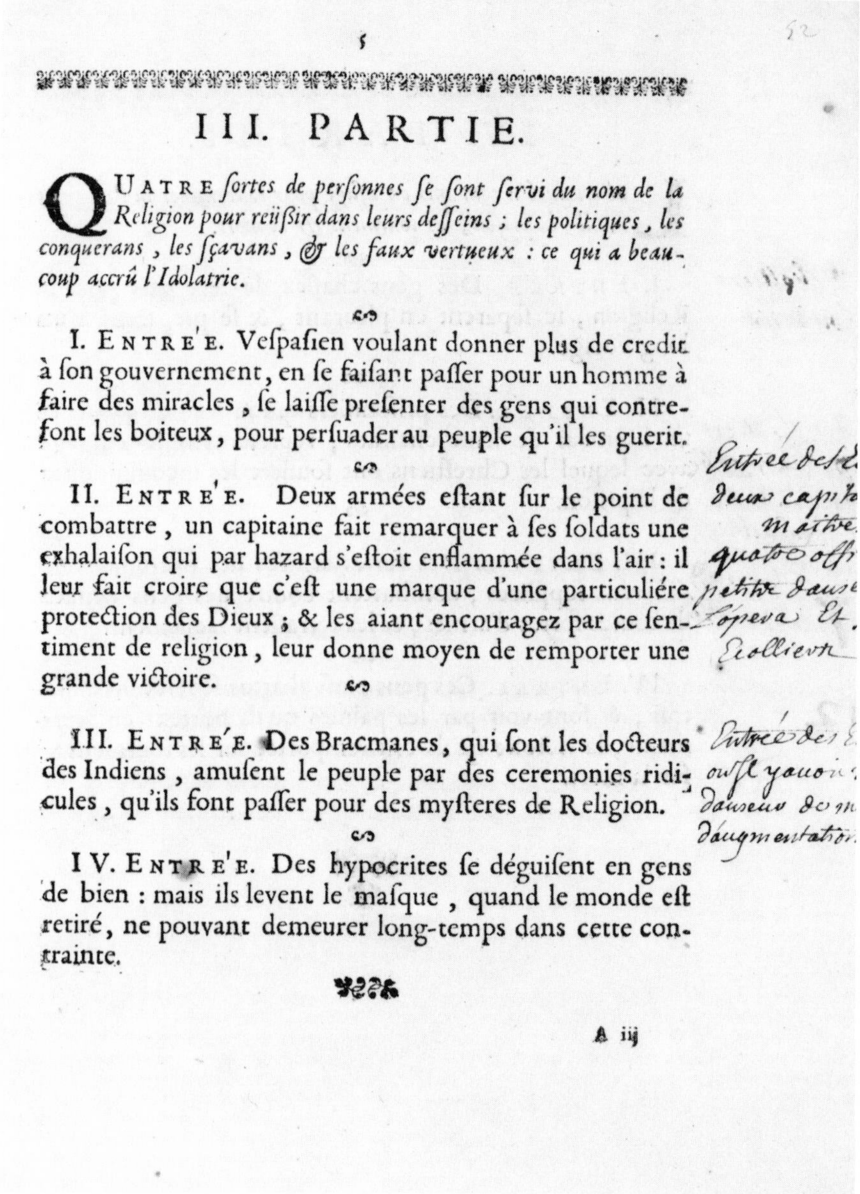

5

III. PARTIE.

QUATRE *fortes de perfonnes fe font fervi du nom de la Religion pour reüßir dans leurs deffeins ; les politiques, les conquerans, les fçavans, & les faux vertueux : ce qui a beaucoup accrû l'Idolatrie.*

I. ENTRE'E. Vefpafien voulant donner plus de credit à fon gouvernement, en fe faifant paffer pour un homme à faire des miracles, fe laiffe prefenter des gens qui contrefont les boiteux, pour perfuader au peuple qu'il les guerit.

II. ENTRE'E. Deux armées eftant fur le point de combattre, un capitaine fait remarquer à fes foldats une exhalaifon qui par hazard s'eftoit enflammée dans l'air : il leur fait croire que c'eft une marque d'une particuliére protection des Dieux ; & les aiant encouragez par ce fentiment de religion, leur donne moyen de remporter une grande victoire.

III. ENTRE'E. Des Bracmanes, qui font les docteurs des Indiens, amufent le peuple par des ceremonies ridicules, qu'ils font paffer pour des myfteres de Religion.

IV. ENTRE'E. Des hypocrites fe déguifent en gens de bien : mais ils levent le mafque, quand le monde eft retiré, ne pouvant demeurer long-temps dans cette contrainte.

A iij

Figure 6: Printed program for the audience at the ballet *Le Triomphe de la Religion*, presented at the Collège de Clermont on August 6, 1681, the year before it came under royal patronage as the Collège de Louis-le-Grand

IV. PARTIE.

L**A cruauté a tout mis en ufage pour exterminer la Religion ;
l'exil, la prifon, les tourmens & la mort.**

de fugillier
jusée fin

    I. ENTRE'E. Des gens chaffez de leur païs pour la Religion, fe feparent en pleurant, & fe preparent à un long voiage.

Del écolliers
en quatre
auteurs de
conducteurs
chaîne
un de m de
un d'augmention

    II. ENTRE'E. Des prifonniers qui fe font un plaifir & un honneur de leurs chaifnes, reprefentent le courage avec lequel les Chreftiens ont fouffert les incommoditez de la prifon.

    III. ENTRE'E. Des furies armées des inftrumens de differens fupplices, combattent contre des gens dénuez de toutes fortes d'armes, & les terraffent facilement.

    IV. ENTRE'E. Ces gens ainfi abattus fe relevent auffi-toft, & font voir par les palmes qu'ils portent en leurs mains, la victoire qu'ils ont remportée fur les tourmens & fur la mort.

A ij

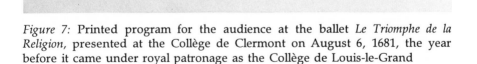

Figure 7: Printed program for the audience at the ballet *Le Triomphe de la Religion,* presented at the Collège de Clermont on August 6, 1681, the year before it came under royal patronage as the Collège de Louis-le-Grand

BALLET GENERAL.

*L*A *Religion triomphe de la Paſſion , de l'Ignorance , de l'Artifice , & de la Cruauté. Toutes les nations de la terre viennent luy rendre hommage.*

DANSERONT AU BALLET

HUBERT DE CHOISEUL DE LA RIVIERE, *de Bourgogne.*   *danſon ſeul*
CHARLES DE LAGNY, *de la Rochelle.*   *danſon ſeul*
WALTER BELLEAU, *de Dublin.*   *danſon ſeul*
ANTOINE LE MOINE, *de Paris.*
ARMAND DOUTÉ, *de Paris.*
CHARLES ESTIENNE RIDELE PUISALOU, *de Paris.*
FRANÇOIS CHARLES BESSET, *de Brie.*
JEAN LAURENT LE NOIR, *de Verneuïl.*
LOUÏS DOMINIQUE DE BIANCOLELLY, *d'Italie.*   *Jouön d'advape*
PHILIPPE DOUTÉ, *de Paris.*   *après le comba*
BARTHELEMI DERLACH, *de Suiſſe.*
HUGUES DE VITRY, *de Châlons en Champagne.*
LOUÏS DALANCÉ, *de Paris.*
PHILIPPE DE SEQUEVILLE, *de Paris.*   *danſon ſeul*
JEAN ESTIENNE CABOUD, *de Paris.*
LOUÏS DE COSSÉ DE BRISSAC, *de Paris.*   *danſon ſeul*
PIERRE PREVOST, *de Paris.*
CLAUDE MICHEL LANGLOIS, *de Paris.*
HENRI JACQUES DE DURAS-FORT, *de Paris.*
PHILIPPE MARIE PRINCE DE MONTMORENCY, *de Flandres.*

Figure 8: Printed program for the audience at the ballet *Le Triomphe de la Religion,* presented at the Collège de Clermont on August 6, 1681, the year before it came under royal patronage as the Collège de Louis-le-Grand

Figure 9: Court ballet costume for female character (Autumn) played by a male dancer

Figure 10: Stage setting and audience in the courtyard of the Collège de Louis-le-Grand for the festivities on August 24–26, 1682, in celebration of the birth of the Duke of Burgundy, son of the Dauphin. The centerpiece of the setting is "the Temple of Apollo . . . newly dedicated to the immortal exploits of Louis-the-Great [Louis XIV] . . . under the patronage of Saint Louis."

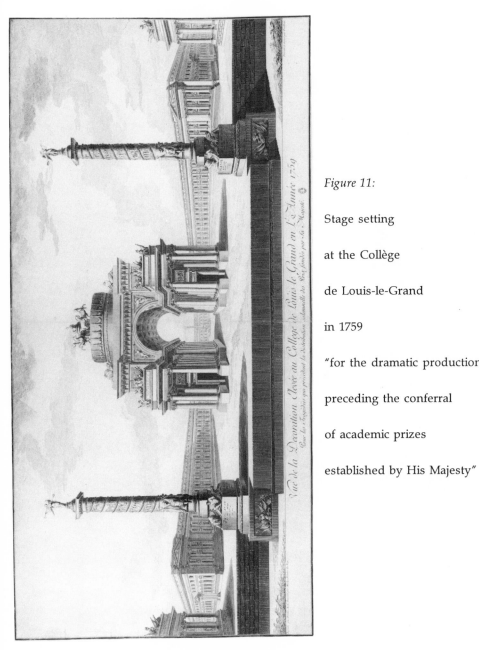

Figure 11:

Stage setting

at the Collège

de Louis-le-Grand

in 1759

"for the dramatic production

preceding the conferral

of academic prizes

established by His Majesty"

four · · · · · · · · · · · · · · ·

THE BALLETS AND
THEIR AUDIENCE

When one announces one of these shows, in which figured and group dances make part of the harmony of the performances, what a concourse of people! What a crowd! What a multitude! What admiration! . . . The spectator no longer breathes, he swoons.

—Charles Porée, S.J.

Theater is made for an audience. Until we know who the audience is, what its concerns are, and how it responds to the show, we have only seen the performance from the wings. The Jesuits believed that theater could be a school for virtue. But ideology always coexists with practicality: theater audiences want to be entertained. In the theater at Louis-le-Grand, these two threads, ideological and practical, continually met and diverged. They exerted more or less tension on each other as the fathers strove to light contemporary events with orthodox Catholic morality, through the time-bound physicality of dance, drama, and music.

It is mainly through surviving programs, period "reviews," chance comments in letters and journals, and rare visual representations that we catch a glimpse of the Louis-le-Grand performances as the audience saw them, and so acquire a context for understanding—and for guessing at—the audience's response.

Three questions can help us in our attempt to see the Louis-le-Grand ballets through their audience's eyes. Who was the audience? What did they say about the ballets? What did the ballets say about them?

Who Was the Audience?

Students in the Audience

Since the Jesuit theater was a college theater, one way to answer the question, "Who was the audience?" is to ask, "Who were the students?" Part of the audience was made up of the students' parents, relatives, and friends. Generally speaking, the students at Jesuit colleges came from all social classes.[1] Tuition was free and scholarships (for living expenses, and so forth) were frequently given.[2] Nevertheless, certain Jesuit schools were known as "grands collèges," which meant that their students were for the most part drawn from aristocratic families and from the upper ranks of the less wellborn but still well-to-do.

Louis-le-Grand was a "grand collège." Though it had scholarship students from "honest and poor families," many of its students were from the upper ranks of the French nobility. A song from the college fête on August 11, 1721, celebrating Louis XV's recovery from an illness, describes the school as "that noble nursery of warriors, magistrates, ministers, prelates."[3] These vocational categories locate Louis-le-Grand alumni in the first two of France's traditional "Estates." The First Estate was defined as "those who prayed," the clergy; and the Second as "those who fought" (and governed), the nobility. (Even after the college became a state lycée, it continued its "grand collège" tradition by recruiting from the "most honorable families" in the army, government, banking, and business.)[4]

Under the Jesuits, de La Tremouilles, Montmorencys, Rochechouarts, Colberts, and de Richelieus appear and reappear in the cast lists of the ballet and tragedy programs as brothers, cousins, and sons followed each other across the stage on the rue Saint-Jacques. Most of the surnames for the "acteurs du ballet" as well as for the "acteurs de la tragédie" include the aristocratic article "de."[5] We find, for exam-

---

[1] Jacques Hennequin, "Théâtre et société dans les pièces de collège au XVIIe siècle (1641–1671)," in *Dramaturgie et société, Nancy 14–21 April, 1967,* ed. Jean Jacquot (Paris, 1968), 1:463.

[2] André Stegmann, "Le Rôle des jésuites dans la dramaturgie française du début du XVIIIe siècle," in *Dramaturgie et société, Nancy 14–21 April, 1967,* ed. Jean Jacquot (Paris, 1968), 1:448.

[3] "Chanson sur les réjouissances." In the fifth verse we read, "cette noble Pepiniere, de Guerriers, de Magistrats, de Ministres, de Prelats."

[4] Emond, *Histoire du collège,* 386.

[5] According to Dupoint-Ferrier, the "de" was not always proof of

ple, not only de Montignac, de La Chassetiere, de Brissac, de Gonthery, and their like ad infinitum, but also de Hautefort de Montignac, de Ligne de May, de Messey de Margival, and other names of that kind. Here and there a performer is further identified as "Prince," "Count" or "Duke."

Because the Jesuit educational system was highly regarded across Catholic Europe and because Paris was a great capital, there were also many foreign students at the college. The cast lists, which often give each student performer's country or city of origin, include boys from Dublin, London, Flanders, Italy, Brussels, Lisbon, Scotland, Martinique, Poland, Cornwall, Seville, Austria, and Switzerland. Other college sources refer to boarders from Canada, India, Armenia, Greece, Syria, and China.[6] Some of these students—especially the English and those from mission countries like China—would have been sent abroad to receive the Catholic education unavailable at home. Others were the sons of ambassadors and other distinguished foreigners living in Paris. In 1686, when the Siamese ambassadors came to the tragedy and ballet, they were fetched by the servants and carriages belonging to Charles II's natural son, the sons of the Grand General of Poland, and the sons of the Grand General of Lithuania.[7] When they arrived, they were ceremoniously greeted in twenty-four languages by the assembled Louis-le-Grand students (34).

Among the students dancing in the 1681 ballet *Le Triomphe de la Religion* (The triumph of religion) was Louis-Dominique de Biancolelly. Ernest Boysse identifies this young dancer as a son of the famous "Arlequin" of the Comédie-Italienne and as a godson of Louis XIV. Both Louis-Dominique and his brother Pierre-François were educated at Louis-le-Grand and made careers in the Théâtre-Italien.[8]

Although his theatrical connections developed later, the young M. Poquelin, who later changed his name to Molière, was also a student at Louis-le-Grand earlier in the century and met his eventual patron there. The young Poquelin's name does not appear in any cast list, however. This is probably because, according to Voltaire, only *pensionnaires*, or boarding students, had roles in the ballets and plays, and many Parisian students, like the future Molière, were externs, or day students.[9] This division of students into boarders and externs

---

nobility in the eighteenth century.

[6] LeBègue, "Ballets des jésuites," 321.

[7] Lowe, *Marc-Antoine Charpentier*, 77f.

[8] Boysse, *Théâtre des jésuites*, 182f.

[9] Dupont-Ferrier, *Vie quotidienne d'un collège*, 297.

meant that at performances, many of the day students would be in the audience, along with their families and friends. This would certainly have been the case at the summer tragedy and ballet, because it was the occasion of graduation and prize giving, and day students were as eligible for those as boarders. In addition, students and teachers from other neighborhood colleges probably attended the Jesuit theater. Academic audiences were apparently demanding. When the Comédie-Française moved from the Saint-Germain neighborhood to the right bank of the Seine in 1770, critics lamented the negative effect that the loss of students in the audience had on theatrical quality.[10]

Loret tells us that the friends and relations of the Jesuits' students included "many of high rank . . . princes, princesses . . . presidents, countesses . . . a bevy of sensitive and intelligent spirits."[11] On several occasions the gazetteer reports that the King himself was there with his royal retinue. Louis XIV began attending the rue Saint-Jacques theater as a boy and continued to come during most of his life. Though Louis XV apparently went less often, he sometimes sent an official representative to the August show.[12] Foreign delegations and exiled royalty were also to be seen. In 1652 the young Duke of Gloucester went to the summer production with the exiled Charles II—who later sent at least one of his natural sons to the college.[13] In August 1697 a Belgian gazette, *Les Relations véritables*, reported that "the English court" (the court in exile of James II) attended the Jesuit theater in Paris with members of the French royal family.[14]

Audience Size

Later commentators describing the crowd often do not mention numbers, contenting themselves with calling it "huge" or "great" or "large"; but Loret's figures for the summer ballet and tragedy audience generally range from thirty-five hundred to seven thousand.[15]

---

[10] Lough, *Paris Theater Audiences*, 201f.

[11] Loret, *Muze historique*, Letter 35, September 3, 1661: "J'y vis des Princes, des Princesses, Des Prezidentes, des Comtesses, Et des Moines plus de deux cents."

[12] *Nouveau Mercure*, August 1719, "Journal de Paris" entry.

[13] Loret, *Muze historique*, August 6, 1652.

[14] Ibid., 76–79.

[15] Loret, *Muze historique*, August 21, 1655; André Stegmann, "Le Rôle des jésuites dans la dramaturgie française du début du XVIIIe siècle," in

Joachim Christophe Nemeitz, who saw a Louis-le-Grand performance in 1713, described the courtyard as "very spacious" and "full of benches for the spectators."[16] As in other theaters, some of the male spectators stood in "the pit," behind which benches were raised on platforms around the sides of the space.[17] Other men and boys sat on the stage itself, as in secular theaters of the period.[18] The dozens of large windows opening onto the courtyard were used as "boxes" for the many women in the audience. Jean La Gravette described them at the windows and sitting on the platforms: "women, girls, rich, good, noble, and beautiful, at the windows and in the courtyard, shining like the daystar."[19] If viewing conditions at Louis-le-Grand were similar to those of other Paris theaters, then even noble theatergoers must have been used to a high level of crowding and discomfort, as well as poor sight lines and acoustics.

Lowe describes the crowd as (at least sometimes) "entirely orderly and serene," behavior that surprised the visiting Siamese in 1686 (78). However, the Court Annals for 1697 and 1698 recount a tragedy performance that was not so serene. For some reason, the musicians refused to play at the beginning of the show, and Le Jay threatened to break their instruments over their heads. Finally, Monsieur, the King's brother, had to intervene. Then, toward the end, several audience members began to fight and were calmed with difficulty, nearly necessitating Monsieur's intervention a second time (81f.).

Although the courtiers among Loret's audience of thirty-five hundred to seven thousand would have been regarded, by themselves and everyone else, as the most important part of the crowd, there were also at least an equal number of the simply well-to-do. (During the seventeenth century, these were in fact probably a great deal better off financially than the courtiers, many of whom were personally impoverished, living at court from hand to mouth.) In his review of the performance in August 1657, though he does not tell us the total number of spectators, Loret states that they included three

---

Dramaturgie et société Nancy 14–21, avril 1967, ed. Jean Jacquot (1968), 1:447.

[16] Astier, "Pierre Beauchamps," 139.

[17] Lough, *Paris Theater Audiences*, 107.

[18] For a recent study of this practice, see Barbara G. Mittman, *Spectators on the Paris Stage in the Seventeenth and Eighteenth Centuries* (Ann Arbor, Michigan: UMI Research Press, 1984).

[19] Lowe, *Marc-Antoine Charpentier*: "Des dames et des demoiselles, Riches, bonnes, nobles, et belles, Aux fenestres et dans la cours Sembloient estre l'astre du jour" (78).

thousand *petits messieurs*, whom he goes on to call "people of the town" *(gens de ville).*[20] It is very difficult to know just what is meant when seventeenth-century writers use words meaning "people" or "populace."[21] *Gens*, though variously translated in modern dictionaries as "persons," "folk," and even "servants," appears to have meant "people in general" in the seventeenth century. *Honnête gens* seems to have been used in relation to persons of reasonably good or at least respectable family. So *gens de ville* would have included various strata of the bourgeoisie. Molière's father, M. Poquelin, third-generation Parisian upholsterer with an appointment to the King, is probably an example of the more prosperous of Loret's *gens de ville*.

At the Jesuit college, then, the two main lay divisions of the audience were the court, *la cour*, and these *gens de ville*. In both ranks, some were there because they were the mothers, fathers, aunts, uncles, friends, and so forth of the performers. Others were there because they were courtiers going where the court went; the most devastating thing that the Sun King could say of someone was "He is a man I never see." Some of the *gens de ville* were no doubt like Molière's *bourgeois gentilhomme*, imitating their higher ranking and fashionable betters. And many people went to the Louis-le-Grand performances simply because they were an irresistible combination of the *haut monde* and theatrical spectacle, those two ruling passions of the Ancien Régime. According to the *Nouvelles extraordinaires* for September 12, 1684, that year's August audience included "many people of the highest quality and an infinite number of the most discriminating connoisseurs and most knowing theatergoers."[22]

Ecclesiastics in the Audience

The audience at Louis-le-Grand, as at all Paris theaters, included ecclesiastics of all descriptions. In 1657 he saw "Cardinal Antoine, crowds of Jacobins, Augustinians, Carmelites, Cordeliers, and Celestines, numerous bishops, four dozen Abbés, and fourteen or fifteen Priors."[23] The papal nuncio was there in 1660, and in 1661 Loret counted more than two hundred monks.[24] The story of Mlle du

---

[20] Loret, *Muze historique*, Letter 32, August 18, 1657.

[21] Lough, *Paris Theater Audiences*, 63.

[22] Lowe, *Marc-Antoine Charpentier:* "en presence de beaucoup de gens de la premiere qualité et de nombre infini de personnes les mieux connaissantes et les plus delicates en spectacles" (77).

[23] Loret, *Muze historique*, Letter 31, August 18, 1657.

[24] Ibid., Letter 33, August 21, 1660; Letter 35, September 3, 1661.

Luc testifies to the continual presence of clerics. The sister of a count, she poured wig powder out of a window onto the tonsured heads of the religious in the courtyard below during the August performance of 1749.[25]

The concourse of clergy and religious in the Jesuits' audience was apparently not there only because the rue Saint-Jacques theater was an educational adjunct of a religious school. In 1702, during Louis's years of a rather evangelical piety when he was less enthusiastic about the theater, his sister-in-law wrote to the Duchess of Hanover that when the King loved the theater, bishops occupied their reserved seats there every day. But now that the King's support had waned, theater going had become "a sin."[26] Of course, she was exaggerating. But, to some extent, both church and society followed the King's example with regard to style, amusement, and opinion. Many clergy understood themselves as supporting blocks in a social pyramid whose pinnacle was the King and his intensely personal rule. Religious orthodoxy and loyalty to the King were both (at least publicly) assumed by the aristocratic "establishment" to be natural hallmarks of the well-born and well-bred.

Many of these members of old families went into convents and became priests with the same inevitability and for the same reasons that their older brothers and sisters inherited the family estate and received a marriage dowry. After the mostly aristocratic political revolt of the Fronde between 1659 and 1653, Louis, on taking the reins of state into his own hands, had excluded the nobility from active government. This decision, together with the country's economic difficulties, meant that the financial burden of maintaining the aristocracy in enforced idleness fell on the Crown. The King desperately needed additional resources to offset this expense, and obtained them by drawing on the possessions of the church. Younger sons and daughters knew from earliest childhood that, any question of religious vocation aside, they would be priests and nuns. Of these, some subsequently developed a genuine vocation, some were diligent though uninspired, and others remained entirely worldly. But for most of those in all three categories, the fact of theater attendance would not have been a litmus test of irreligious worldliness. It was, instead, a natural adjunct of their social class.

One result of this system is that, like the Louis-le-Grand audience, seventeenth- and eighteenth-century literature of all descriptions, including the literature of dance and theater, abounds with

---

[25] Boysse, *Théâtre des jésuites*, 87.

[26] Lough, *Paris Theater Audiences*, 129f.

"abbés." Ernest Boysse draws on Porée's portrait of these worldly abbés, "curled, powdered, pomaded, who peopled the boudoirs of the eighteenth century."[27] Many of these dramatists, librettists, and apologists-critics, like the Abbé d'Aubignac and the Abbé de Pure, were titular abbots, whose family had received an abbey as a financial gift from the King. Once established as a family possession, an abbey could become virtually a hereditary piece of real estate, passed from "Uncle Prior" to one of his nephews. This practice becomes vividly clear in a report in the 1681 *Mercure*. The young Marquis de Louvois gave a rhetoric display at the Jesuit college, and among his *fellow students* participating in the event were the Abbé le Peletier, the Abbé de Charost, the Abbé de Luxembourg, and the Abbé de Vaubecourt.[28] Under the ecclesiastical dress of the nuncios, monks, cardinals, abbés, bishops, nuns, and so forth whom Loret saw at the Louis-le-Grand theater were the brothers and sisters, aunts and uncles, nephews and nieces of the students and the lay members of the audience.

A Sophisticated Audience?

All three divisions of this audience—noble, bourgeois, and clerical—by virtue of their cultural orientation toward the King and court, shared a more or less common intellectual milieu. Because of their commitment to being theatrically au courant, the Paris Jesuits, themselves part of this social and intellectual context, chose tragedy and ballet subjects that harmonized with the moral and intellectual preoccupations and personal sensibilities of their public. The books these theatergoers had at home in their libraries contained the same history, political philosophy, and spirituality that came to life on the Jesuit stage.

When these representatives of royalty, aristocracy, the upper bourgeoisie, and the church met on the rue Saint-Jacques, was it a unique occasion in the pattern of their lives? And especially, to what extent did they go to the Jesuit theater in the same spirit we attend our children's ballet recitals, and to what extent was going to Louis-le-Grand simply another instance of going to the theater? There is a debate among historians about cultural patterns of family feeling and parent-child relationships in the sixteenth, seventeenth, and eighteenth centuries, but this is outside the scope of this book. Still, the opening of Saint-Cyr, Mme de Maintenon's school for the daughters of impoverished aristocrats, has been called the beginning of

---

[27] Hémon, "Comédie chez les jésuites," 533.

[28] Emond, *Histoire du collège*, 357.

the cult of the child, that attempt to take seriously the problems of child welfare and training . . . for before 1686 the only theory entertained about children was that they were a nuisance, so much locked-up capital on which no dividend in the shape of family aggrandizement could be expected for the first 12 or 14 years of the child's life.[29]

It can be argued that the Jesuits anticipated Mme de Maintenon's theories and concerns by at least a century, but nonetheless the popular attitude toward children and their activities appears to have been far less indulgent than our own. Parents and relatives obviously did go to the theater because they wanted to see their young relations perform. But "family aggrandizement" made up a very important part of what they hoped for and expected from the event.

When a student was singled out for notice by a chronicler, the spotlight fell on his family as well. In 1661, during the prize giving at the end of the August performance, the two sons of de Lamoignon, a "Grand Equerrie of France," were honored. Loret extolled them at length as children "worthy of such a father," whom the gazetteer called "a mirror of prudence, knowledge, and law, just as a Solomon."[30] When these two boys received their laurel-crown prizes that day, the audience saw not only two diligent children but the illustrious house of de Lamoignon receiving homage. Families went to see their children perform because they were their children, and also because they expected those children to do them honor. This is one argument in favor of the conjecture that at Louis-le-Grand the audience expected—and generally got—a degree of excellence and polish in the show and in the performers that would be found today only in the recitals of a professional school of the arts. Neither the Jesuits nor their students could afford to give anything less to this high-ranking and theatrically sophisticated audience fiercely bent on "family aggrandizement."

How do we know that the Louis-le-Grand audience was theatrically sophisticated—that is, that it had experienced a large variety of theater and had a context for comparison? In 1653, when Loret described the audience at the *Ballet du Roi* (a court-ballet performance), he found many of the same people, or at least the same kind of people, as at Louis-le-Grand. He saw cardinals, princesses, princes, Parisians, presidents, government officials, financiers; wives of dukes, marquis, and counts; abbés, priors, merchants, and bourgeois. As has been stated, these aristocrats and upper bourgeois made up the core

---

[29] W. H. Lewis, *The Splendid Century* (Morrow, 1971), 241.

[30] Loret, *Muze historique*, Letter 36, September 3, 1661.

of the Paris theater audience from the mid-seventeenth to the late eighteenth century.

In 1733 Voltaire complained that "among the multitude of our inhabitants, there are not four thousand who go [to the theater] frequently."[31] Among these alleged four thousand, there were those whose attendance seems to have been more for social reasons than from serious interest in the theater. Around the middle of the eighteenth century, socialites would drop in on the Paris Opéra, the Comédie-Italienne, and the Comédie-Française during the same evening, catching a favorite chorus here, a tragedy scene there, and the third act of a new ballet elsewhere (233).

Because Paris was still a small city and a large part of the theater audience was drawn from the same social class, the Comédie-Française, the Comédie-Italienne, the Opéra, and the court performances must have numbered many of Louis-le-Grand's thirty-five hundred to seven thousand spectators among their own patrons. It seems reasonable to assume that the performances at Louis-le-Grand must have been on a fairly high artistic level in order to attract such an experienced audience.

We get some idea both of the theatrical experience and the inbred quality of the most influential section of this audience when we realize that the same courtiers danced and acted in court ballets; attended court performances given by visiting companies like Molière's and, during the seventeenth century, performed with the actors in pieces like Le Ballet des Muse (Ballet of the muses), a December 1666 court production; went regularly to the three official Paris theaters; often heard Mass and vespers at the Jesuit church of Saint-Louis in the Marais, where the choral parts were routinely taken by singers from the Opéra and where the music was frequently created by the same composers who wrote the music for the Jesuit ballets; and went together several times a year to the Jesuit theater to see and hear Opéra dancers, singers, and musicians perform alongside their young relatives and friends.

Attracting the Audience

How did people know when theater was being given at the college? And did they pay for admission or were they guests? To begin with the first question, methods of announcing performances changed over time. Publicity for the Jesuit theater seems to have been

---

[31] Lough, *Paris Theater Audiences:* "dans la multitude de nos citoyens, il n'y a pas quatre mille hommes qui les frequentent avec assiduité" (52).

done in much the same way as publicity for the secular theaters. In the sixteenth century, Jesuit college productions had been announced in the town with a crier and a drum. Later, programs or posters were put up at crossroads and on the college gate or door.[32]

In Loret's era, secular-theater posters gave "the place, the hour, the price, and the day" of performances.[33] The names of actors (and presumably dancers) were not added till after 1789. Each Paris theater had its own color for posters: red for the Comédie-Française, green for the Comédie-Italienne, and yellow for the Opéra. Publicity was not done weeks in advance as it is today. The printer delivered the posters the day before the performance, very early in the morning, and the forty or so official bill posters in Paris hurried to put them up at the 175 official bill-posting sites. These included the end of the Pont Neuf and the rue des Mazarines, both fairly near the Jesuit school.[34]

The theaters did not bother to have posters put up in the poorer quarters, like Saint-Marcel or Saint-Antoine, or near Notre Dame or around the University. (The decision not to put posters in the University quarter probably reflects the influential University's attempts to exclude theater personnel and performances from their precincts as much as it does the poverty of the neighborhood.) Posters were concentrated where the well-to-do lived: the Marais, la Ville, around the Louvre and the Palais royale, and in the Saint-Germain and Saint-Honoré quarters. These were the haunts of the nobility, the robe, and the bourgeoisie, who had money to spend and leisure in which to spend it.[35] In these neighborhoods, the official bill-posting places were sometimes at the gates of the townhouses or "hotels" of the wealthy. The inhabitants were jealous of this distinction and complained loudly if they were passed over. In February 1753 the Duke of Gesvres complained to the police that the bill poster was skipping his door, and the bill poster was put in jail.[36]

---

[32] L. V. Gofflot, *Le Théâtre au collège du Moyen Age à nos jours* (Paris: Champion, 1907), 164.

[33] François de Dainville, S.J., "Les Lieux d'affichage des comédiens à Paris en 1753," *Revue d'histoire du théâtre* 3 (1951): 248.

[34] Ibid., 248–51.

[35] Robert Darnton, *The Great Cat Massacre*, Vintage Books (New York: Random House, 1958), 125. "The robe" referred to "magistrates who had acquired nobility through the ownership of important offices as opposed to the older feudal 'nobles of the sword.'"

[36] Dainville, "Lieux d'affichage," 253.

At least one advertisement for a religious-college production has survived. In 1723 a poster was put up in Lot-en-Garonne for *Hercule furieux* (Fierce Hercules), a tragedy "decorated with entrées of ballet," to be performed by the students of the Fathers of Christian Doctrine on July 21 (258). At Louis-le-Grand, students paid for the printing of posters for the college theater. In August 1721 one Charles Armand contributed thirty-nine livres and fifteen sols for twenty-eight dozen "posters for the little tragedy."[37]

There is, however, also some evidence that at least part of the rue Saint-Jacques audience was invited.[38] In August 1655 attendance was by invitation only.[39] Some surviving ballet programs bear hand-written notes "for Father or Mr. So and So"; this may support the thesis that guests were invited to at least some performances. However, it is possible that not everyone had a program—that one reserved them or received them as a mark of special favor. In some years wealthy students paid for the printing of programs, and the numbers suggest either that additional programs came from some other source or that only a few audience members received them. For example, in 1721 the Duc de Tremouille paid for the printing of three hundred programs—which would have supplied barely 10 percent of the audience. The comment of Lang, a German, that "the theater attracts a genteel audience; it is not open to the mob" also suggests an intentional process of audience selection.[40] It is not clear, though, how similar Jesuit theater practices and audiences were from country to country. There is clearly evidence on both sides of the invitation question. In some years in Paris, the August shows were given two or three times because of the number of people who wished to attend.

Scholars generally agree that the Paris Jesuits did not charge admission to their theater and that charges of "profiteering" from theater tickets can be dismissed as Jansenist calumny. However, Loret mentions that on one occasion he gave fifteen sols, the normal seventeenth-century price in Paris theaters for standing room in the pit, to attend the Jesuit ballet and tragedy.[41] The *Nouvelles extraordinaires* for September 12, 1684, recounts how one Noël Falconnet, through the good offices of the gazetteer, got "a ticket" for the tragedy and ballet at Louis-le-Grand from Père Labbé. Other (admittedly questionable)

[37] Gofflot, *Théâtre au collège*, 161.

[38] Lowe, *Marc-Antoine Charpentier*, 85.

[39] Stegmann, "Rôle des jésuites," 447.

[40] Carroll, "Jesuit Playwright," 23.

[41] Lough, *Paris Theater Audiences*, 82; Boysse, *Théâtre des jésuites*, 82.

evidence for ticket selling comes from Jansenist publications. The *Nouvelles ecclésiastiques* for November 27, 1748, for example, states that the workmen who put up the temporary outdoor theater and seating at the college that summer were paid in tickets, which they in turn "scalped" to the public.

Unless further evidence comes to light, it is impossible to draw a definite conclusion about these supposed ticket sales. The actual system may have been some combination of these two methods, as a report in the August 1739 *Mercure* suggests. This article states that the performance was given twice: first on August 2 in the indoor theater for "connaiseurs," and then outside on August 5 for a crowd of four thousand. Of these, many were too far away from the stage to hear and could only watch. If this was or became the normal August pattern, it may be that the outdoor audience paid.

However the August audience got there—by invitation or the purchase of tickets or some combination of the two—the student assigned to make the speech that opened the theater faced hundreds (in the indoor theater) or thousands (in the courtyard theater) of knowledgeable spectators. Nearly all of them danced socially, many had acted, sung, and danced in elaborate private performances at court and elsewhere, and many of them attended the major Paris theaters more or less regularly. This is not to say that their taste was "refined" or "spiritual" in the modern sense. It was in many ways neither, especially in the seventeenth century.[42] But this audience was reasonably au courant with Paris theater, its techniques and controversies. Royalty, aristocrats, government officials, merchants, bankers, students, clergy, religious, and perhaps an undetermined number of random Parisians and visitors to the city: all of these, having thoroughly examined each other and the scenery, either settled themselves in anticipation of the tragedy—or resigned themselves to wait more or less patiently for the ballet to begin.

What Did the Audience Say about the Ballets?

Does a Large Audience Mean an Enthusiastic Audience?

An audience comments on a theater by what it says and writes, and also by attending or staying away. Because the Louis-le-Grand audience can no longer speak for itself and because its recorded responses to the ballets are scarce, indications of who attended and who did not are important. In order to know something of what the

---

[42] Ibid., 121f.

rue Saint-Jacques audience "said" about the ballets, we must take into account all these ways of commenting—attendance, nonattendance, and written responses.

Loret, writing in the mid-seventeenth century, often mentions the large crowd of spectators, numbering them between three thousand and seven thousand at the summer tragedy and ballet; indoor audiences were smaller because of the confines of the theater space. Though some summer shows were given twice because of the large crowds, some spectators were still too far from the stage to hear the speaking and singing.[43] Even so, visitors were (at least sometimes) impressed with the general orderliness of the audience.

Though there are a few references to disappointment with particular performances, there is little evidence that the Jesuits had difficulty attracting spectators. On the contrary, places at their Paris theater and their provincial theaters were prized, according to the evidence supporting some sort of ticket selling and the instances of angling for invitations.[44]

Because Louis-le-Grand gave perhaps seven or eight performances a year, we cannot compare the frequency of college performances and performances given in public theaters. However, we can compare the size of its audience with figures for audience size in the public theaters. In 1672–73 Molière's troupe gave 131 performances for fifty-two thousand audience members, with around four hundred attending any given show.[45] In 1717–18 the Comédie-Française was occasionally closed altogether for lack of an audience, as it also was when a great "personage" arrived in Paris and "everyone" went to wait on him or her (175f.). In May of 1746 a revival of Molière's *Ecole des femmes* played to thirty-five theatergoers, and *Tartuffe*, later that month, to thirty-two. One hundred and seventy Parisians came to see *Le Misanthrope* in June, and in July the double bill of Racine's *Plaideurs* and Molière's *Le Médecin malgré lui* attracted thirty-one spectators. That same month, the Comédie-Française actors were forbidden to give any more of Molière's five-act comedies until further notice, because their production was creating financial disaster (183). Of course, these tiny audiences are partly explained by changes in theat-

---

[43] *La Mercure*, 1739.

[44] There are many references in the literature on the French Jesuit theater to the formal agreements made between the Jesuits and the authorities in provincial towns to ensure that the citizens were invited to the shows. On more than one occasion these citizens broke down the theater doors if they were excluded.

[45] Lough, *Paris Theater Audiences*, 48.

rical fashion from the seventeenth to the eighteenth century. But even a great success of the same period, like Voltaire's tragedy *Merope*, 1743, attracted about one thousand spectators per performance, as opposed to Louis-le-Grand's several thousand (178).

These figures and comparisons underline the continued relative smallness of the Paris theater audience and the fluctuating attendance at the public theater. The Jesuit-theater audience, on the other hand, seems to have remained fairly consistent for several reasons: the family and "special event" nature of the shows, the aura of "court occasion" surrounding them, and the reputation the college maintained not only for excellent music and dance but for re-creating the traditional splendor of court ballet in the time of Louis XIV. The *Mercure* for August 1735 said, before mentioning the large crowd of spectators, that Louis-le-Grand was "perhaps the only place now where one gets some idea of the magnificence of the ballet in the youth of the late king."[46]

Of course, the impression Loret, the *Mercure*, and other gazettes give us of a consistently large audience at the college will only partly support the assumption that people came because they were enthusiastic about what was presented. First and foremost, the rue Saint-Jacques theater was a college theater, and a large proportion of the men and women in the audience were there to see their young family members act, dance, sing, and receive prizes. But in spite of its didactic purpose, the Paris Jesuit theater became and remained a magnet for connoisseurs of music and dance, influencing even the more severe Jesuit authorities at Rome, who refrained from suppressing dance and music at the English College of St. Omers because of the immense public prestige of the Louis-le-Grand ballets.[47]

The picture that emerges is one of a theater whose two distinct elements—drama and intermedes—attracted different audience members for different reasons. The Latin tragedies, the Louis-le-Grand theater's academic raison d'être, were the unaided work of professors and students and, while not without merit, had the theatrical limitations of their creators and interpreters. The intermedes, however, created by outstanding professionals, who often dominated the

---

[46] *La Mercure*, August 1735: "[Le ballet chez les jésuites] est peut-être le seul qui puisse maintenant donne quelque idée de la magnificence des ballets dans la jeunesse du feu roy."

[47] William H. McCabe, S.J., "Music and Dance on a Seventeenth-Century College Stage," *Musical Quarterly* 24 (July 3, 1938).

performance, were of a different order. The latter account for the presence of spectators like the exacting Duc de Saint-Agnon.[48]

Who Stayed Away?

It is equally instructive to ask who stayed away from the college theater, because the refusal of certain segments of Parisian society to attend the ballets is also a comment on the productions. Those most obvious by their absence were the Jansenists, both religious and political. The Jansenist publication *Nouvelles ecclésiastiques,* while not necessarily reliable in its statements about what went on in the Jesuit theater, reflects Jansenist opinion about that theater. Predictably, the Jansenists were scandalized by the Louis-le-Grand shows and by the Jesuit theater in general. Beginning with *Nouvelles*'s first edition in 1728, they cried out against the fraternization of the Jesuit students with Opéra dancers, and against the occasional Louis-le-Grand rehearsals on the Opéra stage. They accused the Jesuits of making money from theater admissions and the rental of costumes, of encouraging vanity and self-love through the theater arts, of disseminating political treason and bad morals through their shows, of demeaning biblical characters by giving them human weaknesses in the tragedies, of creating a theatrical ambience of "scandalous ostentation," and so on predictably over the years. It was especially the dance that drew their fire. "Who would have thought," asks a Jansenist writer in 1732,

> that under the nose of a University where ballets and dance are prohibited in all the colleges, the Jesuits would undertake to give public lessons . . . uniting the theory to the practice of this pernicious art? Nevertheless, it is the history of dance that was this year's subject of the ballet by these so-called Fathers of the Society of Jesus.[49]

However, even the *Nouvelles* writers sometimes grudgingly admired while they condemned. In November 1748, writing on the August ballet and tragedy, they praised the gorgeous scenery even while deploring the production it graced.[50] As usual, they skewered

---

[48] Lowe, *Marc-Antoine Charpentier,* 82.

[49] Pierre Peyronnet, "Le Théâtre d'education des jésuites," *Dix-huitième siècle* 8 (1976): "Qui aurait pensé que, sous les yeux surtout d'une Université ou les ballets et les danses sont interdits dans tous les colleges, les jésuites entreprennent d'en donner des leçons publiques, joignant en quelque sorte la théorie a la pratique de cet art pernicieux? C'est pourtant l'histoire de la danse qui a eté cette année le sujet de ballet des Pères soi-disants de la Compagnie de Jesus" (118).

[50] Dupont-Ferrier, *Vie quotidienne d'un collège,* 300.

the ballet, but for telling reasons. It was "a scandalous spectacle with a cast of buffoons and grotesques comparable to a Saint-Germain Fair." The Latin tragedy was summarily dismissed as simply an excuse for the ballet, which occupied most of the afternoon. This was one of the occasions on which the *Nouvelles* fulminated against the collaboration of "the best dancers and leapers from the Opéra with a very small number of boarding students from the college," the use of masks, and ticket prices.[51] These criticisms suggest that the point of the theatrical occasion was not the Latin drama, which was by now archaic, but the ballet. They also suggest that if the public paid, it did so partly because it would see "the best dancers and leapers from the Opéra."

Jansenist or Jansenist-like condemnation of the Jesuit theater also appears in the unsigned preface to a 1720 edition of an uproarious in-house comedy called *The Monks*. Never intended for public presentation, but only for the amusement of the Jesuits themselves, it was pirated and published by the hostile Archbishop Letellier. The preface's withering contempt for the Jesuits' theatrical enterprise is striking, and the strength of the dislike reflected there hints at disaster to come. First, the author ironically compliments the Jesuits on their dramatic skill. "They have the two ingredients one needs to succeed, inclination and talent. They love comedy, and they are born comedians."[52] Then he complains that a Jesuit school is a stage set.

> No matter where you go—in the courtyard, assembly room, or private chambers—you will always find a show going on, or preparations for one. This, of course, is developing in their students a lifelong habit. Upon quitting their studies, Jesuit students will have grown so used to plot making and to drama that they will find themselves in the world as they were in college: pleasantly disposed to disguise themselves, and to take on any role, for that is what they have been rehearsing for all the time they have been at school. (40f.)

Finally, the author accuses the Jesuits of creating a "carnival atmosphere" from which "these joy lovers will turn the whole year into one uninterrupted Mardi Gras" (41). The preface suggests that the Jesuits' theatrical activities are one source for the late-eighteenth- and nineteenth-century mythology of secrecy, plot, and disguise that grew up around the Society.

Although the Jesuit college was practically next door to the University, the University faculty joined the Jansenists in shunning the Jesuit theater, which was the overt cause of the University's

---

[51] Carroll, "Jesuit Impresario," 4.

[52] Ibid., 40.

major complaints against the Society. Even though the educational programs of the two schools were nearly identical, the Jesuits put enormous energy into amusing their students and creating situations in which learning was fun. The University of Paris had renounced the medieval tradition of school theater, suppressing all stage performances in 1685; the Jesuits, on the other hand, had raised college theater to new heights of éclat.[53] The University faculty banished musicians, dancers, and actors from their neighborhood—all, that is, except the Jesuits. The histrionic students, Opéra professionals, ballet masters, scenery painters, composers, and audiences coming and going must have been a source of perpetual exasperation to the University doctors.

In 1720 a University professor stated that it ill became wellborn youth to perform in a theater; he condemned both tragedy and comedy as an expensive waste of time, "abominable" because of their travesty roles, and dangerous because boys allowed to perform while at school grew up with a love for the public theater.[54] A rector of the Sorbonne, M. Rollins, condemned college theater on the additional grounds that the pressure of production and direction broke down a professor's health—a reason which at times must have sounded convincing to the Jesuits themselves![55]

The University-Jansenist alliance spearheaded the fiercest opposition to Jesuit tragedy, comedy, and ballet. The heaviest attacks on the French Jesuit theater came, not from the Protestants, as one might expect, but from these fellow Catholics. This cannot be taken to mean that the French Catholic church was divided simply into two parties with regard to the theater: the Jesuits versus everyone else. By the eighteenth century the French Catholic church was made up of numerous currents of religious and political thought and feeling, of which the Jesuit and Jansenist streams were the strongest. Precisely because they were the strongest and because it was clear that one or the other must cut the channel into which the religion and politics of France would flow, the Jansenists raised such bitter opposition to the Jesuit theater.

Nevertheless, French Catholic opinion on the Jesuit theater varied, though criticism grew toward the close of the seventeenth

---

[53] Douarche, "Université de Paris," 159.

[54] Bourgoin, *Histoire des représentations*, 18f.

[55] Carroll, "Jesuit Playwright," 37.

century. In the 1660s the Abbé de Pure had written in support of theater, averring that

> [t]he tragedy and the ballet are two kinds of painting where one sees the most illustrious things the world or history has to offer . . . where the most profound mysteries of nature and morality are displayed.[56]

Père Lamy of the Oratory, whose order had rejected school theater, wrote in his 1685 *Entretien sur les sciences* that theater was a waste of time, bad for students, and counter to the Gospel. In the same spirit, Guy de Rochechouart, bishop of Arras, closed the college theaters of his diocese in September 1698 because he felt plays were inconsistent with Christian conduct—and full of loose language.[57] Even the great Bossuet, member of the Academy and friendly to the Jesuits, was ambivalent about their theater because it encouraged "self-love" (36). However, when the violently antitheater *Lettre d'un théologien* was published in 1695 (allegedly by the Theatine Caffaro, though he denied having written it), Bossuet entered the fray on the side of the Jesuits. The anonymous Theologian had asked,

> If it was true that French actors were infamous because they mounted the stage and acted the comedy, I would like to know why the young men at colleges who, for their own pleasure and without scandal, play roles in comedies are not infamous?[58]

Although many religious orders had used and were using theater as part of their schools' educational program, in this period "college theater" is nearly synonymous with Jesuit-college theater, because of the Jesuit theater's reputation for artistic brilliance and good pedagogy, and because of the Jesuits' controversial role in French religious and political life. So when the attacker refers to "young men at colleges" for the most part he means students at Jesuit colleges. Bossuet attempted to bring some tolerance and reason to bear in this recurrent debate over the morality of college and public theater that, fueled by

---

[56] Lowe, "Représentations en musique": "[L]a tragédie et le ballet sont deux sortes de peinture ou l'on met en vue ce que le monde ou l'histoire a de plus illustre, ou l'on étale les plus fins et les plus profonds mystères de la nature et la morale" (28).

[57] Ibid., 36f.

[58] Peyronnet, "Théâtre d'education": "S'il etait vrai que les comédiens français fussent infames pour monter sur le théâtre et jouer la comédie, je voudrais bien savoir en vertu de quoy les jeunes gens des colleges, qui pour se divertir, et sans scandale, representent des personnages dans des comédies, ne sont pas infames" (119 n. 1).

anti-Jesuit sentiment, erupted with new force at the end of the seventeenth century. In his *Maximes et réflexions sur la comédie*, he wrote,

> One does see innocent performances. Who will be so rigid as to condemn college theatricals done by supervised youth, to whom their teachers give such exercises to form their style and action and especially, at the end of the school year, to give them some honest relaxation?"[59]

But a disgruntled father, regretting that he had allowed his son to act in the Jesuit theater at Lyons, complained that the boy had wasted his time at school and afterwards cared only for pleasure.[60] An early-seventeenth-century manuscript in the Arsenal library in Paris contains a more impassioned outcry against the Jesuits and their stage. Part of an anonymous handwritten collection of letters, memoirs, and poems, this letter by its tone suggests that it may have been written by a furious parent.

> Do the Jesuits think they can erase their crimes? This captivating grace [they impart to our sons] cannot do away with our unhappiness, and the laughter of our children cannot stay our tears. These impious Fathers charm the senses so that [our children's future lives are endangered] . . . These foxes enchant our children so that they would kill their own father.[61]

Voltaire, an alumnus of Louis-le-Grand, was on the fence about the Jesuit theater, but for artistic rather than moral reasons. He found the Latin tragedies artistically lacking, although he seemed to consider acting in them good experience for the students. He wrote to Dr. Bianchi that "one of the finest things the Jesuits did at the college where I was taught [Louis-le-Grand] was having the students put on

---

[59] Ibid.: "On voit des représentations innocentes; qui sera assez rigoureux pour condamner dans les colleges celles d'une jeunesse reglée, a qui ses maitres proposent de tels exercices pour leur aider a former our leur style, ou leur actions, et, en tout cas, leur donner, surtout à la fin de leur année, quelque honnête relâchement?"

[60] Carroll, "Jesuit Playwright," 37.

[61] "Sur les Comédies que les Jesuites ont fait jouer ces jours passes dans leur Collège," MS. 4113 (Bibliothèque de l'Arsenal, Paris): "Les Peresz ont fort bonne grace, / De leurs attentats tout Sanglons / Pensent ils effacer la trace? / Faisons badmier[?] nos enfans.

"Cette captieuse souplesse / Ne peut estourdir nos malheurs, / Et le ris de nostre Jeunesse / No tarit le cours de nos pleures.

"En topset[?] les Peres impies / Se laissoient charmer par les sons / Tandis qu'on prinoit de leurs vies / Leurs miserables enfancons.

"Et par un reuvers[?] de misere, / Parces appareils piasons, / Ces renards pipent nos enfans, / Tandis qu'ils font mourir leur pere" (343f.).

plays."[62] But even though he distrusted the Jesuits' dramatic judgment, he presented his *Mort de César* (Death of Caesar) at Louis-le-Grand before showing it in a public theater.

The Gazettes and the Ballets

Though there are many period statements indicating that the Jesuits' *dramatic* efforts may have been artistically mediocre, the ballet was usually regarded differently in the provinces as well as in Paris. For example, around 1748 the dancing master at the Dijon college, M. Cholier, used the public acclaim that had greeted his latest production as his reason for demanding a raise from the Jesuits.[63]

For the most part, the seventeenth- and eighteenth-century gazettes echoed Choliers, calling attention to the public's positive response to Louis-le-Grand's dance and music. Though Loret was essentially a social chronicler–cum–gossip columnist, eager to set down the brilliant social doings of elite Paris, his reports indicate that the intermedes—and the audience itself—were the main attractions. He said much the same kind of thing about the Louis-le-Grand theater year after year, praising the tragedy and the ballet, remarking the presence of any Opéra dancers, enthusiastically lauding the stage decor, enumerating the ranks of society represented in the audience, and recording any little marks of personal favor the Jesuits or noble personages bestowed upon him. He comments most extensively on the ballet, praising the entertaining choreography and the stage presence and skill of the dancers. But his details are reserved for the audience—how many of what rank were there, how many women were beautiful, which religious orders were represented. Though maddening to the contemporary researcher trying to "see" the ballets, Loret's "reviews" remind us that the Louis-le-Grand performances were social occasions of note.

On September 12, 1684, the *Nouvelles extraordinaires*, published at Leyden, reported that the Jesuits had economized on that year's ballet, which so horrified the court and the whole city that the spectators hissed and threw bottles! However, Lowe points out that the ballet that year was *Le Héros*, an allegory about the King, which makes it hard to believe that the performance would have been given with so little éclat.[64]

---

[62] Carroll, "Jesuit Playwright," 42.

[63] Peyronnet, "Théâtre d'education," 117.

[64] Lowe, *Marc-Antoine Charpentier*, 80.

The *Mercure* routinely mentioned the decor and mounting of the Jesuits' productions, printed summaries of and excerpts from the libretti, and published songs from the ballets. In August 1686 the writer praised the grandeur and beauty of the theater, the confidence of the actors, the beauty of the dances, and the skill of the dancers (78). In 1732 the "magnificent decor" was noted, and in 1735 the *Ballet de Mars* was "singularly beautiful, with a great number of spectators and actors." In 1739 the *Mercure* described an entrée of Malter's *L'Origine des jeux* (The origin of games). "The way the stage represented a huge chessboard, with the moves of the young men dressed as the 'pieces' and the little boys dressed as the pawns, appeared most ingenious."[65] In 1744 the skill of the actors in the tragedy *Sesostris* was praised.

> The actors have merited the public's attention. M. de Palacia, playing Sesostris, has responded to the dignity of the character and the character's reputation. M. du Peron has done himself honor by his tender, delicate, and versatile entry into the subtlety of a role difficult to play. . . . What a soul within M. de Farges![66]

Jesuit Response

What about the response of Rome, of the Jesuit superiors, and the wider Catholic hierarchy to the Louis-le-Grand theater and its ballet? The order's superiors were—after early and mostly useless pleas for economy—at least tolerant of the magnificence of the Paris ballets and their hold on the public.[67] At Louis-le-Grand, the fathers had from the beginning given their own broad interpretation to the *Ratio*'s rules concerning theater. Their superiors appear for the most part to have supported them because of the way their theater fulfilled the Counter-Reformation goal of communicating orthodox Catholic morals and values to an influential audience. The college was visited regularly by Jesuit officials who, though occasionally dismayed over

---

[65] Gofflot, *Théâtre au collège:* "La manière dont on representa sur le sol du théâtre un grand echiquier peint avec les evolutions que firent les jeunes guerriers vetus en pièces, et de petits enfants vetus en pions, parut des plus ingenieuses" (138).

[66] *Le Mercure*, August 1744: "Le jeu des acteurs a merité le suffrage du public. M. de Palacia, qui soutenait le rôle de Sesostris, a répondu à la dignité de son caractère et sa reputation. M. du Peron s'est fait beaucoup d'honneur par la manière tendre, delicate et variée avec laquelle il est entrée dans toutes le finesses d'un rôle fort difficule à executer. . . . Quelle âme dans M. de Farges."

[67] Lowe, *Marc-Antoine Charpentier*, 47 n. 19.

expense and uneasy about possible repercussions from the ballets' allegorized presentation of contemporary events and people, were essentially positive in their response. Various cardinals and the Pope's nuncio were also regular audience members, and their accounts of what they saw and heard seem not to have drawn fire from Rome.

The Jesuits themselves were a self-critical part of their own audience. Although they never fundamentally swerved from their humanist conviction that theater was good in itself, they occasionally found themselves in serious public difficulty because of their productions. In 1750 a ballet called *Le Plaisir sage et réglé* (Wise and regulated pleasure) was danced at the Rouen college. A young Jesuit there made what he probably thought was an innocent and orthodox libretto for the annual prize-giving ballet. Its "argument" was based on the Jesuits' Christian-humanist position that pleasure or enjoyment is a gift from God and a better tool than pain for teaching virtue. He must have felt himself on solid ground, as the entire Jesuit theater and much of the Jesuit educational system was oriented toward the enjoyment of learning. However, by 1750 public opinion was turning against the order; and not all Jesuits would defend their "pleasure principle" to the same extent. Those of the Society who forged literary opinion rounded vehemently on the hapless young librettist. In the September 1750 issue of their *Mémoires de Trévoux*, a Jesuit editor named Berthier attacked the Rouen librettist's judgment, orthodoxy, and understanding, repudiating his pedagogical and moral position on behalf of the Society. Of course, *Nouvelles ecclésiastiques* made hay out of the occasion, in turn rounding on Berthier and insisting that his critique had been excessively moderate.

Twenty-four years earlier, Louis-le-Grand's Charles Porée had created a ballet with the same theme as that of his unfortunate provincial brother. Called *L'Homme instruit par les spectacles, ou le théâtre changé en école de vertu* (Humankind instructed by performances, or the theater changed into a school of virtue), it was Porée's staging of Louis-le-Grand's historical attitude toward its own and the public theater. In both his ballet and his famous 1733 speech on the morality of theater, his central question asks whether the theater can become a school for virtue. In both cases his answer is yes. But the burden of the change is placed on the audience, who are motivated largely by curiosity. They are, he says,

> light spirits, butterflies darting here and there, seeing everything except themselves . . . the idle, the professionally lazy, whose principal business is to do nothing . . . going from the table to the club, or to gamble, and from there to the theater . . . without taste, discern-

ment, or benefit. . . . And they are also the overworked . . . who
hasten to the theater as to a port . . . and the domestically harassed . . . who take refuge in the theater and those vague souls . . .
the slaves of custom . . . which sends them to the theater as to
church, to the comedy as to the sermon, with the same attention—that
is to say, an equal indifference.[68]

He concludes with an appeal to all of these, and to his distinguished
ecclesiastical and aristocratic listeners: It is up to them to reform the
theater.

Your indulgence has created the evil, and it is up to you to repair it.
Then a school you have given over to vice will become by your efforts
and insistence a school of virtue. . . . Rescue the stage, innocent in
itself, from the cruel necessity of being guilty of crimes against our
neighbors and the ruin of hearts. You owe it to religion and the stage:
and if it is said that it is wrong to tolerate theater in Christian Repub-
lics, make the theater worthy, insofar as it is possible, of the honest
man, of the Christian.[69]

Porée is talking about the public theater, but he makes his
passionate appeal against the background of at least a hundred years
of "virtuous" theater playing to a packed house at Louis-le-Grand. He
feels that what he appeals for can be done. Although the Jesuit

---

[68] Charles Porée, S.J., *Discours sur les spectacles*, trans. Père Brumoy
(Paris 1733): "esprits leger, vrais papillons voltigeans ça et la sans scavior ou,
faits (ce semble) pour etre spectateurs de toutes chose, excepté d'eux-meme
s. . . . Des oisifs de toute espèce, des paresseux de profession, dont l'unique
affaire est de ne rien faire, l'unique soin celui de n'en point prendre, l'unique
occupation celle de tromper leur ennui; passant de la table aux cercles, ou au
jeu, et de la aux spectacles, pour y assister sans gout, sans discernement,
sans fruit. . . . Des gens plongez dans des emplois laborieux, accablez d'-
affaires soit publiques, soit particulières, agitez par les flots tumultueux de
mille soucis. . . . Ils courent au Théâtre comme vers un Port. . . . Des
hommes fatiguez de querelles domestiques . . . ils se refugient au Théâtre. . . . Des hommes qu'il est impossible de definir. . . . Esclaves de la
coutume . . . qui les mene au Théâtre comme au Sermon, avec une pareille
déférence aux egards, c'est a dire, une egale indifference" (44f.).

[69] Ibid.: "Votre indulgencè a fait le mal; c'est à votre juste severité de la
reparer. Qu'une Ecole, que vous avez livrée au vice, devienne par vos efforts
une Ecole de vertu. Contraignez les Auteurs d'epargner les oreilles pures:
Defendez aux Acteurs de faire rougier un front vertueux, tirez la Scene,
innocente par elle-même, de la cruelle necessité d'être coupable des crimes
d'autrui, et de la perte des coeurs. Vous le devez à la Religion, à la Patrie: et
s'il est dit qu'il faille tolerer les Spectacles dans des Républiques Chrétiennes,
rendez-les dignes, autant qu'il est possible, du Citoyen, de l'honnête homme,
du Chrétien" (48).

theater often called forth the ire of pietists, it was a crucial part of the Jesuits' educational system, because it reached beyond the college walls and into the adult world where decisions and events shaped the political and moral future. The Jesuits' theater was an allegory of Counter-Reformation humanism at work in their audience's world.

But, as always, the audience held the whole enterprise firmly down to earth. Whatever the Jesuits may have wanted from their theater, a wry poem by Porée, found among his papers after his death and published in 1741, leaves us in no doubt about what the audience wanted when they visited the rue Saint-Jacques:

> Musicians, dancers,
> It was only they the audience loved;
> for them the audience hardly had eyes and ears
> enough.
> But during the "piece" [the tragedy]
> they emptied their bottles;
> their shouts and applause
> were only for the leaping.[70]

What Did the Ballets Say to and about the Audience?

The Ballets and Baroque Communication

Faithful to the educational needs of children, [the Jesuit college] could not remain insensible to the political, moral, religious, and spiritual preoccupations of adults. By a continual osmosis, it borrowed the world's culture and styles to show the world the transcendence of the Truth it served.[71]

It is impossible to understand or assess the audience's response to the ballets apart from an examination of the degree to which, directly or indirectly, the ballets reflected the "political, moral, religious, and spiritual preoccupations of adults" in Paris in the seventeenth and

---

[70] Peyronnet, "Théâtre d'education": "menestriers, danseurs, / S'attiraient seuls l'amour des spectateurs; / Pour eux on n'eut assez d'yeux ni d'oreilles. / Mais à la pièce on vidait les bouteilles. / Et commençaient les cris tumultueux / Quand finissaient les bonds hilarieux" (117).

[71] Hennequin, "Théâtre et société": "Fidèle aux besoins pédagogiques des enfants, il ne saurait rester insensible aux preoccupations politiques, morales, religieuses et spirituelles des adultes. Dans un mouvement d'osmose continuelle, ils emprunte à ce monde sa culture et ses modes pour mieux lui manifester la transcendence de la Verité qu'il sert" (467).

eighteenth centuries. That they did reflect these contemporary preoccupations underscores a basic characteristic of the flavor and intent of
Jesuit education and provides a strong contrast with the education
offered by the University and some of the other teaching orders.

> Although the century of Lights introduced natural history and geogra-
> phy (as a result of the taste for accounts of voyages [of exploration and
> trade]) to the program of studies, the other teaching orders, and the
> University itself, in imitation of the monasteries, practiced a scholarly
> life into which few exterior influences came; at the same time the
> Jesuits, by developing their college theater, increasingly opened their
> colleges to the world.[72]

This opening was the practical result of the Society's intention to
shape and influence the world by proclaiming their worldview in
their theater and by training through that same theater boys who
would become the most influential men in France.

For us in the late twentieth century, it is difficult to sense the
political flavor that pervaded the Baroque theater. A legacy from the
Renaissance, this strong relation of theater to current events—commenting on and shaping them—was an essential ingredient of the
Louis-le-Grand ballets. These ballets, so apparently frivolous on the
surface, are the heirs of the tradition that led Essex to commission
Shakespeare's company to revive *Richard II* on the eve of Essex's
march on London, in an attempt to stir up the populace to his cause.
In the Renaissance and baroque centuries, theater was a centrally
important link in the communications system. Baroque ballet has
been called a dialogue between its creators and its audience.

Not only are we not accustomed to think of theater as a vital
and immediate channel of political communication, most of us also do
not associate serious adult concerns and intentions with the word
"ballet." Though many contemporary choreographers have made
dances about life, death, war, love, and a host of specific social and
even religious issues, the word "ballet" still conjures up gauzy sylphs
with little wings, Sugar Plum fairies, and boy-and-girl romances. Like
baroque theater in general, dance on the Jesuit stage carried a high
level of contemporary comment or *actualité*.[73] As Porée's writings

---

[72] Peyronnet, "Théâtre d'education": "bien que le siècle des Lumières
ait introduit l'histoire naturelle et la géographie (consequence du gout pour
les relations de voyages) au program des études, les autres ordres enseig-
nants, et l'Université elle-même, à l'instar des monasteres, pratiquaient une
vie scolaire ou peu de choses venait de l'exterieur; dans le même temps les
jésuites, en developpant le théâtre au college, ouvraient davantage leurs
etablissements sur le monde" (120).

level of contemporary comment or *actualité*.[73] As Porée's writings show, on the Jesuit stage the ballet was a carrier of *actualité* in relation to tragedies that carried political references. But because of the pressure of the academic year, it was not always possible to write a new tragedy for a college performance. When that was the case, a new prologue or intermedes would be added to a standard play to refurbish it and make it current. Therefore, much of the *actualité* of the Jesuit theater is found in the ballets and other intermedes rather than in the tragedies.[74]

Sometimes a clear parallel can be drawn between current political events and the tragedies—not difficult to do with stories about the doings of kings, soldiers, and heroes, and their struggles with other kings, soldiers, heroes, famine, plague, war, and so forth. For example, during the famine of 1709, the August tragedy was about Joseph's brothers going to Egypt to buy grain during a famine in Israel. However, its accompanying ballet, *L'Espérance* (Hope), carried the *specific* references to the social and economic situation in France that year. The *Joseph* play of 1709 was one of a group of Joseph plays and had also been given in 1695, whereas *L'Espérance* was particular to 1709, and was not repeated.

In assessing the *actualité* of Jesuit dance, we are not looking for seventeenth- and eighteenth-century guerrilla theater. The political and social comment of the ballets is neither radical nor immediately recognizable. A stream of references to and comments upon current situations and people is woven into the complex web of classical allegory. Called Hercules and Minerva, dressed like the most fashion-conscious courtiers, moving with precision and self-possession through the small-scale technique of baroque dance, ballet characters do not leap out at us like Ché Guevara from a bush, calling for social change. The Jesuit theater was in no sense a revolutionary theater, and its myths and allegorical conceits are among the ancestors of the sylphs and lovers we associate today with ballet. Its only claim to revolutionary fervor lay in its spiritual dimension; that is, in its commitment to teaching Catholic morals and values. Politically and socially, however, it was for the most part theater as mirror rather than theater as prophet. It reflected contemporary France to the audience by making references to social life and public personalities, and to economics, patriotism, wars, peace treaties, and religious disputes.

Ballets contained the simplest and easiest to read *actualité* when their theme reflected some element of Parisian life or a contemporary

---

[73] Hennequin, "Théâtre et société," 464.

[74] Purkis, "Quelques observations," 197

happening. For example, *Le Ballet des Comètes* (Comets) in 1665 was about the sighting of the great comet in that year. *La Gazette* in 1678 and *Les Nouvelles* (News) in 1703 were about Parisian news networks. It is worth quoting André Maurois at length on this aspect of French society in the late seventeenth and early eighteenth centuries. His description gives a lively sense of the material an acute observer could find here for potential ballets.

> In so centralized a regime, was it possible for any public opinion to take shape? Not only was there a very lively one, but it reverberated; not by means of the press—papers were infrequent and empty—but by means of the newsmongers who in those days created a word-of-mouth journalism. There were state, or political, newsmongers and newsmongers of Parnassus, of letters. It was they who gave reputations their first start in Paris. Their great ambition was to be the first to convey a morsel of information, to explain events, to criticize them; they were strategists, diplomats, theologians. . . . Newsletters, common in English-speaking countries of the twentieth century, existed in France as early as the seventeenth, and weekly their writers, thanks to the Dutch bankers, received war news which the government had not yet made public. Certain groups gathered at designated points, such as under the chestnuts of the Tuileries. Here was a stock exchange for news. Retired field marshals took up their posts there to comment on military operations. Each garden went in for its specialty: at the Palais Royal, internal politics; foreign affairs at the Tuileries; literary news at the Luxembourg. Then private letter writers spread the news throughout the provinces; Madame de Sevigné's letters were copied and circulated all over Provence. Indeed, French public opinion was much more free in 1710 than in 1810.[75]

The alterations in the 1687 production of the fourth part of *La France victorieuse sous Louis le Grand* illustrate the way in which the ballets were part of this communications network, reflecting the events of their year of presentation. When this ballet was first done in 1680, it was a reference to the peace treaty of 1679 and its results in the year that had elapsed since the treaty's signing. For example, the 1680 ballet's fourth part included the characters Hymen, Games, and Laughter to show that the best part of the new peace were the royal marriages of Mademoiselle, Louis XIV's cousin, with the King of Spain, and of the Dauphin with the Princess of Bavaria.

In 1687 the ballet was revived as a double reference to the "cold war" against the League of Augsburg, and the King's 1685 decision to stamp out heresy by revoking the Protestant-toleration act, the Edict of Nantes. The 1687 ballet was the second of a two-part series, follow-

---

[75] Maurois, *History of France*, 225.

ing *Les Travaux d'Hercules* (The labors of Hercules) in 1686, which celebrated Louis's feats on behalf of the well-being of France. In 1687, as Louis struggled against the League of Augsburg, part 4 of the ballet shows the Spirit of France as the bestower of war and peace on Europe. He gives his sword and shield to the god of war, and accepts the olive branch that the goddess of wisdom offers him. In the next entrée "the conquered nations," presumably the Spanish, Germans, and Dutch, whom France had been fighting and who appeared in the third part, ask the Spirit of France for peace. They receive it (his olive branch) and dance for joy. French commerce, damaged as always by war and further threatened by the mass exodus of commercially successful Huguenots from the country as a result of the revocation of the Edict of Nantes, is revived by Neptune and a troupe of ocean gods in the third entrée. In the fourth, Vertumne, the god of gardens, dances with a crowd of French gardeners, indicating the return of fruitfulness to the earth. The next two entrées continue this theme as Abundance and the divinities of the countryside demonstrate the pleasure of rural life in peacetime. The final entrée, whose location renders it the most important, points to the revocation of the edict and its ongoing consequences. The description of this entrée reads, "As the destruction of heresy is the most illustrious effect of peace, this last entrée represents the Furies that Religion forces to return to Hell."[76]

This attitude toward religious differences was present throughout the Jesuit theater, though at Louis-le-Grand the struggle against Protestantism was presented veiled in the usual classical allegory. Colleges in areas with a significant Protestant population dealt more directly and frequently with this issue, sometimes openly satirizing contemporary Protestants. The Paris college, in the heart of orthodox France, played a different role in relation to this issue. Playing to a court audience, it saw itself reflecting and supporting the King as defender of the faith. The upper-class Catholic assumption that orthodoxy and social class were naturally related is apparent. "The Truth" is somehow the birthright of the ruling classes; it is the bourgeois and the peasant who are likely to be seduced by heresy. One provincial college ballet, *Le Triomphe de la Religion sur l'hérésie par la croix d'Aubusson* (The triumph of religion over heresy by the cross of Aubusson), shows a bourgeois and a peasant enticed by Curiosity into

---

[76] *La France victorieuse sous Louis le Grand,* Res. Yf440 (Bibliothèque nationale, Paris): "Comme la destruction de l'Hérésie est le plus illustre effet de la Paix, cette dernière Entrée represente des Furies que la Religion fait rentrer dans les Enfers" (6).

"the heretical party."[77] In the Jesuit theater, "Arianism" is a frequent allegorical cloak for Protestantism; "Arian" often meant "heretical" or "pagan" in the literature of the period. Corneille once speculated that Attila the Hun had been an "Arian" in his religious convictions (463).

Of the ballets at Louis-le-Grand in the second half of the seventeenth century, when the issue of Protestantism in France was once more in the forefront of national events, fifteen titles suggest that in one or more entrées they refer allegorically to the Huguenots and Louis's actions against them. These include

1. Three *Verité* (Truth) ballets, in 1658, 1663, and 1692; "Truth" always referred at least in part to religious orthodoxy;

2. *Le Destin* (Fate) in 1669, a defense of the Jesuit position on free will and an attack on Calvinist and Jansenist predestination;

3. *L'Illusion* (Illusion) in 1672; "illusion" referred to both paganism and Protestantism;

4. *L'Idolatrie* (Idolatry) in 1674, about religious error;

5. *La France victorieuse* in 1680 and 1687, discussed above;

6. *L'Empire du Soleil* (The empire of the sun) in 1673, *Le Héros* (The hero) in 1684, and *Les Travaux d'Hercule* (The labors of Hercules) in 1686, three ballets about the King's heroic exploits for France, a concept that always included his role as defender of the faith;

7. The 1679 and 1698 *La Paix* ballets, because religious harmony was counted as one of the benefits of peace and was especially emphasized in the years when France was embroiled in internal religious disharmony;

8. The 1699 *Les Songes* (Dreams), whose fourth part included an entrée about "false religion" dispelled by the light (the Sun King) of Truth (True Religion, or Louis's orthodoxy);

9. The 1681 *Le Triomphe de la Religion, ou l'Idolatrie ruinée* (The triumph of religion or idolatry destroyed), to which we will return.

A closer look at several of these ballets that include references to heresy gives a clearer idea of the way *actualité* is part of dance on the Jesuit stage. All fifteen occurred between 1658 and 1699, whereas in the eighteenth century, when the heresy issue was less "in the news," there were no Louis-le-Grand ballets whose titles included the words "truth," "illusion," "idolatry," or "religion."

---

[77] Hennequin, "Théâtre et société," 463.

These fifteen ballets presenting the dangers of heresy and the necessity for orthodox religious ideas occur before and after the 1685 revocation of the Edict of Nantes. In 1662 Louis had acknowledged that his Protestant subjects had proved "their affection and fidelity."[78] Nevertheless, encouraged by the upper French clergy, he began to interpret the 1598 edict in the harshest possible way, making life more or less unendurable for the Huguenots, so that many of them fled France. The Jesuits were part of the chorus of clerical voices urging the King to eliminate the Protestants, and their theater in this period reflected their agenda. One Jesuit, Maimbourg, declared to Louis that the King had only to bestir himself one last time, and "the disastrous conflagration which has wrought such ruin in France and of which little more than the smoke remains will soon be utterly extinguished."[79] These fifteen ballets are in part the echoes of the voice of Maimbourg and others urging the King to bestir himself for the faith and praising him when he had done so.

It is probable that the following events and ballets were related. In 1662 Louis declared that the Huguenots had been faithful subjects, and in 1663 the Jesuits produced *La Verité*, which, though it makes no direct reference to religion, can be seen as a challenge to the King's statement. How can heretics be "faithful subjects" of a king who represents the orthodox faith, that is, "the Truth," in his own person? Several entrées in this ballet seem to be echoes of the Jesuits' dissatisfaction with the King's position on the Protestants. The ballet's first part turns on the process of intentionally disguising Truth, as practiced by orators, poets, and, significantly, courtiers—those who had the King's ear and could, to some extent, influence his thought and action. In the second part Truth, chased by the Vices, Falsehood, Error, Ignorance, Deceit, and Slander, hides in a "temple of the false gods." These "furies" finally force her to take refuge in a deep well. At the end of the ballet, the Spirit of the Age pulls her from the pit where she is hidden and proclaims her to the world.[80]

In 1669, largely as a result of Jansenist diplomacy, the King issued the edict of the Peace of the Church, imposing some degree of silence on both Jesuits and Jansenists in their quarrel over the alleged heresy of Jansenist theology. That year the Jesuits produced *Le Destin* (Fate), a ballet about the folly of belief in predestination, a tenet held by both Jansenists and Calvinists.

---

[78] G. R. Cragg, *The Church and the Age of Reason, 1648–1789* (Harmondsworth, England: Penguin Books, Ltd., 1966), 18.

[79] Ibid., 21.

[80] Boysse, *Théâtre des jésuites*, 146f.

Under its cloak of allegory, this ballet is very directly about the issue of free will versus predestination. Predestination is presented as the classical idea of Fate: the evil consequences for humankind of submission to Fate's false rule make up the action. Attended by Ignorance, Falsehood, Imprudence, and Error (nearly the same cast of demons as in the 1663 *La Verité*), Fate is born from hell. Fate's subjects, including misers (commercially successful Protestants?) and disgraced courtiers, appeal in vain to their implacable ruler to save them from death and shame. Mars and Minerva (Louis and, perhaps, his current mistress, Françoise de Montespan), unable to tolerate any longer the decadence of Fate's realm, lead a revolution and thrust him and his Furies back into hell.[81]

In 1681, in addition to his "war" against the Protestants, the King was quarreling with the pope, Innocent XI, over his rights as absolute ruler in relation to the French church. The ballet that year was *Le Triomphe de la Religion*, in which Constantine's establishment of Christianity appeared as the emblem of Louis's defense and spread of "the true faith." Ballets glorifying the King and all his exploits appeared in 1684, 1686, and 1687, the years immediately before and after the 1685 revocation of the Edict of Nantes—an act to which at least some Jesuits were urging him.

Story and Current Reality

If current events prompted allegorical ballets, how did those ballets communicate their political and social references through idea, character, and theatrical sequence? It is helpful here to restate part of the process of ballet composition. First, the librettist selected a subject of "general truth," often inspired in his choice by contemporary events. Then he gave it the "prestige of fiction," which meant that he searched through his library of history and fable for stories and characters whose "essence and moral" were similar to his real-life people and happenings. He then used them as allegorical veils for his *actualité*.[82] Skillful veiling was essential; many writers on the theater stressed that one should never *openly* mix

> ancient history/fable/myth with contemporary events. We do not want Floridor [a seventeenth-century actor], in playing Cinna, to speak of his domestic affairs, . . . or to mix the barricades of Paris with the laws of the Triumvirate, or, in Cinna's harangue to the Romans, to address his reflections to the Parisians listening to him. . . . in other words, to confound the city of Rome with that of Paris . . . and the day of that

---

[81] Ibid., 157f.

[82] Dainville, "Allégorie et actualité," 1:435.

speech with a public divertissement sixteen hundred years later . . . is against common sense. (437)

In the ballet it was politically prudent, socially graceful, and, for the Jesuits, professionally required by their authorities at Rome not to represent real people or their actions on the stage. But because allegory and its related mazes of metaphor and indirect reference were visually and verbally everywhere and everywhere understood by educated Europeans, contemporary people and events danced their way across the Louis-le-Grand stage with impunity.

A closer look at the 1681 *Le Triomphe de la Religion* helps to show how the ballets mixed story and reality, and also raises tantalizing questions. The ballet program contains a paragraph stating the ballet's design or plan:

> When Idolatry ruled the world, she was destroyed at one blow by Constantine's victory over Maxentius, and by his conversion to Christianity. This is the design of this ballet, which will be explained by an entrée that will serve as a prelude to the four Parts which follow.[83]

This is followed by the somewhat unusual element of a prelude entrée, in which the demons of hell, apprehensive about the Christian hero (Louis under the emblem of Constantine) who will one day destroy Idolatry (Protestantism), appear in the world as pagan divinities whose servants are Passion, Ignorance, Cunning, and Cruelty. The ballet unfolds through the usual four parts, each with four entrées. Each part is ruled by one of the four evil servants of Idolatry presented in the prelude. In the concluding *ballet général*, Religion dances, triumphing over Passion, Ignorance, Cunning, and Cruelty. As usual, all the nations of the world pay homage to the victor.

We do not know who wrote the libretto or composed the music for this ballet; but to judge from the partially legible handwritten notes on the edges of pages 3 and 6 of the program preserved in the Bibliothèque nationale, its dances (and perhaps its music) may have been by Beauchamps, who was ballet master for the 1680 and 1682 Louis-le-Grand productions.[84]

---

[83] *Le Triomphe de la Religion, ou l'Idolatrie ruinée*, Res. Yf 2699 (Bibliothèque nationale): "Lorsque l'Idolatrie regnoit dans le monde, elle si vit tout d'un coup detruite par la victoire que Constantin remporta sur Maxence, et par son entière conversion au Christianisme. C'est la dessein de ce Ballet, qui sera expliqué par une entrée qui servira comme de prélude aux quatre parties suivantes" (2).

[84] Most unfortunately, the edges of this program (Res. Yf2699, in the Bibliothèque nationale), have been cut, probably to make it a more convenient size for storage. The handwriting on the outside edges, which appears

The first clue that this ballet is, on one level, about current events is its double title: *Le Triomphe de la Religion, ou l'Idolatrie ruinée.* The first part of a Jesuit ballet's double title gives its reference in history or fable (in this case Constantine's establishment of Christianity) and the second part gives the clue about the allegory it presents (here the destruction of Protestantism). In 1681 because of his quarrel with the Pope over control of the French church, Louis was anxious to present himself as an orthodox and pious ruler. In 1681 he also officially sanctioned the forcible "conversion" to Catholicism of Protestant children aged seven and older. Soon after this decree, the infamous dragonnades against the Huguenots began.

The verbal statement of the ballet's argument or design and its prelude entrée seem straightforward settings of the scene for a tirade against heresy and a vindication of orthodoxy. "Idolatry," her manifestation as "pagan divinities," and those divinities' four attendant monsters—Passion, Ignorance, Deceit, and Cruelty—are probably a triple reference to Protestantism, the non-Christian religions the Jesuits were encountering in their foreign missions, and Catholic Jansenism. By suggesting that these three kinds of "false religion" are cut from the same cloth, the condemnation of all three is strengthened.

The ballet's first part, about the passions and desires which create idolatry, suggests that human beings make gods in their own image and according to their own needs; that is, both pagans and Christian heretics create useful cosmologies to further their own purely human ends. The first entrée shows Nebuchadnezzar making his subjects worship a statue of himself. The second shows the poor and miserable making the evils of their lives into gods, and then propitiating them. In the third, a crowd of young men follow the riotous Momus and Bacchus, because personal pleasures are their gods. This first part closes with sailors worshipping Neptune to ensure a successful voyage in search of wealth.

If the figures under these allegorical veils are Huguenots, what are we to conclude about them? That they are proud, like Nebuchadnezzar, and that, by setting up in the world a theology made in their own severe image, they are treasonously rivaling the King himself.

---

to be notes about who danced when in the ballet, is now only partly legible. Page 3 carries the note: "Entrée des [illegible] de Monsieur Beauchamp." Page 6 includes what may be a reference to the appearance of a nephew of Beauchamps as an extra dancer, probably a professional, in the ballet: "neveu de M De——amp d'augmentation." Beauchamps' name was sometimes written de Beauchamps.

Where the King represents orthodoxy in his own person, heterodoxy is treason. Having brought the evils of persecution on themselves by their willfulness, they have to some extent created a miserable and false theology out of that experience. The last two entrées seem at first glance less likely to apply to Huguenots: carousing young men and opportunistic sailors do not seem obvious symbols for sober seventeenth-century Protestants. The link here may be that the Huguenots were among Louis's most solid and prosperous citizens, and that their enemies denounced Protestant theology as a convenient cloak for worldly "pleasure" and "profit."

The ballet's second part, about Ignorance as the creator of Idolatry, is a series of entrées ridiculing other religions. "Egyptians" worshiping pumpkins and onions find themselves in a town where these vegetables are sold in the market. The outraged faithful want to attack the sellers, and finally buy all the pumpkins and onions at an outrageous price. Next, a group of obstinately superstitious people decide to believe that the earth is a god, and refuse to walk on it for fear of dirtying it with their feet. Then sun worshippers, "Persians," insist on gazing so fixedly at their god that they become blind; finally, Idleness and Sleep overtake a group of travelers who lie down, are lulled asleep, and led astray. (The French verb for "to lead astray," *égarer*, also carries the sense of "to impair one's intellect.") In this second part of the ballet, idolatry is the result of stupidity, ridiculous notions, stubborn persistence in error, and mental laziness. The message is that those who believe strange things do so for silly reasons, and that those who are led into error have only themselves to blame. The heterodox are figures of fun and contempt.

Part 3 of *Le Triomphe de la Religion*, presided over by Deceit, shows four kinds of people whose "religion" serves their own ends. The pagan emperor Vespasian, trying to consolidate his rule, presents himself as a worker of miracles. The captain of an army on the eve of battle, hoping to spur his soldiers to victory, convinces them that an unusual cloud formation in the sky is a sign of God's favor toward their cause. Indian Brahmans "amuse" their people with ceremonies that they have convinced the worshippers to accept as the true mysteries of religion. Finally, some hypocrites, having disguised themselves as *honnête gens*, take off their masks in private, escaping their pretended respectability. All these figures are deceitful and self-serving, protecting their own social credit and position. None really believe the false religion they foist on others. All can be seen as a comment on the Protestant leaders who were not allowed to settle in any one location during this period, but were forced to move at short intervals lest they gather strong communities around themselves by their "deceitful" methods.

The material in these first three parts of the ballet seems predictable, reflecting the Jesuits' anti-Protestant convictions. The fourth part, however, is more startling. This section is about cruelty used to exterminate true religion. Its first entrée shows people forced to leave their homeland because of their faith; they are weeping and preparing for a long voyage. The second scene is of prisoners who count it an honor to wear chains for their faith; according to the program, this scene "represents the courage with which Christians suffered the discomforts of prison."[85] Next we see Furies armed with instruments of torture terrorizing unarmed people. In the final entrée, the persecuted victims of the preceding scene, triumphant and carrying palms, are the symbol of the faithful martyr's victory over suffering and death.

It is possible, and probably necessary, to read this fourth part as an allegory for the persecuted Christians of the Church's early years, an affirmation of "the faith of our fathers and mothers," and a call to follow their example in defending "true religion" and resisting heresy. But it seems scarcely credible that in 1681 any aware French person, Catholic or Protestant, could have watched this part of the ballet without thinking of the Huguenots.

In another four years, the Edict of Nantes, revoked in all but name during the preceding fifteen or twenty years, would be declared officially null. The Huguenots' suffering had increased proportionately.

> In 1681 the tide of persecution rose higher. . . . Had Louis had eyes to see, the most significant events of this year were the large-scale emigration of his northern subjects, and the speed with which the Lord Mayor of London collected 25,000 pounds for the distressed Huguenots in England.[86]

In Poitou, this year was the beginning of the dragonnades, though in 1681 they were still unauthorized. During these escapades by the army

> the King's soldiers were to be seen torturing the King's subjects in order to force them to become Catholics. Such cruelty was employed that many of the reformed abjured their creed in dismay and proceeded from torture to Communion.[87]

---

[85] Ibid., 6: "representent le courage avec lequel les Chrestiens ont souffert les incommoditez de la prison."

[86] Lewis, *Splendid Century*, 109f.

[87] Maurois, *History of France*, 222.

Many, however, did not give way, and it is as easy to see the third entrée as an emblem of their commitment as it is hard not to see emigrating Huguenots in the first entrée. The second entrée, that of the prisoners, recalls the thousands of Huguenots jailed as a result of the proliferating laws made to harass and exclude them from national life. The dignity and humility of these prisoners and their willingness to suffer for their beliefs, both before and after 1685, often elicited the respect and good-will even of their Catholic jailers.[88]

It is unlikely that the Jesuits, vowed to counter the Reformation, would have been the ones to call official Catholic France to account for the sufferings of the French Protestants. But in view of the likelihood that a contemporary audience watching this part of the ballet would have thought of the Huguenots, is it possible that some Jesuit librettist, revolted by all the suffering inflicted in the name of truth, set out to create a double-edged allegory? Interpreting the allegory of the fourth part as the persecution of the early Christians, though admittedly that interpretation makes sense on the level of the ballet's "story" link to its accompanying tragedy, leads to a problem: it leaves us without a level of *actualité*, without a reference to current events. It may be that we are meant to see in these persecuted believers English Catholics who had been in jeopardy three years earlier as a result of the "Popish Plot." It is also possible that the Jesuits were making a reference to Jesuit missionaries persecuted in the course of their evangelical duties. Nonetheless, those four final entrées may have raised disquieting questions for some in the Louis-le-Grand audience.

Dainville has made a very detailed study of the *actualité* in the 1686 ballet, *Les Travaux d'Hercule*, presented the year after the revocation of the Edict of Nantes. He identifies the contemporary references under the ballet's allegory so that the program suddenly reads like a newspaper—as it must have done for those who sat reading it at Louis-le-Grand before the show and in the intervals of tragedy that interrupted the dancing. His painstaking work to match contemporary names with their allegorical figures and events makes an important contribution to this discussion of Jesuit ballet *actualité*.[89]

One important fact which emerges from this analysis is that the contemporary event implied by the allegory need not be taking place in the year of the ballet. For example, the entrée about the Affair of the Poisons refers to the trials and executions that took place in Paris

---

[88] Lewis, *Splendid Century*, 220f.

[89] See the table on pp. 150f., based upon Dainville, "Allégorie et actualité," 436f.

ALLEGORY	ACTUALITÉ
PART I	
Hercules dismays the Nemean lion	Flanders
Hercules routs a troupe of pygmies	various victories and troubles inside and outside France
Geryon, with his three bodies, fails to overcome Hercules	The Triple Alliance
Hercules crosses the river Alphaeus	Louis's armies cross the Rhine
Hercules enters the Hesperides	Louis invades Holland
PART II	
Hercules restrains the violence of the Lapithes	Louis outlaws duels in France
Hercules discovers that Cerberus hoards secret poisons	The discovery in 1676 of the Affair of the Poisons, in which courtiers were involved
Hercules assembles the Argonauts for the conquest of the Golden Fleece	Louis encourages French commerce
Hercules makes a passage between two mountains	Louis captures territory between two seas
PART III	
Hercules prevents the conquest of Thrace	recalls Louis's aid to Hungary in 1664
Hercules blasts the sons of Neptune who have insulted him	Louis attacks the pirates of Algeria and Tripoli

ALLEGORY	ACTUALITÉ
Hercules helps Theseus against the Furies	Louis delivers the pirates' captives
Hercules breaks Prometheus' chains	Louis helps his allies
PART IV	
Hercules throws down the giants trying to scale heaven	refers to Louis's piety
Hercules ruins Troy	Louis destroys Protestant churches
Hercules helps Atlas hold up heaven	Louis defends religion
Hercules destroys the Hydra	Louis revokes the Edict of Nantes

in the summer of 1676, as this exposé of black magic and murder at court unfolded. Likewise, the entrée about Louis's aid to the King of Hungary refers to the year 1664, and the two entrées about Mediterranean pirates would have been relevant during most of the second half of the seventeenth century and into the eighteenth.[90]

Identifying the particular personages represented by the ballets' gods and heroes is difficult at this distance in time and is, for the most part, outside the scope of this study. But it is important to remember that contemporary people *were* meant by the mythological figures. It is usually safe to assume that Hercules, Jupiter, Mars, and Charlemagne refer to the reigning king and, from the 1680's until 1715, Minerva often means Mme de Maintenon, as does *La Raison* (Reason), one of Louis's pet names for his morganatic wife. Similarly, Jason, in the 1701 Golden Fleece ballet, stands for the Duke of Anjou, who had just gained the throne of Spain.

Occasionally, in provincial colleges, the librettist listed in the program whom he meant by his mythological characters. In 1666, the year of the Queen Mother's death, the Toulouse college gave *Astrée ou l'apothéose d'Anne d'Austriche* (Astrea, or the apotheosis of Anne of Austria). The program tells us that Astrée is Anne of Austria, Astreide is her son Louis XIV, and Francion is Louis's young son, the Dauphin; Aurele is Louis's brother, and Gothargne is the Prince of Condé. In Paris there were undoubtedly hundreds of specific ballet references to particular members of the nobility and their exploits. However, painstaking study of each ballet in relation to political and social history and in the light of letters, journals, period gazettes, and court annals is needed to reveal most of these references.

A new theme, exoticism, emerged in the ballets' *actualité* during the reign of Louis XV. Like the tragedies, the ballets had sometimes referred to the Jesuits' activity in foreign missions and presented Asian characters, especially after the 1686 visit of the Siamese. Now the ballets also contained many references to France's involvement in world exploration, colonization, and trade. In doing so they mirrored what had become not only a French but a European preoccupation. France, her allies, and her enemies "were discovering credit and the colonies."[91]

Trade and finance were inseparable from issues of colonial expansion in these years. Soon after Louis XIV's death in 1715, Louis

---

[90] In the course of this research, I found repeated references in the *Muze historique*, the *Mercure*, and the *Journal de Trévoux* to these hostage-taking pirates and European efforts to free their captives.

[91] Maurois, *History of France*, 229.

XV's regent, Philip of Orleans, recalled John Law, the Scots financier (expelled from France by the old monarch), and Law set up the French General Bank. Financial schemes at home and abroad created great prosperity until the inevitable crash—which affected the state as much as private persons—and which was followed by deep national discontent. But although Law's Indies-related bank failed in 1720, the public fascination with wealth from France's "empire" remained.

> [T]he colonies or, as people called them, "the Islands," were in fashion. Coffee from the Isles of Bourbon, Martinique, and Saint-Domingo (Haiti) briskly cheered . . . spirits. In Canada the Couriers des Bois were exploring the Great Lakes area. . . . The colonial epic seemed to partake at once of the Lives of the Saints and the courtly novel.[92]

During the Regency the Jesuit librettists were undoubtedly influenced by Law's flamboyant financial advertising: by the Indians "bedecked with gold" who were marched through the streets of Paris, and by engravings that showed Louisiana's "silver mountains" and "emerald cliffs" (232). However, this theme of trade and colonization does not seem to appear in the pieces from other college theaters during the same period.[93]

This vein of exoticism was a natural addition to the Jesuit ballets, because it emphasized their picturesque and fantastic element. It was an excuse for rarely or never seen animals, people, and costumes, and for spectacular stage effects; and it called for movement that provided a stylistic contrast to the usual noble or court-derived style of baroque dance. Eighteenth-century ballets with exotic characters included

- 1709 (pre-Regency): Mexicans fill the empty French treasury with gold from the new world. (*L'Espérance*).
- 1720: Inhabitants of the New World give gold to France (*L'Industrie*).
- 1728: French merchants trade with Africans, Asians, and Americans; dancers appear dressed as monkeys, parrots, and pagodas (*Les Voeux de la France*).
- 1736: Mexicans give Europe gold ingots in exchange for useful iron objects (*L'Ecole de Minerve, ou la sagesse*).

New World exoticism, however, was not the only change in the ballets' *actualité* in the eighteenth century. The changing nature of the government, and ultimately of the King's role, produced others. Councils were created by the regent (though they lasted only a short

---

92 Ibid., 231.

93 LeBègue, "Ballets des jésuites," 322.

time), and the nobility once again had some influence on policy. The Jesuits, supported by the old king, now found themselves opposed by Philip, the regent. In this new atmosphere, more favorable to the Jansenists, the old theological quarrels were quickly renewed. But as the Regency passed into the reign of Louis XV, the Jesuits seemed to be winning once more against their adversaries. This was a misleading appearance, because their insistence on pressing the operation of the anti-Jansenist *Unigenitus* bull did much to turn public opinion against them, as Jansenism developed into a political party.[94]

During Louis XV's reign, the *gloire* associated with the Sun King became much less a part of the monarchy. The new Louis was thought by many to be uninterested in government or war or anything else requiring much effort. There were four wars during the reign, but the public attitude, even toward the disastrous Seven Years War, was mostly one of indifference.[95] The Louis-le-Grand ballets after 1715 reflect this apathy toward military exploits. There are no *Peace* ballets to celebrate the four major treaties of the reign. However, during the five-year War of the Polish Succession, in which France was entangled because one of the Polish protagonists was Louis's father-in-law, there was a ballet called *Mars* (1735) and another called *Le Portrait de la nation française* (The portrait of the French nation) in 1738, the year the war ended. In 1745, when the French won the significant victory of Fontenoy during the War of the Austrian Succession, a ballet called *La Renomée* (Reputation) was produced at the Jesuit college. The indolent king had been, for once, present at the fighting with his army, which made the victory especially important and, above all, publicly "presentable." Many in France, including the Jesuits, repeatedly tried to salvage some reputation for their generally unpopular sovereign. In 1748, the year of the treaty of Aix-la-Chapelle after the Austrian war, the Jesuits produced *Le Portrait du grand monarque* (Portrait of the great king). Their final effort was *Le Tableau de la gloire* (The scene of glory) in 1756, near the beginning of the Seven Years War. After that, they apparently gave it up, leaving the King's reputation to languish as they attempted to salvage their own.

---

[94] In 1713, the Pope issued the Bull *Unigenitus*, which condemned over one hundred and one propositions in *Réflexions morales*, written by the Jansenist leader Quesnel. Though there was bitter controversy about this bull in and of itself, the debate reached explosive proportions in the context of the practice enforced by some bishops and clergy that the last rites could be administered only to those who had confessed to a priest who accepted *Unigenitus*.

[95] Albert Guerard, *France: A Modern History* (Ann Arbor: The University of Michigan Press, 1969), 197.

Meanwhile, before the downfall of the French Jesuits in 1762 and the obliteration of the French Empire with the Treaty of Paris in 1763 at the end of the Seven Years War, the rue Saint-Jacques ballets caught up and reflected back the fortunes and fashions of Parisian life. Exotic ballets and obligatory attempts to cast a little reflected glory around the unsatisfactory king shared the stage with ballets which seem to show a new strain of domesticity, that is, ballets whose allegory veiled an *actualité* focused less on the *gloire* of particular persons and more on the fortunes and life of France and the French. Ballets had been staged that did this, notably *L'Espérance*, which painted such a graphic picture of France's misfortunes in 1709. The difference is that, in the earlier ballets, the assumption is that Louis XIV, "Jupiter," is *personally* responsible for France's fate. He, with his direct line to God and the gods, is at the center of the physical and emotional reality which is France. His successors were not to follow in his footsteps.

Social and Political Change

Since the sixteenth century, court ballet had reflected current conceptions of the King's relationship to the state and had also helped to create those conceptions. Before the 1620s, ballets at court presented the King as the symbol of national harmony and order— usually a longed-for rather than an accomplished harmony. But by the 1620s, under Louis XIII (known, like his son, by the symbol of the Sun), the ballets were oriented toward the King as an isolated personality, unapproachable because of his grandeur, and the sole source of well-being for his people. Throughout the seventeenth century, under both Sun Kings, the royal person rather than the political system became increasingly the point of the ballets.[96] In a profane sense, these ballets were sacramental: that is to say, they made the King's glory, his all-important *gloire*, apparent to the senses of the participants and spectators.

With the advent of Louis XV, two factors prompted baroque ballet's entry into the third and final phase of its relationship to the state and its ruler. One was the general climate of social change which began slowly to manifest itself after Louis XIV died, and the other was the early evidence that Louis XV would not be a king in the tradition of his fathers. In August 1722 the *Mercure* printed the program of *Les Couronnes* (Crowns), which had been danced on August 5 at Louis-le-Grand, as an early celebration of the twelve-year-old Louis's approaching coronation. The gazette gives a synopsis

---

[96] McGowan, *Art du ballet*, 174.

of the librettist's intentions in presenting *Les Couronnes* some months before the actual event to which it referred. It is allowed, says the ballet's author, to rejoice over the *idea* of events which have not yet happened. Therefore we can celebrate "the coming coronation of a king crowned already by his virtues."[97] The librettist then begs the reader to remember that this is a ballet and not a scholarly treatise on kingship.

Though not a treatise on kingship, its allegory allows us to see that we are now in a different reign in a different France. The ballet is made to honor and please a child. It contains entertaining elements of exoticism, and there is little of the majesty of Olympus. After the instrumental overture, there is a prelude entrée. Bacchus, the inventor of crowns—which, we are told, were first made of ivy and then of grape leaves—enters in a chariot drawn by tigers, attended by his satyrs and the people he has defeated in battle. (The War of the Spanish Succession had ended in 1720.) He presides over a dance of satyrs, captive Indians, and Indian ambassadors. The ballets' first part has four entrées whose connecting idea is crowns as prizes awarded to the best "combatants" in the arts. These entrées seem to be about the arts in France and about the Jesuits' professional attitude toward the arts. No allegorical Louis appears. There is an ensemble piece in which dancers follow a violinist and a flautist, competing for crowns of flowers. Singing poets and dancing poets compete for ivy crowns. A tragic poet and a comic poet, each with his followers, compete for crowns of laurel and tinsel. Acrobats vie with each other for wreaths of tinsel and pine boughs.

The second part is about military prizes. A Roman soldier fighting Africans saves a fellow soldier's life and receives an oak-leaf crown. A Roman officer relieves a besieged town and is given a crown of grass by its inhabitants to show that they are indebted to him for saving their land. A victorious naval officer receives a gold crown decorated with sails and other marine symbols. The last entrée in this section shows a Roman general carried in triumph after a great victory; first he is crowned with laurel and then with "the purest gold." The Roman soldiers are allegories for French soldiers and military might, and the last, the Roman general, is a hopeful reference to Louis. But the allegorical figure that represents the King is not a young god or a mythological hero, or even a great king from France's past. He is simply a competent Roman general.

---

[97] *Le Mercure,* August 1722: "Nous pouvons donc temoigner notre joye à l'approche du Couronnement d'un roy déjà couronné par ses vertus" (159).

The third part of the ballet is called "Crowns Given to Royal Virtues" and is intended as a "school of virtue" for the young king. This theme must have seemed especially necessary after the vaunted immorality of the Regency and Louis's dismaying lack of interest in either effort or virtue. Here he is allegorized as a series of heroes, who demonstrate particular traits desirable in a sovereign. As Telemachus he wins the crown of Crete because of his wisdom. As David the shepherd boy he tears in pieces a bear and a lion who threaten his flock, and then is chosen king by the other shepherds because of his courage. As the emperor Titus, he bitterly regrets the bloodshed to which a war has forced him, and receives a crown of olive branches for his moderation. (This is a negative reference to his great-grandfather's unending series of financially and socially devastating wars in the service of his personal *gloire*.) As the crusader Godfrey de Bouillon, his piety and courage in "the Holy War" (the fight against Protestantism) are honored by five nations, France, England, Germany, Italy, and the Low Countries.

The last part of the ballet is about crowns bestowed because of birth. Somewhat oddly, it is about the *variety* of ways in which a king's successor is chosen, instead of being simply a eulogy of the French way. One cannot help wondering whether this willingness to notice other ways of choosing a sovereign might not reflect the Jesuits' misgivings about young Louis. In any case, this apparent affirmation of plurality drew criticism from the Jansenists, who charged that the ballet undermined the monarchy. In the first two entrées, succession in China (a major scene of Jesuit missionary activity) and in Spain (whose throne a Frenchman now occupied) is shown. The last two entrées are about French succession: the first about the Salic Law, which barred women from succeeding, and under which the four sons of Clovis divided the realm; and the second about the modern custom of the oldest male heir inheriting the throne. In this last entrée, which describes contemporary France, Louis XV is crowned; Hymen brings in the portrait of the Spanish infanta, the little girl who has been chosen for his bride; and the Spirits of France and Spain decorate genealogical trees for each of them, showing their royal descent.[98]

The ballet closes with a two-part *ballet général*. First, the Virtues and the Arts present the new king with the crowns he merits now

---

[98] In fact, the infanta, who was brought to France to be educated, was subsequently sent home for political reasons, and Louis married the much older princess of Poland.

and will merit in the future of his reign. Then the various provinces of France pay homage to him with their regional dances.

The ballet is a eulogy of the King, like so many of the ballets under and about Louis XIV. But it is a eulogy with a wholly different flavor. Throughout, one senses that it is addressed to a boy, and to a not altogether satisfactory boy at that. This is no *Ballet of Night*, in which the teenaged Louis XIV was, with utter confidence, presented to France as her Rising Sun.[99] It has a schoolmasterish air about it, almost as though Louis XV is just another recalcitrant adolescent who needs to be licked into shape and given a good dose of classical and Christian exhortation. This Louis has been described as "the absentee king," and, in spite of this ballet's hopeful ending, one gets a sense that France is now on her own.

In the opening years of the reign, the Jesuit ballets remained hopeful about the King. Beginning in 1721 with *Le Parfait Monarque* (The perfect king), there was a series of eulogies: *Les Couronnes*, the ballet just described, in 1722; *Le Temple de la Gloire* (The temple of glory), 1723; and *Le Mariage de Thesée et d'Hippolite* (The Marriage of Theseus and Hippolyta), 1725, to celebrate the King's wedding. But as the reign continued, the ballets seem to focus less on the court and more on French identity and life. The 1728 *Les Voeux de la France* (The desires of France), whose third part is about the French economy, points to this subtle shift, as does the ballet's fourth part, though it is about an impending royal birth. In the fourth entrée of this fourth part, it is not gods and goddesses who dance around the royal cradle, but "people of different states, conditions, and professions."[100]

These real people from a real France dancing around the cradle of the King's child foreshadow the events of 1789, when their dance became for the monarchy a dance of death. But more immediately, they are indicative of the new sort of *actualité*, seen also in ballets like *L'Industrie* (Industry) in 1720, and *La Prosperité* (Prosperity) in 1755, with their entrées about finance, trade, colonization, and internal affairs. This new kind of *actualité* suggests that France is a state, a day-to-day place where people live, rather than an idealized realm embodied in the person of the King.

---

[99] In 1653 Cardinal Mazarin produced *Le Ballet de la Nuit* (Ballet of night). The ballet was a response to the political disturbances of the Fronde, and presented the fifteen-year-old Louis XIV in the role of France's Rising Sun. *Night* was part of Mazarin's strategy to strengthen the monarchy and inspire loyalty to the King's person.

[100] Boysse, *Théâtre des jésuites:* "des personnes de differents états, conditions, et professions" (286).

Many of the ballets between 1715 and 1762 were what came to be called "moral ballets." Not only were these much less often about the sovereign, they also turned less often around direct theological issues—like Protestant heresy—than around social and moral questions. Two frequent themes were the immorality of society and the potential morality of the arts. The relative moral severity of Louis XIV's final years had been followed by the licentiousness of the Regency and then by the rather bored immorality of Louis XV. The Jesuits, historically identified in Paris with the outlook of the court, found themselves with a new need to defend their educational practices—especially theater. The ballet titles and libretti suggest that the Jesuits were simultaneously attempting to justify their activities and to address what they perceived as a general social need for moral reform, while at the same time strengthening their audience's personal moral fiber and sense of identity.

Titles that point to this attempt to shore up individual morality in an immoral society include *L'Art de vivre heureux* (The art of living happily), 1718; *L'Ambition* (Ambition), 1727; *L'Empire de la mode* (The empire of fashion), 1731; *L'Envie* (Envy), 1733; *Les Tableaux allegoriques de la vie humaine* (Allegorical pictures of human life), 1734; and *Le Monde demasqué* (The world unmasked), 1740.

The Jesuits' zeal for defending the morality of the arts in these years, especially through their spokesman Porée, who wrote many ballet libretti before his death in 1741, is seen in a series of ballet titles about the arts as moral teachers. The first of these was Porée's 1726 *L'Homme instruit par les spectacles, ou le théâtre changé en école de vertu* (Humankind taught by theatrical productions, or the theater changed into a school of virtue). This ballet appears to have been a preliminary version in dance of Porée's 1733 rhetorical tour de force that framed and answered the question whether the theater was or could become a school of virtue. The 1730 ballet *Le Ridicule des hommes donné en spectacle* (The silliness of humanity shown in the theater) continued this theme, proclaiming that the theater arts are good because by showing humanity its faults, these arts pleasantly invite human beings to reform. Two years later, Porée's *L'Histoire de la danse* (The history of dance) affirmed the morality of dance, as usual under Jansenist attack, by showing its ancient uses and demonstrating that these were the forerunners of dance in eighteenth-century France. The theme of the arts as a school of virtue is also present in *Les Tableaux allégoriques de la vie humaine*. After Porée's death, these apologies for the arts continued with *La Poésie* (Poetry), 1742; *Les Merveilles de l'Art* (The wonders of art), 1744; *Le Pouvoir de la fable* (The power of

fable), 1752; and *Les Spectacles du Parnasse* (The productions of Parnas
sus), 1754.

The *Mercure*'s recounting of the 1724 ballet *Le Génie françois*
(The French spirit) throws light on the changes in self-understanding
France was experiencing in the first half of the eighteenth century.
Although Louis XIV during much of his reign had been revered as
the supreme symbol of France, there were many who rejoiced at his
death because of France's economic suffering under his passion for
defending his *gloire* by waging war. Saint-Simon wrote that when the
King died,

> the provinces, in despair at their own ruin and prostration, trembled
> with joy. The people, bankrupt, overwhelmed, disconsolate, thanked
> God with scandalous rejoicing for a release of which it had forsworn
> all hope even in its dearest dreams.[101]

During the winter of 1709, a satire on the Lord's Prayer had gone the
rounds in France:

> Our Father who art in Versailles, thy name is no longer hallowed; thy
> kingdom is diminished; thy will is no longer done on earth or on the
> waves. Give us our bread, which we lack. (226)

There is an echo of these currents of feeling in the 1724 *Le
Génie françois*. The first sentence of the *Mercure*'s account of the ballet
reads, "Grace and delicacy, *rather than magnificence*, characterize
French celebrations, and this truth is shown by contrasting today's
customs with those of the ancient Gauls" (emphasis added).[102] Magnificence had been the hallmark of Louis XIV; grace and delicacy are
what we still associate with the arts of the eighteenth century. Perhaps, under the allegory of the ancient Gauls, we are meant to see
not only remote times and customs but the reign of the old king. The
new king was also Louis, and the Jesuits at Louis-le-Grand needed,
for political and philosophical reasons, to move with the times. The
Mercure continues, probably quoting the program, "Cruelty and
rudeness reigned at the fêtes of our fathers . . . instead of the elegance and politeness that mark our own."[103] The ballet that is then
described presents four kinds of French fêtes: those at court, those of
the bourgeois, those of the peasants, and—oddly—those at sea. We

---

[101] Maurois, *History of France*, 227.

[102] Boysse, *Théâtre des jésuites:* "Comme le gracieux et le délicat caracte-
risent encore plus les fêtes des François que le magnifiques, on met cette
verité en son jour par l'opposition des moeurs d'aujourdhui avec celles des
anciens Gaulois" (273).

[103] Ibid.: "La barberie et la rudesse regnoient dans les fêtes de nos
Pères; au lieu que l'élégance et la politesse se font remarquer dans les nôtres."

know that we are in the eighteenth century in this ballet, because not only are the three traditional "estates" of noble, bourgeois, and peasant presented, but peasants are not presented as they were in the ballets of the preceding century. Earlier, when they appeared at all, they were a foil for courtiers or a romanticized symbol of rural France. Here they are somewhat more realistically presented as a group that has its own customs and is a part of France.

Did the educated French at the end of the Regency see the previous reign, which was probably better at fêtes than at anything else, as characterized by rudeness and cruelty? If the ancient Gauls and their fêtes are an allegory for a more or less contemporary reference, whom was the audience meant to see, if not Louis XIV and his magnificent "spectacles"? Conceivably, the reference could be a less specific one, pointing to a general improvement in French manners and the morality of the theater, both of which themes recur in the Jesuit libretti. In either case, the message is that the times have changed. The artistically discerning now look for "grace and delicacy" and not for "magnificence," and they live in a France where the bourgeois and the peasants have their fêtes as well as the nobles.

Magnificence did not disappear from the rue Saint-Jacques. Until 1762 the King is still praised and the gods and goddesses still appear on the Louis-le-Grand stage. As the *Mercure* said, it was on the rue Saint-Jacques that Parisians could still see ballets that recalled the great productions of Louis XIV's court. Nonetheless, the Jesuit theater did not become a museum. It reflected the world of a new century to new generations of audience members. The ballet titles and programs communicate a new sense of this audience. Though still upper-class, still full of clerics, it also had its investments in trading schemes, and its family members engaged in commerce or evangelism in the West Indies, Mexico, and China. It had had a new taste of power under the regency after long years of decorative dependence on the King. It was thinking about morality and the existence of God because the philosophes and the Jansenists between them were pushing it to recognize the extremes of belief and disbelief. It probably had to make at least standing room for more members of the bourgeoisie when it went to the ballet. It is as though, when the audience seated itself in the theater, the supremely self-confident king no longer sat at the points of origin of the lines of perspective. What was on the stage began to be made less for the monarch and his entourage and more for "France," for the audience in general, whose point of view would become increasingly important as the century progressed.

It is no accident that toward the middle of the eighteenth century, theater costumes and scenery began to be more historically realistic.[104] Their irrelevance to historical period, which had increased earlier in the century, became a matter of heated debate among critics, dancers, and actors. Individual artists, like the dancer Marie Sallé, had already initiated reforms in their own personal repertoires. But by the 1740s the practice was becoming widespread. It is as though the production—the ballet or the play itself—and its own internal world became increasingly the focus and the point of theater. Internal coherence became more important than external spectacle, just as the state of France ultimately became more important than the *gloire* of the monarch. The Louis-le-Grand audience experienced a change of address during these years. As Louis XV ceased to support thousands of aristocratic families at court, they found that they lived in France rather than at Versailles. The Louis-le-Grand ballets reflected their discovery.

---

[104] Aghion, *Théâtre à Paris*, 416.

five ·

THE "MARRIAGE"
AT LOUIS-LE-GRAND

Terpsichore and the Heroes

The heavens rejoice in motion, why should I
Abjure my so much lov'd variety?
Pleasure is none, if not diversified.

——John Donne, *Variety*

B rigid Brophy's remark that the two most interesting things in the world are sex and the eighteenth century might well be applied to the study of women and the feminine in relation to the ballets at Louis-le-Grand. One scholar's assertion that "the Jesuits sought every means of exalting women" overstates the case, at least for the researcher with a feminist perspective.[1] By presenting strong female characters, however, with the classical feminine virtues of courage and modesty and showing these characters shaping destinies and wielding power, the Jesuit producers did at least attempt to entertain and hold the interest of the women in their theater audience. These women accounted for some of the college's benefactors, a significant portion of the court, and half the relatives of the Jesuits' students.

However, the most important key to understanding the treatment of female roles on the Rue Saint-Jacques stage does not lie in documenting an "exaltation" of women by the Jesuits, but in considering the way in which the "masculine" Latin tragedy was paired with the "feminine" ballet. The star feminine "role" in the Louis-le-Grand theater was played by the ballet itself.

---

[1] Dainville, "Allégorie et actualité," 1:449.

with the "feminine" ballet. The star feminine "role" in the Louis-le-Grand theater was played by the ballet itself.

Women at Louis Le Grand, in the Audience and Onstage

That we can even raise the question of the feminine in relation to the Jesuit college stage is surprising. It suggests that almost from the beginning the Jesuits recognized the importance of tempering the austerity of their tragic theater with more generally appealing elements. Although the *Ratio studiorum* of 1599 directed that no female characters or costumes should appear in college productions, this rule, like many others, was being sidestepped or ignored in Paris very soon after the *Ratio's* publication.

Even though the Jesuit theaters in Germany and in the French provinces offered separate performances for men and women, the Paris college audience was mixed, at least by the 1650s. The Louis-le-Grand theater functioned in some ways as an annex of the court theater, attracting numbers of courtiers to its productions; this contributed to the presence of women in the audience, in spite of the *Ratio's* directive that women not attend the college theater.[2]

When Loret saw the tragedy *Tartaria christiana* on August 18, 1657, he counted four hundred women in an audience of around four thousand.[3] Ladies of the court, mothers, grandmothers, sisters, aunts, and cousins of the students, together with some female religious, attended the performance with male religious, civic dignitaries, court gentlemen, and the students' male relatives.

In August 1651 Loret saw the queen mother, Anne of Austria, with the thirteen-year-old Louis XIV and his brother at the Jesuit tragedy. Because the queen mother was there, at least some of her ladies in waiting must also have been present; in any case, Loret described eating the preperformance buffet luncheon "with beautiful creatures."[4] In 1653, he enthusiastically remarked, "I see beauties shining everywhere, as many blondes as brunettes."[5] Eight years later

[2] Victor R. Yanitelli, S.J., "The Jesuit Theater in Italy from Its Origins to the Eighteenth Century" (unpublished M.A. thesis, Fordham University, 1943), 11.

[3] Loret, *Muze historique*, Letter 32, August 18, 1657.

[4] Ibid., Letter 32, August 13, 1651.

[5] Ibid., August 1653: "Je vis briller en plusieurs lieux / Des beautés tout blondes que brunes."

he commented on the princesses and countesses who flocked to the August performance.[6] On July 7, 1718, Madame, mother of the regent, wrote a letter describing a visit the day before to Louis-le-Grand to see her young cousin de Tremouille perform. She began, "At three o'clock, I got into my carriage, with the Duke of Chartres, Mlle de Valois, and my ladies, to go to the Jesuit college."[7] We have already met Mlle du Luc, sister of the Count du Luc and niece of an archbishop of Paris, who created havoc in the audience during the 1749 ballet and tragedy by pouring wig powder from a window onto the heads of the clerics below.

It may be that Mlle du Luc was bored by the Latin tragedy, because, like Loret, she did not know Latin. But the Jesuit college was part of a social world that included many educated women, especially during the seventeenth century. Some women of this class, like Mme de Sevigné, the Countess de LaFayette, the popular novelist Mlle de Scudery, and Mme de Maintenon, morganatic wife of Louis XIV, were as well educated as their brothers. Mme de Sevigné, for example, was taught not only singing, dancing, Latin, Spanish, Italian, and French literature but also rhetoric. She was part of the group of intellectual women who significantly shaped the manners and language of France in the great salons of the time.

It was not unusual for the women of Louis XIV's court to know Latin; early in the reign, one could quote a Latin verse to either a man or a woman without seeming pedantic. The story is told of women of Louis's court going to congratulate a newly elected archbishop of Paris. When they entered the room, the gallant archbishop paid them a Latin compliment, and the Duchess of Bouillon extemporaneously replied in kind.[8] The salutation to female theatergoers printed in a French-language program from the Jesuit college at Toul in 1653, however, seems to belie this portrait of educated and serious-minded women. Addressing the audience at the college of Saint-Léon's February performance of the tragedy *Pietas*, an anonymous Jesuit writes, "We have abandoned Latin in favor of *the women,* in the hope that they will approve of our efforts and will find themselves here precisely at mid-day, to hear us in *complete silence.*"[9]

---

[6] Ibid., Letter 35, September 3, 1661.

[7] Boysse, *Théâtre des jésuites:* "A trois heures et demie, je montai en voiture, avec le duc de Chartres, Mlle de Valois, et mes dames de compagnie, pour me rendre au collège des jésuites." (86).

[8] Emond, *Histoire du Collège,* 122.

[9] Hennequin, "Théâtre et société": "Nous avons oublié le latin en faveur *des dames,* ce qui fait esperer qu'elles agreeront nos efforts et se trouve-

This touchily polite directive may reflect any one of several things: men's assumptions about women, a lower degree of education on the part of provincial women, or an audience of a somewhat lower social class than the audience at Louis-le-Grand. But it also reflects the general rowdiness of baroque theatergoers of both sexes. In any event, during the seventeenth century, the Paris college began to use French programs for the convenience of those—male as well as female—who did not know Latin. During the next century, proficiency in Latin declined among both women and men. By Mlle du Luc's time, there were probably many spectators who either did not know Latin at all or who could not understand it well enough to follow the dialogue of the tragedy. The shift in emphasis from the tragedy to the ballet that took place in practice, though not in theory, was partly the result of this decline in the knowledge of Latin.

When the women at the Louis-le-Grand theater consulted their programs and watched the action onstage, what sort of female characters did they find? Probably the first thing they noticed is that there were relatively few female roles compared with the number of male roles, especially in the tragedies. Many tragedies had no female characters at all, and three or four seems to have been the maximum—and an unusual number—in any single play. Women's roles in tragedy were usually limited to a mother, sister, or wife of one of the classical heroes or other male characters. There were several ingenious alternatives to the direct appearance of female characters. Women were sometimes "disguised" as men; or they could be "present," though offstage, important in the development of the plot and collaborating with other characters in various actions, but for one plausible reason or another speaking their lines unseen. A third possibility was to build the plot around the positive or negative influence of a woman who, dead or absent, was never directly part of the action, either onstage or off.

In a few tragedies, female characters played central parts. Six tragedy heroines had major roles on the Louis-le-Grand stage between 1656 and 1692. Women either played minor roles or were absent from the other thirty tragedies in this thirty-six year period. Loret's letter for August 19, 1656, described going to see *Cyané*. He found the play "touching and tragic," and its heroine, a young Persian princess, "beautiful and charming, pleasing everyone." *Athalie* was the August tragedy in 1658; of its four principal roles, Athalie, Joas, Jozaba, and Mariane, three were female. Loret described the crimes of the title character:

---

ront precisement a midy, pour nous entendre avec *grand silence*" 1:462 n. 14.

> A long-ago Judean queen,
> who feared to lose her throne and crown,
> killed all the Royal House but one,
> And him she raised tenderly.
> But he undid her subtlety,
> surviving all her cruelty,
> and became the Hebrews' king.[10]

Of the pretty Mariane, he wrote,

> As for the young Mariane, no one thought
> that Cypris, Pallas, or Diana,
> was as pretty and sweet as she.[11]

The next tragedy about a woman was *Caterina*, in 1672. Then came *Erixana* in 1680 and 1687, *Jephté* in 1686 (around whose daughter the action turned), *Idomenée* in 1691, and *Sophronie* in 1692.

The Machiavellian Athalie and the sweetly charming Mariane represent two of the several types under which women appeared in the tragedies. They tended to be either very unscrupulous or else very virtuous. Chastity, conjugal faithfulness, love of children, long-suffering, and support and inspiration for the exploits of their sons, brothers, fathers, and husbands were, predictably, among the traits of the "good" characters. Reaching for traditionally male power, as did Queen Athalie, or seeking revenge, as did Queen Constance of Naples in *Clementia christiana* (1660), characterized the "bad" ones.

But women acting courageously and independently for the good of their souls or family or country also appeared from time to time on Jesuit stages. Suzanna, who refused to worship false gods; Editta, daughter of an English ruler who disguised herself as a warrior and captured the fortress of London; and the biblical Judith and Esther are examples of such characters. Of these four valiant women, however, only Suzanna was presented at the Paris college. Cecilia, Theodora, Helena, Joan of Arc, Jezebel, Mary Stuart, and St. Agnes (the last-named in a tragedy called *St. Agnes Rescued from a House of Ill Fame*, at Caen in 1682), also appeared outside France and in the French provinces, but not on the Rue Saint-Jacques.

---

[10] Loret, *Muze historique*, letter for August 19, 1656: "Reyne, autrefois, de la Judée qui pour n'etre deposedée / de la supreme autorité, fit mourir, avec cruauté, / par une trame deloyale tous ceux de la Maizon Royale, / un excepte, tout seulement, que l'on sauva, subtilement, / l'élevant comme une Pucelle, et qui, malgré cette Cruelle, / apres pluzieurs dangers scabreux, fut coronée Roy des Hebreaux."

[11] Ibid.

The absence of these characters probably reflects the Louis-le-Grand Jesuits' interests as classicists as well as their attitude toward women. The French colleges, and especially Louis-le-Grand, drew most heavily on what might be called the humanist cycle of Jesuit plays, with their overwhelming emphasis on the Greek mythological hero and his relationships with homeland, comrades, and quest. Women, if they appeared at all, were mostly adjuncts to his actions.

But when the first act of the tragedy ended, and the ballet began, the spectators found themselves in a different world. The loosely constructed ballet plots and the nature of the ballet as a genre offered a wider scope for the inclusion of female characters. A ballet had many more roles than a tragedy, and though the majority of these were still masculine, there were often proportionately more feminine roles in the ballet than in the tragedy.[12] A sampling of ballets from 1697 to 1709, the approximate middle of our period, yields a surprising number and variety of goddesses and feminine personifications.

La Jeunesse (Youth), produced in 1697, with dances by Beauchamps, had several characters who were clearly female, and a swarm of personified feelings, arts, and ideas which were almost certainly cast as women. In the third entrée of *La Jeunesse*'s first part, La Verité (Truth) appears to Plato, Aristotle, Democrites, Epicurus, and their suite of modern philosophers. Not content simply to see her, each wants her for his own and tries to grab her. But "she escapes from their hands, not without losing pieces of her clothing, which they treasure."[13] Minerva, goddess of wisdom, presides over the ballet's third part, educating the youth of France, and reappears in the final *ballet général*. In the second entrée of the second part, the women of Thrace, egged on by La Dépit (Spite), La Colère (Anger), and La Haine (Hate), tear Orpheus to pieces. The third part, under the auspices of Mars, god of war, has no female roles, though Theseus is shown preparing his soldiers to fight the Amazons.

In this and other ballets, La Poésie (Poetry), La Chicane (Trickery), La Fourbe (Deceit), L'Avarice (Greed), La Justice (Justice), La Jurisprudence (Law), La Dépit (Spite), La Colère (Anger), La Haine (Hatred), L'Oisiveté (Idleness), La Molesse (Indolence), La Volupté (Voluptuousness), and some of the Pleasures were probably presented as women. In the books of emblems, personifications were

---

[12] Hennequin, "Théâtre et société," 462.

[13] *Ballet de la Jeunesse,* program, Jesuit Archives, Chantilly, France: "[E]lle s'echappe de leurs mains, non sans perdre quelque chose de ses vestements, dont ils font trophée."

presented as feminine or masculine according to their grammatical gender, and the same was probably done in the ballets. All of the above characters, except for Les Plaisirs (The Pleasures), are grammatically feminine. The Jesuit librettists, professors of rhetoric and grammar, who drew on Ripa's book and others like it for characters and costumes, would have taken the gender of words into account in deciding how to personify them onstage.

The participation of both women and men in various cultural pastimes, as well as the tendency of men to associate women with seductive leisure, suggests that some of the Pleasures would have been female as well. On the other hand, La Musique (Music), L'Oisivité (Idleness), and La Molesse (Indolence), in spite of being grammatically feminine, may not have been cast that way. Though Ripa presents Music as a woman, the Jesuits seem more often to have identified that art with the god Apollo; and Idleness and Indolence offered obvious comic opportunities for satirizing the behavior of idle and indolent boys at the college.

The 1701 ballet *Jason* presents Jason consulting Themis, goddess of Justice, whose oracles are the most revered in Thessalonica. Minerva directs events in the ballet's second part, appearing in three of five scenes. The female Harpies attack Jason in scene 2 of the third part, and in the next scene, La Discorde tries to discourage him. Characters in the *Récits en musique*, which served as intermedes for this ballet, included two Furies with their nemesis, the goddess Pallas Athena, and two Pleasures employed by Indolence to persuade Jason to stay at home. One Pleasure sings to him, "A little repose is good for Heroes," sounding like the stock stage seductress, and also like everyone's protective mother.[14]

In *Jupiter, vainquer des Titans* (Jupiter, conqueror of the Titans), 1707, with dances by Pécour, La Terre (Mother Earth) is the principal character of the ballet's second part, but she bears little resemblance to her benevolent modern counterpart. Mother of the evil Titans who are trying to oust Jupiter from the throne of the gods and replace him with their own leader, Titanus, she appears in each of part 2's four scenes, doing everything in her power to help her children. In the third scene, she gives birth to a daughter, L'Envie (Envy), who comes into the world accompanied by goblins. L'Envie and her attendants help La Terre by smashing Jupiter's statue. In the fourth scene, La Terre places a statue of her son Titanus on an altar and summons all

---

[14] *Récits en musique*, program, intermedes for the *Ballet de la conquête de la Toison d'Or*, 1701, part 3 (Jesuit Archives, Chantilly, France): "Un peu de repos sied bien aux Héros."

earth's people to worship him. The third part of the ballet presents the goddess Hebe and her suite, forced by the Titans to serve them nectar intended only for the gods. Pallas Athena is a main character in the ballet's final part, reassuring the gods that they can overcome the Titans. The ballet also includes various feminine divinities of the earth and the countryside. It is surprising, considering the sensuality of baroque art and the relatively benign Christian humanism of the Jesuits, that in this ballet the feminine earth is evil.

The female characters in *L'Espérance*, 1709, include Flore, Pomone, and Vertumne (goddesses of the countryside), Pandora, Ceres, Terpsichore (goddess of dance), La Discorde, the Muses, La Paix (Peace), and the title character, the goddess Hope. In this ballet these last two divinities are heaven's gift to beleaguered France. Hope replaces the male Apollo on Parnassus, and when Peace descends on her cloud to rule the earth in Hope's place, she and L'Espérance exchange recitatives like two female courtiers exchanging compliments at Versailles.

When the Jesuits cast these female characters in tragedies and ballets, they were played *en travesti* by boys or young men in female dress. The practice of travesty roles had been common in earlier secular theater and court ballet, as well as in college theater. Loret's description of Suzanna in *Suzanna christiana* (August 4, 1653), by Jourdain, gives us a glimpse of a seventeenth-century travesty representation of a female Christian martyr:

> A virgin, young and wise, with a pure and holy heart, having beauty patches on her cheek, round ones and long ones, the same as coquettes wear . . . the aforesaid saint, in one bloody blow, lost her pretty head because she wouldn't worship false gods. I saw, with my own eyes, that those little black miracles stayed fast on her cheek even so.[15]

The students playing women's roles were fully dressed for their parts according to current fashion, so that, as Loret reports, an early Christian martyr appeared looking like a lady at court. Theater costumes made little historical reference to a character's actual time and place. Though Suzanna would probably have carried the martyr's palm and worn white as a symbol of her virginity, her costume would have been heavy and elaborate, with corset, petticoats, hoops,

---

[15] Lowe, *Marc-Antoine Charpentier:* "Une vierge, jeune et sage, dont le coeur etait pur et saint,avoit des mouches sur son teint, de formes rondes et longuettes ainsi qu'on voit aus coquettes. . . . Ladite saint, d'une sanglante epée, sa belle teste fut coupée pour n'adorer pas les faux dieux. J'apercus, de mes propres yeux, les miracles, de couleur de more, qui, sur sa joue, etoient encore" (40f).

panniers, heels, wig, jewelry, beauty patches, and fan, according to the fluctuations of fashion.

Were all the feminine roles on the Louis-le-Grand stage played by boys? The unhesitating answer in Jesuit-theater research has been "Yes, of course." However, until existing cast lists for the Paris college ballets are compared with corresponding personnel records for Opéra dancers, we should maintain an open mind on this question. The list of the surnames of eighteen Opéra dancers who appeared in the 1698 *Ballet de la Paix* (Ballet of peace) includes the names Guyot and Dumoulin.[16] M. Dumoulin and Mlle Guyot (also spelled Guiot) were two of the most famous Opéra dancers at the end of the seventeenth century, and were often seen in duets.[17] It does not seem impossible that these famous partners appeared together at the Jesuit college, where so many Opéra dancers performed. As has been said, dancers were sometimes masked and costumes were voluminous.

Of course, the Guyot in the Louis-le-Grand cast list may have been a male dancer of that name. Professional performers in this period often belonged to dynastic theater families, with an array of performing brothers, sisters, cousins, and so forth. But the possibility of the occasional appearance of professional female dancers in the Paris college ballets is an intriguing one and cannot, at this point, be ruled out on the basis of direct evidence.

Women, the Feminine, and Sexual Entanglement

Although contemporaries delighted in making much of the travesty characters on the Jesuit stage, the Jesuit theater was probably relatively restrained in this area—though perhaps less restrained in Paris than in the provinces, especially in the earlier years of Louis XIV's reign. One obvious limit to the travesty possibilities offered by this all (or mostly) male theater was the difficulty of persuading adolescent boys to face their peers as a Hebe or a Minerva. Another was concern for the students' chastity. Jouvancy warned, "Fire, even when banked, cannot be touched without harm."[18]

---

[16] *Ballet de la Paix*, program, Rondel Collection, Bibliothèque de l'Arsenal, Paris.

[17] The *Nouveau receuil de dance de M. Pécour* (Paris, 1712) includes an "Entrée d'un pastre et d'une pastourelle" danced by M. Dumoulin and Mlle Guiot in *Les Fêtes venitiennes;* the note about Dumoulin's career under the dance score also refers to his frequent appearances with Mlle Guiot.

[18] Carroll, "Jesuit Playwright," 34.

As he implied, the Jesuits saw feminine characters as posing the threat of romantic and sexual entanglements. Myths or other stories which included a strong love interest were suitably expurgated for the Jesuit stage, or presented so that romantic passion served as an object lesson consistent with the Jesuit point of view. The 1699 *Les Songes* (Dreams) had an entrée called "Love" in its third part. In this scene Orpheus, still longing for Eurydice whom he has lost, dreams that he sees her in Hades. He tries to call her back with his enchanted music, but fails. When his hopes are disappointed, his romantic passion becomes a passion of anger. The moral warning is that romantic love leads to illusion, disappointment, and the loss of self-control.

It is in their handling of romantic love, that the Jesuit theater appears most clearly as the theater of a celibate male religious order. It is here that the theatrical need was created which the ballet filled so admirably. Although in nearly every other area of theatrical production the Paris Jesuits in particular accommodated their rule and their stage to prevailing artistic taste and court fashion, when it came to romantic love, they held the line. Le Jay wrote, "The emotions and frivolous woes of lovers have no more place on a Jesuit stage than they did in Greek tragedy."[19] Their desire to emulate the ancient Greek theater was a powerful reason for the rarity and severity of love scenes on their stage. Porée said, in his speech on the morality of the theater, that Aeschylus never dealt with romantic love, Sophocles presented it only once, and Euripides included it two or three times. And then, so cautiously—and plainly—that it disappeared, "trailing after itself horror and punishment."[20]

What the Jesuits deplored in the secular theater was not its secularity, but its endless exaltation of romantic passion—which, in this era of marriages arranged for practical reasons, often meant illicit passion. The Jesuits' exasperation with the growing storm of "amours" on the French stage mounted during the eighteenth century. In the 1680s Menestrier could still pass with no apparent prejudice or discomfort from describing college ballets to describing *Les Amours déguisez* (Loves disguised), in which the King danced in 1664. Its titillating characters, among others, were Venus, Marc Antony, and Cleopatra. Although he probably would not have countenanced them on the college stage, he felt that the wedding of Peleus and Tethys and the birth of Venus were especially good ballet subjects. In

---

[19] Ibid., 31.

[20] Porée, S.J., *Discours sur les spectacles:* "en trainant aprés lui l'horreur et le châtiment" (33).

August 1660, with Menestrier's and the other professors' approval, the students at Louis-le-Grand had themselves performed the *Ballet du Lys et d'Imperiale* (The ballet of the lily and the bearded iris), an allegory about the wedding of Louis XIV.

The problem was not the existence of romantic love as a fact of life. The Jesuits' objection was to the secular theater's increasing glorification of illicit relationships, and its placing feeling and pleasure (not considered in themselves bad or wrong) at the center of the moral universe. As Porée cried out, it seemed as if Venus had become "the only divinity."[21] He went on to complain that in the contemporary theater the destructive consequences of illicit love were never presented. Instead, audiences were shown Love

> with his retinue of Graces, with his snares of delicate sentiment, with all the poison of enchantment. Arrows in hand, he shows us his wounds, sighing: but they are mostly self-inflicted. . . . If he deplores his ills and torments, it is to excite, not repentance, but desire.[22]

What is being deplored here is not so much sexual love in itself as the popular attitude that the state of being in love excuses all actions and renders moral decision making impossible. Then as now, this attitude struck at the heart of Christian ethics and moral theology. Christian humanism affirmed that human beings are capable, with God's help and by virtue of being created in God's image, of making good moral choices. Any philosophy or theology which denied or minimized that assumption was to be denounced.

The Jesuits' point, in their own theatrical practice and in their writing on the theater, was that if men and women chose to do so, they could make the theater—including tragedy, comedy, and the theater forms built around music and dance—into a "school" for virtue. But that could not happen as long as the riot of romantic love on the stage made it a school for thoughtless and illicit pleasure. The contemporary theater already had, Porée said, several famous "schools" in which boys and girls were being educated. In an implied attack on the Jesuits' former student, Molière, he pointed out that there were, among others, the famous *School for Husbands,* and the even more famous *School for Wives.* What will you say, he asked,

---

[21] Ibid.: "passe enfin pour l'unique Divinité?" (32).

[22] Ibid.: "avec tout le cortège des Graces, avec tous les pièges des sentimens délicats, avec tout le venin de l'enchantment. Les fleches à la main, il nous montre ses blessures en soupirant: mais beaucoup moins pour etre guéri que pour blesser lui-meme. . . . S'il déplore ses maux et ses tourmens, c'est pour exciter non pas le repentir, mais le désir." (34).

if in these vaunted schools all the refinement of vice is taught at the expense of virtue? What if the youth of both sexes forget antique simplicity in order to learn to escape the most enlightened vigilance, and to follow a blind passion? . . . What if the claims of a sacred bond are on the one hand betrayed for outright flirtation and libertinism, for furtive ruses, a thousand strategies; and on the other, sunk in confusion, ignominy, and blame?[23]

As he drove home his point that romance had become the scourge of the French theater, Porée painted a rhetorical picture of Voluptuousness enthroned among a swarm of cupids. This image, which could be a canvas by Watteau, could also be an entrée in almost any baroque ballet that presented romantic love. Imagine it, he urged:

> Voluptuousness enthroned on a lawn, crowned with rosebuds, her lyre in one hand, and her honeyed cup in the other. A thousand cupids armed with their quivers fly around her. Reason, drunk on her deadly brew, lies at her feet, almost asleep and chained with flowers. From every quarter, a crowd of Heroes and Heroines arrive, all in a silly languor of love. Gods and Goddesses, victims of Cupid, make a brilliant assembly. Between these two groups we imagine many students of both sexes, all young, uneducated, and therefore susceptible to all sorts of lessons, especially lessons of pleasure. Voluptuousness seems to tell them, "Gather the flowers of spring: twine them in your hair: never mind that they fade: don't worry about the future; enjoy the present. . . . Close your ears to carping Reason, follow your heart. Love is the only good in life." These maxims are expressed in delicate verse, taken up by a consort of instruments, sung by Sirens in an artless dance, and resound, like echoes, from the mouths of Shepherds and Nymphs. Fauns and Dryads leave their woods and take them up; Naiads and Tritons come up from the water; Gods of the Heavens and the Underworld leave their realms; all hasten to revive their senseless loves. All wait, all sigh: birds, zephyrs, streams, even rocks, all learn to love.[24]

---

[23] Ibid., 36.

[24] Ibid.: "la Volupté assise sur un Trone de gazon, couronnée de roses naissantes, tenant sa lyre d'une main, et une coupe emmielée de l'autre. Mille Amours armez de leurs carquois voltigent çà et lá au-dessus et autour d'elle. La raison enyvrée par le breuvage funeste, presqu'endormie et enchaînée de las fleurs est couchée a ses pieds. On voit arriver de toutes parts une foule de Héros et Héroïnes, tous connus par leurs folles languours. D'autre part, Dieux et Déesses, . . . victimes de Cupidon, forment une Assemblée brillante. Entre ces deux groupes, imaginons quantité d'eleves des deux sexes, jeunes surtout, peu instruits, et par la susceptibles de toutes sortes de leçons, surtout de celles du plaisir. La Volupté semble leur tenir ce langage. 'Cueillez les fleurs du Printems: ornez-en vos têtes: n'attendez pas qu'elles se

Outside the college theater, the professional theater's gorgeous marriage of dance and music was certainly a dazzling "school" of visual, musical, and kinetic pleasure; and on the college stage the ballet, though it did not present the sweets of romantic love, was the chief attraction of the Louis-le-Grand productions. The Jesuits were justly renowned for their contributions to the pleasure garden of the ballet, but what were they doing in this illusory realm of enchantment and feeling?

The Marriage at Louis Le Grand

Since only God could rightfully occupy the center of the universe, romantic love morally acceptable to the Christian humanist was love that contributed to the right ordering of God's creation by affirming and urging the other virtues. *Cyrus*, the 1679 tragedy at Louis-le-Grand, contains a love scene between Cyrus and Palmyra that illumines this point. In the midst of his war against the Medes, Cyrus is urging Palmyra to marry him. She reminds him that the war is not yet won and could still go against him. He accuses her of only loving him for his reputation as a soldier and not wanting to marry him yet, in case he loses. She hotly denies his charges in a speech that ends with these lines:

> It is not the scepter, it is not the double laurel wreath crowning your young head that make you dear to Palmyra; *it is your passion for honor, justice, and virtue.* That is the glory which has earned you my heart, just as it has won you the admiration of men and gods.[25] (emphasis added)

---

fanent: ne portez point des yeux inquiets sur l'avenir; jouissez du présent...Fermez l'oreille a l'importune raison, suivez la pente du coeur. La tendresse fait l'unique bonheur de la vie.' Ces maximes exprimées in Vers delicats, relevées par un concert d'instrumens, chantées par des Syrenes au milieu d'une danse naïve, passent, comme par échos, dans la bouche des Bergers et des Nymphes. Pour les redire, Faunes et Dryades sortent de leurs bois; Nayades et Tritons s'élevent des eaux; Divinitez du Ciel et des Enfers quittent leur séjour; tous font revivre leurs amours insensées. Tout s'attendrit, tout soupire: oiseaux, zéphyre, ruisseaux, rochers même, tout apprend à aimer" (39f.).

[25] Boysse, *Théâtre des jésuites:* "Ce n'est point le sceptre, ce n'est point le double laurier qui coronne votre jeune tête, qui vous ont rendu cher à Palmyre; c'est votre passion pour l'honneur, la justice et la vertu. C'est cette gloire qui vous a merité mon coeur, comme elle vous a valu l'admiration des hommes et des dieux" (173).

Seen in this light, prohibitions and refusals that at first appear simply as prudish, defensive, and misogynist reactions against sexual love become visible as—at least in part—something more. The ball and chain and water snake of Lang's allegorical costume for Marriage notwithstanding, the Jesuit theater at least sometimes tried to offer a moral and ethical challenge to both sexes. At its best, the challenge of the Jesuit stage was not a simple rejection of passion, but an admonition to lovers to love for the good of each other's immortal souls. Perhaps not a popular suggestion in any period, it was nevertheless a profoundly Christian one, and one that contained within it a certain respect for women as decision makers and independent thinkers, capable of challenging the assumptions of men.

In the broader context of Paris theater, the Jesuits set themselves up as the austere masculine antidote to the secular theater's eternal *tendresse*. But within the confines of their own stage, they understood that the high-minded love of a Palmyra and a Cyrus, although it embodied their own justification of romance, offered little relief from the severe atmosphere of the tragedy. The Jesuit producers at Louis-le-Grand were too theatrically expert not to realize that their elegant and worldly audiences wanted something more enticing to the eye and diverting to the heart. They found it in the ballet. Without focusing its energies on sexual entanglements, the ballet, by its unabashed appeal to the senses, filled the emotional and sensual gap that the avoidance of all but the most rigorously moral romantic love (seen only in its most presentable public moments) left in the Jesuit theater. By skillfully manipulating the ballet's kaleidoscope of characters, costumes, props, scenery, French songs, dances, and instrumental music, the Jesuit librettists created the balance—which the contemporary observer may call masculine-feminine in a Jungian sense—so necessary to good theater. "Masculine" and "feminine" as used here indicate contrasting *human* capacities, not traits normative for men or women. However the Jesuit producers may have thought about the characteristics of real men and women, they understood the importance of contrasting emotional dynamics: severe-tender, judging-loving, conquering-receiving, working-playing, static-changing, and others similar.

The world of the ballet was a world essentially more feminine in conception and impact than that of the tragedy, if "feminine" is understood typologically, as simply the reverse of the traditionally "masculine" qualities of logic, severity, and aggressiveness. Unlike the analytic tragedy, which presented the inexorable consequences of moral choices, the ballet's construction was synthetic, depending on constantly changing and loosely related characters, events, scenery, and costumes. Not bound by the classic unities of time, place, and action, the ballets unfolded imaginatively, with an emphasis on playfulness and feeling. Although, to our twentieth-century eyes, baroque dance may seem to be a formal and demure technique, we will misunderstand both it and the Jesuit ballets if we forget that, in its own time, its point was the communication of feeling. Loret's description of La Verité, the title character in the 1658 ballet by that name, evokes this "feminine" spirit of the ballet and the sensual and emotional relationship between dancer and audience.

> [T]hen La Verité came on,
> and with her steps and her pirouettes,
> she *ravished* the audience,
> both Prudes and Coquettes.[26] (emphasis added)

To say that the Jesuits turned to the ballet to provide the missing feminine element of their theater is neither to make them out as seventeenth-century Jungians nor to minimize the anti-feminist bias that can be found in some of their rule, writing, and theater. From a present-day perspective—and no doubt from the perspective of a seventeenth- or eighteenth-century woman in the Paris college audience—it is a serious flaw if Voluptuousness, Envy, and Idleness are always female, if daughters always obey their fathers, and if queens are always vengeful usurpers. Nevertheless, the audience at Louis-le-Grand was not presented with either a misogynist or a monastic theater. Female characters and the feminine ballet spoke with a variety of voices, for and about a range of ideas, decisions, experiences, and feelings shared by both women and men. Though the ballets' and tragedies' statements and implications about women and the feminine reflected a male perspective and carried the limitations of their time and place, the world presented in the college theater was a world in which moral decisions were made by both sexes, and a world that offered delights to both.

In pairing the classically rooted moral tragedy with the still moral but contemporary and flamboyant ballet, the Jesuits attempted to create a rightly ordered theatrical universe. They put God and God's commandments, embodied in the baroque version of antique tragedy, at the heart, and let the physical universe, including feelings, sorrows, and pleasures, dance around the divine center during the intermedes. This universe's center was "masculine," but its liveliness—its movement—was in its "feminine" element.

---

[26] Loret, *Muze historique*, Letter for August 24, 1658: "La Verité sortant d'un puis, / Par ses pas et ses pirouettes, / Ravit et Prudes et Coquettes."

What became of this mating of opposites, this theatrical "marriage" at Louis-le-Grand? By the end of the seventeenth century, as we saw in chapter 1, the ballet, originally intended as light and colorful interludes in the serious business of classical tragedy, was beginning to have its *own* intermedes. The wry poem found among Charles Porée's papers after his death lamented that, on the Louis-le-Grand stage, only the dancers were loved by the crowd; during the tragedy, the audience drank![27] As far as the audience, at least, was concerned, the center of the Jesuits' theatrical cosmology had shifted. Terpsichore upstaged the heroes.

---

[27] Lowe, *Marc-Antoine Charpentier:* "menetriers, danseurs / s'attiraient, seuls, l'amour des spectateurs, / pour eux, on n'eut assez d'yeux ni d'oreilles, / mais, à la pièce, on vidait les bouteilles, / Et commençaient les cris tumultueux / quand finissaient les bonds hilarieux" (39).

Conclusion · · · · · · · · · · · · ·

THE FINAL CURTAIN

[A]ll the misfortunes that histories
are so full of, the blunders of politicians,
the miscarriages of great commanders—
all this comes from want of skill in dancing.

————Jean Baptiste Poquelin (Molière)

Thousands of pages have been written about the fall of the Society of Jesus from favor and power in Europe in the eighteenth century. Even so, the fate of the Old Society remains somewhat mysterious. Though their ballets lost none of their éclat, the Jesuits themselves, to borrow Molière's conceit that public disaster is the result of "want of skill in dancing," lost step in the dance of power. From the 1750s until its dissolution by Pope Clement XIV in 1773, the order suffered a series of reverses in Catholic Europe that would have seemed unthinkable at the beginning of the century. Many contemporaries of the Jesuits' downfall, enemies as well as friends, were shocked and outraged at the manner of events, if not at the matter. Prince Hohenlohe wrote of the order's destruction as "an infernal cabal"; and Theiner, a sworn enemy of the Society, said that the suppression was "a disgraceful warfare, a deplorable drama, in which too many impure elements played a leading part."[1]

The elements of this final drama were many and varied; in France, the declining influence of the aristocracy and a steadily growing negativity toward the clergy both played a part. By the 1760s, the clergy were in many places neither esteemed nor influential in daily affairs.[2] As the century progressed, many of the clergy themselves, most of the bourgeois of Paris, and the majority of those in govern-

---

[1] Robert Schwickerath, S.J., *Jesuit Education* (St. Louis, Missouri: B. Herder, 1903), 173.

[2] Darnton, *Cat Massacre*, 124.

ment positions opposed the Jesuits.[3] These symptoms of social change were part of the background for what happened, but the immediate causes were international and complex.

The curtain began to fall in Portugal. In 1757 the Jesuits there were accused of illegal commercial activities, and their colleges were closed. In 1759 they were expelled from the country. France was the next scene of disaster. In 1755 a French Jesuit, Lavalette, the superior of the Martinique mission, contracted extensive debts because of his unauthorized business ventures. Without the knowledge of his superiors, he risked large sums of money, which he lost as war loomed between Britain and France. The Society refused to pay his debts, and Lavalette's creditors took the case to court. During the trial Jansenists and Gallicans, old and bitter enemies of the Society, united to investigate the Jesuit statutes; and they recalled to mind that the order was legally present in the country only on sufferance. Vindictive legal proceedings snowballed, and on October 1, 1761, barely two months after what would be the last tragedy and ballet performance at Louis-le-Grand, the Parlement of Paris forbade the Jesuits to receive novices or to run their schools in places where other schools existed. In towns where there was no other school, the Jesuit schools were allowed to operate until April 1, 1762. In August of that year, Parlement, in opposition to the King, dissolved the Society of Jesus in France. Finally, in November 1764, Louis XV, succumbing to a long campaign by the Jesuits' enemies, ratified the Parlement's action and proscribed the Society in his realm. Expulsion of the Jesuits from Spain and its dominions followed in 1767. In 1773, after intense pressure by the Bourbons and others, the Pope followed suit and issued the brief, *Dominus ac Redemptor*, which dissolved the Society throughout the world. Because of unforeseen circumstances, however, the Society continued to exist legally in Prussia for a few years under Frederick the Great and in Russia under Catherine the Great and her successors until 1820.

Although the order would be restored universally in 1814, its theater never returned to anything like its former glory. Dramatic theater remained as a minor part of the Society's educational tradition, but the ballets were ended forever. When the order was reborn in 1814, the face of European government and society had been permanently changed. There was no place for the court ballet; many countries no longer acknowledged a monarch to glorify. The anticlassicist aesthetic, championed by the philosophes during the eighteenth century, had replaced the baroque classical principles for the creation

---

[3] Douarche, *Université de Paris*, 308f.

of art. Latin, though still the basis of "classical education," was a dead language in public life. Dance itself had changed radically, as baroque technique and style began to be replaced by the preclassical ballet; within twenty years or so, the ballet stage would be dominated by romanticism's ballerina in blocked-toe shoes and gauzy white tutu. A few years after that, Victoria would ascend the throne of England, becoming the symbol, in Europe and the United States, of a sober piety and domesticity that had more in common with the Jansenists than with the Jesuits who had produced the college ballets.

When Louis-le-Grand was emptied of its faculty, students, and servants, the college property went to the University of Paris. Anticipating the 1765 action of Parlement, which officially forbade all college theater—a largely redundant measure after the expulsion of the Jesuits—the University rector took possession of the college, making a speech in its empty theater. He quoted from the eighteenth chapter of Revelation, which describes the fall of Babylon. "The music of harps and of human voices, of players of the flute and the trumpet, will never be heard in you again!"

Directions for Further Jesuit-Ballet Research

Aside from the probably vain hope of discovering baroque notation for the dances from the college ballets, there are many avenues of research to be explored and tasks to be undertaken as we increase our knowledge about the ballets and their place in the Jesuit theater. One of the most important among such tasks is the translation into English of the main Jesuit treatises on dance. The four central documents are Menestrier's *Des Ballets anciens et modernes*, Le Jay's *De choreis dramaticis*, Lang's *De actione scenica*, and parts of Jouvancy's *Ratio discendi et docendi*. Because it is in French, Menestrier's book is more accessible to the majority of readers than are the other three works, which are written in Latin; but lively and readable translations of all four would give a larger number of scholars more tools for understanding the Jesuit theater. Greater availability of the information in these books would help researchers to compare ballet production among the Jesuit colleges in different countries, and to get a clearer picture of the similarities and differences between Jesuit and other baroque ballet.

Perusal of the financial records for baroque Paris, the royal accounts of Louis XIV and Louis XV, and the financial records for Louis-le-Grand would help to clarify remaining questions about ballet finances at the Paris college. For example, exactly how much did the

King contribute? How did the contributions change from year to year, and from reign to reign?

Inventories taken when Louis-le-Grand was closed as a Jesuit school would cast light on the number and kind of theater costumes the college owned, and on its store of stage settings and machinery. Likewise, the library inventory taken at that time would yield important information about the extent of the college's collection of theater books and about the classical and other authors the Jesuit producers routinely consulted. One such catalogue exists in the Bibliothèque Sainte-Genevieve in Paris: *Catalogue des livres de la bibliothèque des ci-devant soi-disant jésuites du Collège de Clermont* (1763).

Once a basic picture of ballet at a particular college has been constructed, the researcher can seek the letters and journals of people who were involved—as producers, dancers, patrons, and spectators. In the course of preparing this book, I learned of two such sources (which I was not able to consult) for the Louis-le-Grand ballets: the letters of Nicolas Talon, S.J., in the archives of the Duc d'Aumale, preserved in the library of the Conde's chateau in Chantilly; and the journals of Charles Porée, S.J.

In addition, the regular reports (in Latin) sent from Louis-le-Grand to Rome should be read to further elucidate how the college faculty saw their ballets, and how they interpreted them to their superiors. Period cast lists for the Paris Opéra need to be consulted, and compared with college-ballet programs to find out more about the professional dancers who appeared at Louis-le-Grand and about the ballet masters who staged the dancing. Opéra archives may also yield information about the formality or informality of the ongoing relationship between the Opéra and the college.

With regard to the many postsuppression Jesuits who went to Poland and Russia, the fascinating question whether their presence had any influence on the subsequent development of the Russian ballet needs to be raised and pursued. This research would require, of course, facility in Russian and Polish as well as French and Latin. And, finally, more Jesuit ballets, especially those whose musical scores exist, need to be studied, restaged, and presented at universities and seminaries; at conferences on dance history, religious history, and theology and the arts; and in theaters. This, in my opinion, is both the point and the cutting edge of Jesuit-ballet research. Production tests the conclusions of research and raises further questions. Successive productions cast light on one another. The current wave of reconstruction and restaging of baroque dance and opera, along with the vastly increased understanding of period-music performance makes the time absolutely right for contemporary presentation of the

Jesuit ballets. Because research in this area is inseparable from restaging, it seems essential that those who want to do serious work on the Jesuit-college ballets be both dancers and scholars; this is a field in which the facts make sense only if they make sense in the body and on the stage.

The Curtain Rises

In 1985, at the Jesuit School of Theology in Berkeley, California, the 1709 *L'Espérance* from the Louis-le-Grand repertoire was restaged. This small-scale shoestring production raised as many questions as it answered, but the experience of translating the two-hundred-and-seventy-six-year-old ballet onto a stage for a 1985 audience was the invaluable backdrop for this study of the Jesuit theater. Dancers, actors, musicians, costumer, music director, and artistic director all worked to recreate not only a theater piece, but at least the echo of its original social and historical context.

This collaboration emphasized for me the profoundly social and political web from which the ballets arose in the first place. In any era, a theater piece finally lives and becomes what it is meant to be in relation to its audience. Many in the audience for that production of *L'Espérance* commented after the performance that they had come for social reasons or out of historical curiosity, but had stayed to be delighted and entertained by the ballet on its own terms. Created as physical rhetoric, the ballets finally speak to us only when they are embodied in the theater. This study will have fulfilled one of its purposes if many more researchers will unite to "raise the curtain" once again on these ballets, artifacts of an urbane and unusual relationship between theology and the arts.

appendices · · · · · · · · · · · · · · · · ·

1. Titles of Ballets Performed at Louis-le-Grand, 1638–1761

This ballet repertory list for Louis-le-Grand is based on the lists created by Robert Lowe, Ernest Boysse, and Régine Astier, supplemented by research for this present volume. All the ballets are referred to by their titles, except in cases where the title is unknown. Where the ballet master for a production is known, his name is given after the work. Unless otherwise indicated, the ballets listed were performed in August, as part of the college commencement ceremonies. Reference citations for these ballet programs and libretti may be found in Lowe's repertory and tragedy list, in his *Marc Antoine Charpentier et l'opéra de collège*, 175–95, and in Régine Astier's "Pierre Beauchamps and the Ballets de Collège," *Dance Chronicle* 6 (1983): 139–63.

1638: (October) Ballet to celebrate the birth of Louis XIV

1650: Intermèdes dansés

1651: Ballet

1653: *Ballet des jeux*

1654: Ballet

1657: *Ballet sur les fausses expériences des mortels*

1658: *La Verité*

1659: Ballet

1660: *Ballet du Lys et de l'Impériale* to celebrate Louis XIV's marriage

1661: *L'Impatience*

1662: *La Destinée de Monseigneur le Dauphin* to celebrate the birth of Louis XIV's son

1663: *Ballet de la Verité*

1664: *Ballet de la Haine*

1665: *Ballet des Comètes*

1666: *Ballet du Temps*

1667: *Ballet de l'Innocence*

1668: Ballet

1669: *Le Destin* (Beauchamps)

1670: *Ballet de la Curiosité*

1671: *Ballet des Songes* (Beauchamps)

1672: *Ballet de l'Illusion*

1673: *L'Empire du Soleil*

1674: *Ballet de l'Idolatrie*

1675: *Ballet de la Mode*

1676: *Ballet des Jeux*

1677: *Persée*

1678: *Ballet de la Gazette*

1679: *Ballet de la Paix* (Beauchamps) to celebrate the treaty of Nijmegen

1680: *La France victorieuse sous Louis le Grand* (Beauchamps)

1681: *Le Triomphe de la Religion, ou*

l'Idolatrie ruinée (Beauchamps)

1682: *Plutus, dieu des richesse* (Beauchamps)

1683: Death of Queen Marie-Thérèse; no ballet

1684: *Le Héros, ou les Actions d'un grand prince, representées dans celles de Louis le Grand*

1685: *Ballet des Arts* (Beauchamps)

1686: *Les Travaux d'Hercule* (Beauchamps)

1687: *La France victorieuse sous Louis le Grand*

1688: *Ballet des Saisons*

1689: *Sigalion, ou le secret*

1690: (February) *Le Triomphe de Thémis*
Orphée (Pécour)

1691: *Ballet des Passions*

1692: *Ballet de la Verité*

1693: *Romulus*

1694: Year of economic and agricultural hardship; no ballet

1695: *Comus, ou l'origine des festins*

1696: *Ballet de Mars, ou de la Guerre*

1697: *Ballet de la Jeunesse* (Beauchamps) for the young Duke of Burgundy

1698: *Ballet de la Paix* (Blondy) to celebrate the treaty of Ryswick

1699: *Les Songes* (Pécour)

1700: *La Fortune*

1701: *Jason, ou la conquête de la toison d'or* (Pécour) to celebrate the Duke of Anjou's ascension to the throne of Spain

1702: *L'Empire de l'imagination* (Pécour)

1703: *Les Nouvelles* (Pécour)

1704: *La Naissance de Monseigneur le Duc de Bretagne* (Pécour)

1705: *L'Empire du Temps* (Pécour)

1706: *Feste des Dieux, ou l'origine des Ballets* (Pécour)

1707: *Jupiter vainquer des Titans* (Pécour)

1708: *Le Triomphe de Plutus, dieu des richesse*

1709: *L'Espérance* (Pécour)

1710: *L'Empire du monde partagé entre les dieux de la fable* (Pécour)

1711: *Apollon législateur, ou le Parnasse reformé* (Blondy and Pécour)

1712: *L'Empire de la Folie*

1713: *Ballet de la Paix* (Blondy) to celebrate the treaty of Utrecht

1714: *Le Tableau allégorique des moeurs* (Blondy)

1715: *L'Empire de la Sagesse* (Blondy)

1716: No August ballet is recorded by Lowe or Boysse. No indication was found of reasons—economic difficulties or royal deaths—that would have prevented a production. A comedy, which could have contained dance, was performed as intermedes for the August tragedy.

1717: No ballet or other intermedes for the August tragedy are recorded by Lowe or Boysse. As in the case of 1716, there is no obvious reason for omitting the ballet. This gap in the repertory list probably reflects incomplete archives rather than the absence of intermedes.

1718: *L'Art de vivre heureux*

1719: *La Jeunesse d'Achille*

1720: *L'Industrie* (Froment)

1721: *Le Parfait Monarque*

1722: *Les Couronnes* (Froment)

1723: *Le Temple de la Gloire* (Froment)

1724: *Le Génie François, ou les Festes Françoises* (Froment and Opéra dancers)

1725: *Le Mariage de Thesée et d'Hippolite* (Opéra dancers) to celebrate Louis XV's marriage

726: *L'Homme instruit par les spectacles, ou le théâtre changé en école de vertu* (Laval and Malter, the elder)

1727: *L'Ambition* (Laval and Malter, the elder)

1728: *Les Voeux de la France* (Laval and Malter, the elder)

1729: *Les Aventures d'Ulysse, ou le Génie vainquer des obstacles* (Laval and Malter, the elder)

1730: *Le Ridicule des hommes donne en spectacle*

1731: *L'Empire de la Mode* (Blondy and Malter, the elder)

1732: *L'Histoire de la Danse*

1733: *L'Envie*

1734: *Les Tableaux allégoriques de la vie humaine* (Malter)

1735: *Mars* (Malter, the elder)

1736: *L'École de Minerve, ou la Sagesse* (Malter, the elder)

1737: *La Curiosité* (Malter, the elder)

1738: *Le Portrait de la Nation Française* (Malter, the elder)

1739: *L'Origine des Jeux* (Malter, the elder)

1740: *Le Monde demasqué* (Malter, the elder)

1741: *Les Aventures de Télémaque, ou le Prince instruit par la Sagesse* (Malter, the elder)

1742: *La Poésie* (Malter, the elder)

1743: *Les Caprices* (Malter, the elder)

1744: *Les Merveilles de l'Art* (Malter, the elder)

1745: *La Renomée* (Malter, the elder)

1746: *Portrait de la Jeunesse*

1747: (July) *L'Imagination*

1748: *Le Portrait du Grand Monarque* (Dupré)

1749: *Les Héros* (Dupré)

1750: *Le Temple de la Fortune* (Dupré)

1751: *Le Génie* (Dupré the younger)

1752: *Le Pouvoir de la Fable*

1753: No August performance of tragedy or ballet is recorded by Lowe or Boysse.

1754: *Les Spectacles du Parnasse*

1755: *La Prosperité* (Dupré)

1756: *Le Tableau de la gloire d'après les fastes du peuple François, ou l'établissement de la monarchie françoise* (Dupré the younger)

1757: *L'Invention, ou l'origine des arts* (Dupré)

1758: Intermedes for the tragedy of *Astyanax*

1759: (July) *Entr'actes en ballet* (LeVoir)

1760: Ballet (LeVoir)

1761: Ballet

2. PERIOD WORD LIST

The definitions of the words in this list are translations by the author of definitions found in Antoine Furetière's *Dictionnaire universel* (The Hague and Rotterdam, 1691), and François Pomey's *Grand Dictionnaire royal*, 7th ed. (Cologne and Frankfort, 1740).

1. *Abbé:* An *abbé* can be of three kinds: a priest and member of a religious order, a secular priest, or an *abbé commendataire*. This last kind is sometimes a cardinal, and also someone who has been given several abbeys, usually by the king. *Abbé de cour:* a young ecclesiastic, polite in manners and dress, leading a worldly life. One expects a certain degree of delicacy, voluptuousness, and gallantry . . . and more knowledge of the world than of theology. (Furetière)

2. *Acte:* A term of physics. The *acte* is the doing of a thing. In poetry, one uses it of the divisions or principal parts of a dramatic poem, in order to allow the actors and the spectators to rest. In a college, one uses it of the public defense of theses. (Furetière)

3. *Arguments:* A term in philosophy; to pose certain principles from which one draws out consequences; a rhetorical term. Old usage: said of prologues: they contain the *argument* of the comedy. (Furetière)

4. I. *Ballet:* "A harmonious representation of figured dance with music, done by several masked persons, who represent by their steps and postures various natural things or actions, or who imitate other people. For example, 'The *ballets* of the king are very magnificent.' 'A *ballet* is made up of several entrées.' 'One produces verses for *ballet* in order to explain the characters played or the actions done by those who dance; these verses, which together are a kind of dramatic poem, support the title of the *ballet*'; 'Benserade has made many of these *ballets*, and Father Menestrier has written a learned treatise about them.' One says proverbially that someone makes a *ballet* entrance when he comes brusquely and without ceremony into a group." (Furetière)

    II. *Ballet:* To dance. (Pomey)

5. *Baroque:* A jeweller's term used only of pearls not completely or perfectly round. (Furetière)

6. *Bienséance:* That which is fitting, which gives a thing grace and agreeableness. (Furetière)

7. *Comédie:* An artfully composed theater piece, in prose or verse, representing some human action; used in this sense of serious and humorous pieces . . . especially used of pieces which represent things which are pleasant and not cruel, and persons of an ordinary station in life. . . . Comedy is an image of ordinary life . . . also, the art of composing and presenting comedies. (Furetière)

8. I. *Danse:* Some ancient authors say that Minerva invented *danse* in her joy over the defeat of the Titans. Jumps and measured steps in time to the

music, movements of the disciplined body, made with art, to the sound of violins or the voice. Aerial *danse* is what professional dancers and acrobats do, with cabrioles and gambades [jumping steps]. Earth-bound *danse* is that which is done modestly, without leaving the ground, as well-bred persons do. (Furetière)

II. *Danse:* The action of dancing; serious *danse*; grotesque *danse*; a *danse* called the *branle*; to *danse* with measured steps; whoever leads the *danse*; to *danse*; to *danse* a *branle*; to *danse* "les matassins"; to *danse* to the music of violins; to *danse* on the tightrope; a male dancer; a good dancer; a dancer who dances out of time to the music; a dancing master; a female dancer. (Pomey)

9. *Danser:* To bend the knees and rise onto the balls of the feet, in time to the music, at the beginning of the measure of an air; to make regular steps and move the body in an agreeable manner to the sound of the voice or instruments. (Furetière)

10. *Dance types listed by Furetière:*

Gaillarde: Old dance also called Romanesque, because it comes from Rome. [He then gives Thoinot Arbeau's description of the *gaillarde* from the 1588 dancing-instruction book, *Orchesography*.]

Chacone: A musical form or dance from the Moors.

Branle: An air or dance with which all balls are begun, which many people dance in a circle, holding hands. . . . First the *branle simple* is danced, and then the *branle gay*, and it is called that because one has always one foot in the air. It doesn't stop. [He again cites Arbeau as a reference.] *Branles* of Burgundy go right and left, for a double measure, quickly and lightly. . . . *Branles* of Poitou, always left. In the *branles* of the washerwomen, the dancers make noise by clapping their hands; in the *branles* of the wooden shoes, noise is made with the feet. In the *branle* of the torch, the dancer carries a torch. The exit *branle* is danced at the end of a ball.

Gavotte: A gay dance with three steps and an assemble. In the old *gavottes*, one kissed and gave bouquets of flowers. [He cites Arbeau.]

Menuet: A dance with quick small steps; it is composed of a couppé, a relevé, and a balance. It begins *en battant* and is in three-quarter time.

Sarabande: Music or dance in triple time, which usually ends with a rise, in contrast to the *courante*, which ends in kissing the hand. . . . It comes from the Saracens, like the *chacone*. It also takes its name from a comedienne named Sarabanda, who first danced it in France. Some think the name comes from *sarao*, which means "ball" in Spanish. One usually dances it to the guitar or castanets. It has a gay and amorous feeling.

11. *Dance types listed by Pomey:*

Sarabande: A metered dance that they call the sarabande. A dance art.

Courante: A kind of dance.

12. *Distribuer:* A preacher, a dramatic poet, and an orator all distribute

[effectively organize according to the principles of rhetoric] their material. (Furetière)

13. *Entr'acte:* A term from poetry. A ballet, music, or other divertissement which is given between the acts of a comedy, to entertain the spectators by its diversity, or to give the actors a chance to change their costumes, or to give an opportunity for changing the stage decorations. (Furetière)

14. *Entrée:* Each scene performed by the dancers in a ballet. (Furetière)

15. *Figure:* [This word is followed by five columns of entries and definitions, among which are the following:]

With respect to dances and ballets, the word is used of steps performed by the dancers in different formations and cadences, which make a variety of *figures* on the floor. In rhetoric, an ornament or turn of speech different from what one would use in ordinary unemotional speech. For example, "the metaphor is the queen of *figures*"; "allegory is a *figure* which is dominant throughout *The Song of Songs.*" *Figures* serve to disturb the soul and to impart the truth with greater force. (Furetière)

16. *Gens:* People and nations . . . many persons who make up a group . . . an indeterminate number of persons . . . a division of persons distinguished according to their profession and their good or bad qualities . . . either masculine or feminine. (Furetière)

17. *Honnesté:* That which merits esteem or praise, because it is reasonable or according to good manners. One uses it especially of the well-bred man, of the gallant man, who has a wordly air, who knows how to live. Often it is used of what is mediocre, for example, "This boy is of *honneste* birth"; that is to say, he is of mediocre family. (Furetière)

18. *Jansenisme:* The doctrine of grace according to St. Augustine. *Jansenisme* has strongly divided us in these later years. (Furetière)

19. *Janseniste:* Those who are of the party and doctrine of St. Augustine. Also said of those who affect a great fervor in their way of life, and a great austerity in their manners and doctrine. Thus, many devoted and reformed persons are called *Jansenistes* who do not know Jansenius's work at all. Women are called *Jansenistes* who, for modesty, cover their arms. (This last sense is not current usage.) (Furetière)

20. *Jésuite:* A member of the order of religious founded by St. Ignatius of Loyola, also called the Company of Jesus. It is the order with the highest standing, with the most imposing reputation, and which has rendered the most service to the Church by its missions to the Indies, and by the pains it takes in the instruction of youth. (Furetière)

21. *Mouvement/Mouvemens:* [This word is followed by more than four columns of entries and definitions, among which are the following:]

The word is used figuratively of moral and spiritual matters, and means thought, feeling, and will; that is, "It only needs one good *mouvement* to convert a sinner." "One never resists the *mouvemens* of grace." One uses the word in this sense when one says that someone make his *mouvement,* in the sense that he does something willingly, by his own choice, without being urged.

In the arts: in rhetoric and poetry, one is said to excite *mouvemens* when the passions of the hearer are affected by the force of eloquence. One says also that a theater piece is full of great *mouvemens* when it has many vehement and pathetic figures and expressions.

Of keeping time in music: it is the *mouvement* that makes sarabandes, gavottes, bourrées, chacones, and so forth different from each other. One uses the word also in dance to mean the various agitations of the body that one makes in order to move pleasingly in time to the music. "This girl dances badly, because, however she makes the steps, they are never accompanied by the suitable *mouvement* of the body." (Furetière)

22. *Nouvelles:* Information, by speaking or writing, about the state of a thing, an action, or the way of life of a person. One gives one's *nouvelles* to one's friends. One is not welcome when one brings bad *nouvelles*. The people are very curious for *nouvelles*, *nouvelles* of the gazette. . . . I wait for *nouvelles* of my letter, that is, a response to what I have sent. To be at the source of *nouvelles* is to be where the most important things are happening, and where one receives the first word about everything.

In royal warfare, there are ships of information, to carry *nouvelles.* To have *nouvelles* is to have precise information. It can also mean to know gossip about someone, as in, "Ah, monsieur, I know your nouvelles."

In law, it can mean the Constitutions of various emperors. It also means an agreeable and intriguing story, for example, the *Nouvelles* of Cervantes, de Scarron, or Queen Marguerite.

Point de *nouvelles* means "nothing doing." For example, "You think you are going to convert that heretic, but nothing doing; you will not achieve your goal!"

Nouvelle convertie: A girl or woman of the Reformed religion who has embraced or been forced to embrace the Roman faith. The clergy take great pains to convince these *Nouvelle* converties. Also, a convent where these are instructed. For example, it is necessary to send her to the *Nouvelles*-Converties. (Furetière)

23. *Opéra:* A public spectacle; a magnificent representation on the stage of a dramatic work, whose verses are sung and accompanied by symphonies, dances, and ballets, with superb costumes and decorations, and astonishing machinery. *Opéra* is a whimsical mixture of poetry and music in which the poet and the musician both put themselves out. (Furetière)

24. *Pastorale:* A theater piece or dramatic poem about the loves of shepherds, whose characters are dressed as nymphs and shepherds; it takes place in the countryside and in forests. Also called a *bergerie* or a *pastoral amoreuse.* (Furetière)

25. *Personnage:* A male role in a theatrical production. (Furetière)

26. *Personne:* A female role in a theatrical production. (Furetière)

27. *Poème:* A fairly long work or composition in verse. True *Poèmes* are epic, dramatic, or heroic (describing one or more actions of a hero). Lyric

verse, sonnets, epigrams, and songs do not merit the name of *poème* except as a strong term of abuse. (Furetière)

28. *Poésie: Poésie* is a speaking painting. It must be free without effrontery, ornamented without affectation, and speak the language of the gods without committing excesses. (Furetière)

29. *Program:* [The only definition given for this word.] A college term: a handbill or reminder that one posts and gives out, inviting people to a rhetoric display or college ceremony, and containing the subject or whatever is necessary to understand the event. Those in colleges give out *programs* to assist the audience at their declamations and tragedies. (Furetière)

30. *Temple:* Nowadays we use this word for the building where the Protestants gather to practice their religion. Under the edicts of pacification, the Reformed in France had the right to a certain number of *temples* in each province; but all these were destroyed under various laws, and finally under an edict given in 1685.

    It is used sometimes in very formal speech to refer to Christian churches. For example, "This Prince has defended the honor of our *temples,* subduing the rebels who profaned them."

    It is used sometimes in a poetic way to refer to those imagined *temples* that exist only in fiction and thought; for example, the *Temple* of Glory. One also says, "This Prince deserves to have *temples* and altars built to him," as a way of saying that he deserves praise, that one would wish to erect monuments to his glory. (Furetière)

31. *Théâtre:* The raised place where tragedies, comedies, and ballets are presented. *(Dictionnaire de l'Académie, 1694)*

32. *Tragédie:* A dramatic poem in the theater that represents some important action of illustrious persons, the result of which is often disastrous. (Furetière)

33. *Tragi-comédie:* Another theater piece, presenting something that happens among important persons, of which the result is neither sad nor bloody, and in which one occasionally includes less serious characters. The ancients knew nothing about these sorts of pieces, in which one mixes the serious and the comic. (Furetière)

34. *Trousser:* To pick up, fold up, place higher, as one does with long clothing or skirts, for fear of mud. (Furetière)

3. NAMES OF BAROQUE-THEATER FORMS

A table of theater forms recognized in the eighteenth century. From De Beauchamps, *Recherches sur les théâtres de France.*

Ballet	Mistère
Bergerie	Opéra
Comédie	Opéra comique
Comédie allégorique	Parodie
Comédie ballet	Pastorale
Comédie facétieuse	Pastorale bocagère
Comédie héroïque	Pastoral héroïque
Comédie satirique	Poème dramatique
Églogue	Tragédie
Farce	Tragi-comédie
Idille	Tragi-comédie héroïque
Moralité	Tragi-comédie pastorale
Mascarade	Tragédie sainte

4. MYTHOLOGICAL BALLET CHARACTERS

Achilles: Hero of the Iliad, son of Peleus and Thetis, a Nereid (sea nymph). He was slain by Paris. Paris, the son of Priam and Hecuba, had eloped with Helen of Troy.

Aesculapius: God of healers and medicine.

Ajax: Son of the king of Salamis and a hero of the *Iliad*, second only to Achilles in bravery.

Alcyone (also Halcyone): Daughter of Aeneas. When her husband, Ceyx, drowned, she flew to his floating body, and the gods changed them both into kingfishers, who are said to nest at sea during a certain calm week in winter, "halcyon weather."

Apollo: God of music and singing, whose symbol is the lyre.

Atlas: One of the Titans, condemned to carry the heavens on his shoulders as his punishment for opposing the gods.

Aurora (also Eos): Goddess of the dawn.

Bacchus (also Dionysus):
God of wine and ecstatic celebration.

Bellerophon: Slayer of the Chimera, a fire-breathing monster whose body combined the characteristics of a lion, a dragon, and a goat.

Ceres (also Demeter):
Goddess of marriage and human fertility.

Ceyx: King of Thessaly (see Alcyone)

Chimera: See Bellerophon.

Cupid: Son of Venus and god of love.

Cyclopes: Homer's lawless Sicilian giants with circular eyes, who ate human beings and helped Vulcan forge the thunderbolts of Zeus under Mt. Aetna.

Diana (also Artemis): Goddess of the moon and the hunt, daughter of Jupiter and Latona.

Dryads: Wood nymphs, Pan's dancing partners.

Esculapeius: See Aesculapius.

Eurydice: Wife of Orpheus. She was killed by a snake and taken to the underworld. Orpheus came to find her and was told he could take her back to the upper world if he would not look back at her as she followed him on the journey. But he did, so she returned to the dead.

Fauns: Minor woodland divinities, companions of Pan. Represented with small horns, pointed ears, a goat's hind legs, and a tail.

Flora: Goddess of flowers and spring.

Furies (also Erinyes and Eumenides):
Alecto, Megaera, and Tisiphone, the three punishers of crime, especially of those who escaped public justice; represented as snake-haired old

women.

Harpies: Creatures with the head and bust of women, depicted with wings, legs, and tail of birds. They snatch the souls of evildoers or punish them by taking or defiling their food.

Hebe: Daughter of Juno and the gods' cupbearer.

Hercules: A Hero, son of Jupiter and Alcmena, wearing a lion skin and carrying a club, famous for his successful completion of twelve impossible labors and other deeds.

Hippolyte: Queen of the Amazons, wife of Theseus, slain by Hercules.

Icelus: Member of the suite of Morpheus, the god of dreams who takes the shapes of animals in human dreams.

Jason: Leader of the Argonauts, who sought the Golden Fleece.

Juno: Wife of Jupiter, queen of the gods, guardian of women.

Jupiter (also Jove): Son of the Titans Saturn and Rhea; king and father of the gods.

Mars: Son of Jupiter and Juno, god of war.

Mercury (also Hermes): Son of Jupiter, messenger of the gods; god of commerce, science, eloquence, trickery, theft, and skill.

Midas: The earthly king who asked Bacchus that all he touched might turn to gold, then repented of his greed when his food turned to gold and was inedible. Bacchus released him from his gift, and Midas left his palace and lived in the country, worshiping Pan.

Minerva (also Pallas Athena): Daughter of Jupiter, who sprang fully armed from his forehead; goddess of wisdom, learning, and health. Her symbols are the owl and the olive tree.

Momus: God of laughter, also said to jeer bitterly at gods and human beings.

Morpheus: Son of Sleep and god of dreams.

Muses: The nine goddesses of the arts: Calliope, epic poetry; Clio, history; Erato, love poetry; Euterpe, lyric poetry; Melpomene, tragedy; Polyhymnia, oratory and sacred song; Terpsichore, choral song and dance; Thalia, comedy and idyls; Urania, astronomy.

Neptune (also Poseidon): God of the sea.

Nymphs: Lesser divinities of nature, personified as beautiful young girls: Dryads and Hamadryads, tree nymphs; Naiads, nymphs of springs, brooks, and rivers; Nereids, sea nymphs; Oreads, mountain or hill nymphs.

Orestes: Son of Agamemnon and Clytemnestra; after murdering his mother, he was chased by the Furies until he was absolved and purified by Minerva.

Orpheus: Son of Apollo and Calliope, who could move stones with his music.

Pallas Athena (see *Minerva*):

Pan (also Sylvanus and Faunus): God of nature and the universe, whose favorite dwelling was Arcadia.

Pandora: The first woman, made by Jupiter, with a gift from each god. (Her name means "all-gifted.") Curious, she opened a magic box and released all the ills of humanity; but she also found Hope in the box, and that goddess remained on earth with mortals.

Patroclus: Friend of Achilles, killed by Hector.

Phantasus: Son of Sleep, bringer of strange dream images.

Pluto: God of the netherworld

Plutus: God of wealth.

Polyphemus: A Cyclops and giant son of Neptune, whose fierceness was somewhat tamed when he fell in love with the sea nymph Galatea, whose lover, Acis, he killed.

Pomona: Goddess of fruit trees, who fell in love with Vertumnus, god of the changing seasons.

Prometheus: One of the Titans, who, with his brother Epimetheus, created man. Epimetheus had given all his gifts to the animals and had nothing left for man, so Prometheus went up to heaven and brought back fire as the gods' gift to man.

Proteus: Son of Neptune, known for wisdom, able to predict the future and change his shape at will.

Saturn (also Cronos): A Titan, son of Earth and Heaven, grandson of Chaos, father of Jupiter.

Satyrs: Forest divinities, half man, half goat.

Sirens: Sea nymphs, whose singing caused sailors to plunge into the sea. When Ulysses passed their island, he closed his crew's ears with wax and tied himself to the mast to escape the spell.

Terpsichore (see Muses):

Themis: One of the Titans, she was the legal counsel of Jupiter.

Titans: Sons and daughters of Uranus (Heaven) and Gaia (Earth), who opposed the gods and were finally defeated by them.

Triton: Son of Neptune and Amphitrite, demigod of the sea, Neptune's trumpeter.

Ulysses (also Odysseus): King of Ithaca, husband of Penelope, hero of the *Odyssey.*

Venus (also Aphrodite): Daughter of Jupiter and Dione (though some said she sprang from the sea foam), goddess of beauty and love.

Zephyrs: Gentle winds, companions of Zephyrus, the west wind.

5. SELECTED FRENCH BOOKS ON DANCE, 1623–1760

1623: de Lauze, François. *Apologie de la Danse.* Trans. Joan Wildebloode. Reprint ed., Geneva: Minkoff, 1977.

1636: Mersenne, Père Marin. *Harmonie universelle.* [Contains several chapters on the ballet.]

1641: de Saint-Hubert. *La Manière de composer et faire réussir les ballets.*

1657: d'Aubignac, L'Abbé. *La Pratique du théâtre.* Amsterdam.

1658: Menestrier, Claude François, S.J. "Remarques pour la conduite des ballets." In *L'Autel de Lyon consacré a Louis Auguste.* Lyon:Jean Molin.

1668: de Pure, L'Abbé Michel. *Idée des spectacles anciens et nouveaux.* Paris.

1681: Menestrier, Claude François, S.J. *Des Représentations en musique anciennes et modernes.* Paris.

1682: ———. *Des Ballets anciens et modernes selon les règles du théâtre.* Paris.

1700: Feuillet, Raoul Auger. *Chorégraphie, ou l'art décrire la dance.* Paris.

1723: Bonnet, Jacques. *Histoire générale de la danse.* Paris: Chez d'Houry fils. Reprint ed., Geneva: Slatkine, 1969.

1725: Le Jay, Gabriel, S.J. "Liber de choreis dramaticis." *Bibliotheca rhetorum.* Paris.

1725: Rameau, Pierre. *Abrégé de la nouvelle methode dans l'art décrire ou de tracer toutes sortes de danses de ville.* Paris: J. Villette.

1725: ———. *Le Maître à danser.* Paris: J. Villette. Reprint ed., Gregg International Publishers Limited, 1972.

1750: Riccoboni, François. *L'Art du théâtre.*

1760: Noverre, Jean Georges. *Letters on Dancing and Ballets.* Lyons. Reprint ed., Trans. Cyril W. Beaumont. Dance Horizons, Inc., 1966.

For collections of notated dances, the reader is referred to Wendy Hilton's list of choreographic collections published in France between 1700 and 1725. Twenty-eight of these collections include choreography by Pécour, Blondy, or both, and are, together with Feuillet's *Chorégraphie,* the best available sources of choreography for use in restaged ballets from the Paris college. The list is found in Hilton's *Dance of Court and Theater,* 335–37.

bibliography · · · · · · · · · · · · · · · ·

Primary Sources on French Jesuit Baroque Dance and Theater

Ballet de la Jeunesse. Jesuit Archives, Chantilly, France.

Ballet de la Paix. Rondel Collection, vol. 32, *Théâtre des jésuites.* Bibliothèque de l'Arsenal, Paris.

Les Ballets des jésuites composées par Messieurs Beauchant, Desmatins et Collasse recueillie par Philidor l'aisne en 1690. Res. F. 516. Bibliothèque du Conservatoire (Bibliothèque nationale), Paris.

Chanson su les réjouissances faites au Collège de Louis-le-Grand, le lundy 11 aoust 1721 au sujet de l'heureux retour de la santé du Roy. Jesuit Archives, Chantilly, France.

Du Cerceau, Jean Antoine, S.J. *Théâtre de Père du Cerceau a l'usage des collèges.* Paris, 1822

L'Empire de la Sagesse. Res. Yf 2678. Bibliothèque nationale, Paris.

L'Espérance. Yf 2571, 2572. Bibliothèque nationale, Paris.

La France victorieuse sous Louis le Grand. Res. Yf 440. Bibliothèque nationale, Paris.

Intermèdes chantez a la tragédie de Joseph vendu par ses frères. Jesuit Archives, Chantilly, France.

Le Jay, Gabriel, S.J. "Liber de choreis dramaticis." In *Bibliotheca rhetorum.* Paris, 1725.

———. *Le Triomphe de la Religion sous Louis le Grand.* Paris: Gabriel Martin, 1687.

Jouvancy, Joseph, S.J. *Ratio discendi et docendi.* Paris: Fratres Perisse, 1685.

Des Magnificences des honores funèbres de M. le cardinal de La Rochefoucault: Description de la Pyramide dressée en son honneur, 1645. Bibliothèque de l'Arsenal, Paris.

Menestrier, Claude François, S.J. *Des Ballets anciens et modernes selon les règles du théâtre.* Paris, 1682.

———. "Remarques pour la conduite des ballets." In *L'Autel de Lyon consacrée à Louis August.* Lyon, Jean Molin, 1658.

———. *Des Représentations en musique anciennes et modernes.* Paris, 1681.

Porée, Charles, S.J. *Discours sur les spectacles.* Translated by Père Brumoy. Paris, 1733.

Le Portrait du grand monarque. Res. Yf 2790. Bibliothèque nationale, Paris.

Récits en musique. Intermedes for the *Ballet de la conquête de la toison d'or.* Jesuit Archives, Chantilly, France.

"Sur les comédies que les jésuites ont fait jouer ces jours passés dans leur collège." MS 4113. Bibliothèque de l'Arsenal, Paris.

Le Triomphe de la Religion, ou l'idolatrie ruinée. Res. Yf 2699. Bibliothèque nationale, Paris.

Primary Sources on Secular Baroque Dance and Theater

Cochin, Charles-Nicolas. *Projet d'une salle de spectacle pour un théâtre de comédie.* London, 1765.

Beauchamps, Pierre François de. *Recherches sur les théâtres de France.* Paris, 1735.

Danchet, Antoine. *Le Théâtre de M. Danchet.* 4 vols. Paris, 1751.

Feuillet, Raoul Auger. *Chorégraphie, ou l'art décrire la dance.* Paris, 1700.

Lambranzi, Gregorio. *New and Curious School of Theatrical Dancing.* Nuremberg, 1716; reprint ed., Brooklyn, N.Y.: Dance Horizons, 1966.

Lavallière, Louis-César de La Beaume-le-Blanc. *Ballets, opéras, et autres ouvrages lyriques.* Paris: J. Baptiste Bauche, 1760; reprint ed., London: H. Baron, 1967.

Noverre, Jean Georges. *Letters on Dancing and Ballets.* Lyon: 1760; reprint ed., Brooklyn, N.Y.: Dance Horizons, 1966.

Secondary Sources on French Jesuit Baroque Dance and Theater

Astier, Régine. "Pierre Beauchamps and the *Ballets de Collège.*" *Dance Chronicle* 6 (1983): 138–63.

Blocq, Hippolyte de. "Lieux du théâtre dans les collèges des jésuites." *Revue d'histoire du théâtre* 2 (1950): 468–69.

Bourgoin, Aubin. *Histoire des représentations théâtrales dans les lycées et collèges.* La Roche-sur-Lyon, 1897.

Boysse, Ernest. "La Comédie au collège." *La Revue contemporaine* 72 (1869): 656–82; 73 (1870): 33–57.

———. *Le Théâtre des jésuites.* Paris, 1880; reprint ed., Geneva: Slatkine, 1970.

Carroll, William, S.J. "The Jesuit Impresario." Unpublished paper.

———. "The Jesuit Playwright." Unpublished paper.

———. "Repertory of Biblical Drama, with *Ballets d'attache,* performed at Clermont/Louis-le-Grand." Papers presented at the Seminar on the Bible in Dance. Jerusalem, 1979.

Dainville, François de, S.J. "Allégorie et actualité sur les tréteaux des jésuites." In vol. 1 of *Dramaturgie et société, Nancy 14–21 April, 1967,* 433–43, ed. Jean Jacquot. 1968.

———. "Decoration théâtrale dans le colléges des jésuites au XVIIe siècle." *Revue d'histoire du théâtre* 4 (1951): 355–74.

———. *L'Education des jésuites.* Paris: Minuit, 1978.

——. "Lieux d'affichage des comédiens à Paris en 1753." *Revue d'histoire du théâtre* 3 (1951): 248–60.

——. "Lieux de théâtre et salles des actions dans les collèges des jésuites de l'ancienne France." *Revue d'histoire du théâtre* 1 (1950): 185–90.

Desgraves, Louis. *Répertoire des programmes des pièces de théâtre jouées dans les collèges en France, 1601–1700.* Geneva: Librarie Droz, S.A., 1986.

Emond, G. *L'Histoire du Collège de Louis-le-Grand, ancien collège des jésuites à Paris, depuis sa fondation jusqu'en 1830.* Paris, 1845.

Gofflot, L. V. *Le Théâtre au collège du Moyen Age à nos jours.* Paris, Champion, 1907.

Griffin, Nigel. *Jesuit School Drama: A Checklist of Critical Literature.* London: Grant and Cutler, Ltd., 1976.

Hémon, Félix. "La Comédie chez les jésuites." *Revue politique et literaire* 17 (1879): 529–34.

Hennequin, Jacques. "Théâtre et société dans les pièces de collège au XVII siècle, 1641–1671." In vol. 1 of *Dramaturgie et société, Nancy 14–21 April, 1967,* 432–62, ed. Jean Jacquot. 1968.

LeBègue, Raymond. "Les Ballets des jésuites." *Revue des cours et conferences.* April 30, May 15, May 30, 1936, pp. 127–39, 209–22, 321–30.

Le Jeaux, Jean. "Les Decors de théâtre dans les collèges des jésuites." *Revue d'histoire du théâtre* 7 (1955): 305–15.

Lowe, Robert. *Marc-Antoine Charpentier et l'opéra de collège.* Paris: Maisonneuve et La Rose, 1966.

——. "Les Représentations en musique au Collège Louis-le-Grand, 1650–1688." *Revue d'histoire du théâtre* 10 (1958): 21–34.

——. "Les Représentations en musique au Collège Louis-le-Grand, 1689–1762." *Revue d'histoire du théâtre* 11 (1959): 205–12.

McCabe, William H., S.J. "An Introduction to the Jesuit Theater." Unpublished Ph.D. dissertation, Cambridge University, 1929. St. Louis University Microfilm, 1958.

——. "Music and Dance on a Seventeenth-Century College Stage." *Musical Quarterly* 24 (July 1938): 313–22.

Misrahi, Jean. "The Beginning of the Jesuit Theater in France." *The French Review* 16 (January 1943): 239–47.

Peyronnet, Pierre. "Le Théâtre d'education des jésuites." *Dix-huitième siècle* 8 (1976).

Purkis, H. M. C. "Quelques observations sur les intermèdes dans le théâtre des jésuites en France." *Revue d'histoire du théâtre* 18 (1966): 182–98.

Schnitzler, Henry. "The Jesuit Contribution to the Theater." *Educational Theater Journal* 4 (1952): 285–92.

——. "The School Theater of the Jesuits." *The Theater Annual* (1943): 46–58.

Sommervogel, Carlos, S.J. *Bibliographie de la Compagnie de Jésus.* 10 vols. Brussels and Paris, 1890–99. Index s.v. "Ballet." Vol. 11 edited by Pierre Briard, S.J. Paris, 1932. Vol. 12 edited by Ernest M. Rivière, S.J. Louvain, 1960.

Stegmann, André. "Le Rôle des jésuites dans la dramaturgie française du debut du XVIIIe siècle." In vol. 1 of *Dramaturgie et société Nancy 14–21 April, 1967*, 445–56, ed. Jean Jacquot. 1968.

"Un Collège des jésuites en 1713: Le Collège de Louis-le-Grand." *Revue internationale de l'enseignment* 5 (1892).

Vial, Fernand, S.J. "The Jesuit Theater in Eighteenth-Century France." *Jesuit Educational Quarterly* 19 (1957): 197–207.

Yanitelli, Victor, S.J. "The Jesuit Theater in Italy from its Origins to the Eighteenth Century." Unpublished M.A. thesis. Fordham University, 1943.

Secondary Sources on Secular Baroque Dance and Theater

Aghion, Max. *Le Théâtre à Paris au dix-septième siècle*. Paris, 1926.

Christout, Marie-Françoise. *Le Ballet de cour de Louis XIV, 1643–1672*. Paris: Picard et Cie, 1967.

Hilton, Wendy. *Dance of Court and Theater: The French Noble Style, 1690–1725*. Princeton Book Co., 1981.

Kirstein, Lincoln. *Dance, a Short History*. 1935; reprint ed., Brooklyn, N.Y.: Dance Horizons, 1969.

Kunzle, Regine. "Jean Loret, a Pioneer of Seventeenth-Century Criticism." *Dance Scope* 10 (1976).

Lough, John. *Paris Theater Audiences in the Seventeenth and Eighteenth Centuries*. London: Oxford University Press, 1957.

MacGowan, Margaret. *L'Art de ballet du cour en France, 1581–1643*. Paris: Centre national de la recherche scientifique, 1963.

Mittman, Barbara. *Spectators on the Paris Stage in the Seventeenth and Eighteenth Centuries*. Ann Arbor, Michigan: UMI Research Press, 1984.

"Problèmes de la mise en scene de chefs d'oeuvres classiques. II: La tragédie classique." Comments of Jean Louis Barrault, 7 and 14 April 1951. *Revue d'histoire du théâtre* 3 (1951): 281–87.

Ranum, Patricia. "Audible Rhetoric and Mute Rhetoric: The Seventeenth-Century French Sarabande." *Early Music* 14 (February 1986): 22–36.

Winter, Marian Hannah. *The Pre-Romantic Ballet*. Brooklyn, N.Y.: Dance Horizons, 1974.

Jesuit Education, Rhetoric, and the Counter-Reformation

Bangert, William V., S.J. *A History of the Society of Jesus*. 2nd ed. St. Louis, Mo.: The Institute of Jesuit Sources, 1986.

Chadwick, Owen. *The Reformation*. Harmondsworth, England: Penguin Books Ltd., 1964.

Cragg, G. R. *The Church and the Age of Reason, 1648–1789*. Harmondsworth, England: Penguin Books Ltd., 1960.

Dainville, François de, S.J. "L'Evolution de l'enseignment de la rhétorique." *Revue de la dix-septième siècle* 80–81 (1968): 19–43.

Dinouart, L'Abbé. *L'Eloquence du corps dans la ministère de la chaire.* 2nd ed. Paris, 1760.

Douarche, A. *L'Université de Paris et les jésuites XVI et XVII siècles.* Paris, 1888.

Dupont-Ferrier, Gustave. *La Vie quotidienne d'un collège parisien pendant plus de 350 ans: Du Clermont au Lycée Louis-le-Grand.* 3 vols. Paris: De Brocard, 1921–1925.

Evennet, H. Outram. *The Spirit of the Counter-Reformation.* London: Catholic Truth Society, 1954.

Fleischer, Manfred P. "Father Wolff: The Epitome of a Jesuit Courtier." *The Catholic Historical Review* 64 (October 1978): 581–613.

Fouqueray, H. *Histoire de la Compagnie de Jésus en France des origines à la suppression, 1528–1762.* 5 vols. Paris, 1910–1925.

Fumaroli, M. "Théâtre, humanisme, et contre-reforme à Rome, 1591–1642." *Bulletin de l'Association Guillaume Bude* 33 (1974): 399–412.

Lamy, Bernard. *La Rhétorique, ou l'art de parler.* Later ed. Paris, 1740.

———. *Nouvelles réflexions sur l'art poétique.* Paris, 1668.

Le Jay, Gabriel, S.J. "Discours sur les avantages de l'eloquence, addressé aux jeunes élèves en rhétorique." In *A la jeunesse françoise.* Paris, 1835.

Morel, Jacques. "Rhétorique et tragédie au XVIIe siècle." *Revue de la dix-septième siècle* 80–81 (1968): 89–105.

O'Malley, John, S.J. "The Jesuits, St. Ignatius, and the Counter-Reformation: Some Recent Studies and Their Implications for Today." *Studies in the Spirituality of Jesuits* 14 (January 1982).

Schwickerath, Robert, S.J. *Jesuit Education.* St. Louis, Mo.: B. Herder, 1903.

Snyders, Georges. "Rhétorique et culture au XVIIe siècle." *Revue de la dix-septième siècle* 80–81 (1968): 79–87.

Van Kley, Dale. *The Jansenists and the Expulsion of the Jesuits from France.* New Haven, Conn.: Yale University Press, 1975.

Yanitelli, Victor, S.J. "Jesuit Education and the Jesuit Theater." *Jesuit Educational Quarterly* 11 (1948–49): 133–45.

Art History

Bazin, Germain. *The Baroque: Principles, Styles, Modes, Themes.* Translated by Pat Wardroper. Greenwich, Conn.: New York Graphic Society, 1968.

Knipping, John B. *Iconography of the Counter-Reformation in the Netherlands.* 2 vols. Nieuwkoop, Netherlands: B. de Graaf, 1974.

Nugent, K. "The Jesuit Influence on Early Baroque." *Month* 23 (1960): 89–104.

Raspa, Anthony, S.J. *The Emotive Image.* Fort Worth, Tex.: Texas Christian University Press, 1983.

Ripa, Cesare. *Baroque and Rococo Pictorial Imagery.* The 1758–60 Hertel Edition of Ripa's *Iconologia.* Edited by Edward A. Maser. New York: Dover Publications, Inc., 1971.

Tartarkiewicz, Ladislas. "L'Esthétique du Grand Siècle." *Revue du dix-septième siècle* (1966): 21–35.

Wittkower, Rudolf, and Irma B. Jaffe, eds. *Baroque Art: The Jesuit Contribution.* New York: Fordham University Press, 1972.

French History

Braudel, Fernand. *Civilization and Capitalism in the Fifteenth through the Eighteenth Century.* Vol. 1, *The Structures of Everyday Life.* New York: Harper and Row, 1979.

Charlton, D. G. *New Images of the Natural in France.* Cambridge: Cambridge University Press, 1984.

Darnton, Robert. *The Great Cat Massacre.* New York: Random House, 1958.

Guerard, Albert. *France: A Modern History.* Ann Arbor: The University of Michigan Press, 1960.

Maurois, André. *A History of France.* Translated by Henry L. Binnse. Minerva Press: 1960.

Mossiker, Frances. *Madame de Sévigné.* New York: Alfred A. Knopf, 1983.

Russell, John. *Paris.* New York: Harry N. Abrams, 1983.

Other

de Rochefort, Jouvin. Map of Paris drawn by, 1672. Estampes. Carnavalet Museum, Paris.

"Feu d'artifice et decoration au Collège Louis-le-Grand." Estampes 97. Dossier Louis-le-Grand. Carnavalet Museum, Paris.

Furetière, Antoine. *Dictionaire universel.* The Hague and Rotterdam: 1691.

Loret, Jean. *La Muze historique.* Edited by C. L. Livey. Vichy, 1878.

Les Memoires de Trévoux. Jesuit Archives, Chantilly, France.

Le Mercure de France. Bibliothèque de l'Arsenal, Paris.

Le Mercure Galant. Bibliothèque de l'Arsenal, Paris.

Le Nouveau Mercure. Bibliothèque de l'Arsenal, Paris.

Pomey, François, S.J. *Le Grand Dictionnaire royal.* 7th ed. Cologne and Frankfort: 1740.

index ·

After the titles of works listed below, the following abbreviations are employed:

(tr)	=	tragedy	(p)	=	pastoral
(b)	=	ballet	(c)	=	comedy
(op)	=	opera			